EUROPE 1870 - 1980

An Analysis of European History

Martin Collier

GREENWICH EXCHANGE
LONDON

Greenwich Exchange

First published in Great Britain in 1996

Europe 1870 - 1980 - An Analysis of European History © Martin Collier 1996
All rights reserved

Printed and bound by Priory Press, Holywood, N. Ireland.

ISBN 1-871551-04-8

DEDICATION

For Alli, Tom and Anna

ABOUT THE AUTHOR

Martin Collier

Martin Collier studied Modern History at St. John's College, Oxford.
He is presently Head of History and Humanities at Weavers School, Wellingborough.
He is also an Assistant Examiner for 'A' Level History

CONTENTS

LIST OF PICTURES AND MAPS

Photo Credits:

Reproduced by kind permission of "The Illustrated London News"

Photographs - Giolitti; Mussolini; Stresemann; Hitler; Speer; Stalin; Franco; Briand.

Reproduced by kind permission of Hulton Deutsch: *Photograph* - Khrushchev in London 1956

Photographs of D'Annunzio and Witte - private collection.

INTRODUCTION

To all readers.

This book attempts to deal with some of the relevant questions of the last hundred years of European history. In doing so, each chapter has been broken down into narrative and analysis sections. That is not to suggest that there is no overlap between the two - in fact the contrary is true. However, there is a clear distinction between the value of each. Any individual who wishes to answer a historical question needs to know what happened. Yet knowing what happened is not enough. Questions can only be answered with analysis. Structuring an analytical answer is a process. At the beginning one must look to simplify, to clarify what the issue is and the important themes around which any answer revolves. The analysis then takes the form of an explanation. It should cover the main points - although what constitutes the main points will always be a matter of choice. The narrative now becomes important as the source of evidence which can verify the explanation.

The last hundred years of European history are of significance because they are so close and still so relevant. As contemporary society attempts to re write the history of continental Europe for political ends, we should be wise enough to note that there are themes which run through this book which are also applicable to Britain. The fact that Britain escaped the horrors of dictatorship in the past hundred years is a fact in which we all rejoice. Yet our history shares so much in common with that of our neigbours that we are foolish to be either sanctimonious or wilfully ignorant about their recent past. For better or worse our future lies in Europe. So for that reason if no other - we must aquaint ourselves with the developments and changes which influence European culture today.

There are themes which run through the history of most of Europe in the last hundred years or so. The tensions created by industrialisation, the resultant social change and threat posed to the ruling classes is a constant factor for change. Overshadowing this period was the Great War of 1914-'18. It destroyed the foundations and certainties of the 19th century and acted as a catalyst for revolution and upheaval. Throughout Europe, the ruling establishments attempted to cling on to power in the wake of such change - in Germany, Italy, Spain - and resorted to extreme measures to do so. What also becomes apparent is the ruthlessness with which power has been gained and consolidated. It is wrong to blame this wholly on ideological considerations - such ruthlessness is a shared trait of regimes of all persuasions. Individual countries develop their own distinct identity, e.g. French economic and industrial change being of a very different character to that in Spain or Britain. Yet there is much which is common to many countries, the trauma of war comes to mind.

There are some important subjects which have been omitted from this volume - it is hoped that this omission be addressed at a later date. Some chapters have been included because they fill a gap for students. I believe that the topics which are debated in this book are of central importance to our understanding of European history as a whole.

To the teacher and the student.

This book is intended to be a text book. It is not a work book in that exercises are not provided. The aim of the text is twofold.

i. To give students of history sufficient information/detail for them to answer questions with confidence.

ii. Even more importantly, this book aims to provide students with examples of lines of arguments/themes which they can then use to analyse historical questions.

A common frustration of history examiners and teachers is that students fail to analyse. In response to questions, they take refuge in what is perceived as an easier option, that of narrative - of telling the story. Too frequently this automatically constitutes a weaker answer and the student fails to do him/herself justice. It is hoped that this book will help students to find analysis easier.

Suggestions.

a. Students can be asked to read sections of the narrative. There are many different ways of dealing with the narrative, the most obvious is to ask students to take notes from it. This exercise is often self defeating as it is difficult to take notes without knowing the criteria on which selction of information is to take place. Therefore, the teacher might want to give various pointers to the themes/areas which students can discuss/write down after reading all or part of the narrative section. An example is from the narrative on the Spanish Second Republic, 1931-'39. After reading the first few pages, the students might be asked to note down/discuss: 'The main divisions in Spain' or 'The extent of reform 1931-'33'. Out of this should come the key themes/concepts/ideas which will form the basis of any analysis.

b. What the student should look for are the main themes of a topic which can be used to form the basis of an answer to a variety of questions. These themes are the topic simplified, the basic ideas. Again, using the Spanish Second Republic - the narrative produces these basic ideas:

- The Republic was born against a background of division.
- Through reform, the Republic accentuated ideological and social polarisation.
- The Civil War was a stuggle of ideologies. That the Nationalists won was due to the ideologically inspired foreign aid and unity.

So the student can bring away the key themes of division, ideology, polarisation. In any essay about the Second Republic, these are points around which an argument can be based.

The analysis is the explanation of these points using information from the narrative. When the student reads through the analysis section of any chapter, it is hoped that he/she will try to pick out the main points which have been suggested. Then they should try other questions about the topic and try to use those points. Of course, some points will not be relevant to a different question - but some most probably will. If a student can gain a fundamental understanding of a topic, then they will find it easier to expain. Once a student is armed with an understanding, so will follow the confidence which is such an important element of historical writing.

Acknowledgements.

I would like to thank Dr Ross McKibbin of St Johns College, Oxford for his teaching and encouragement. The teaching of history in schools can be a exciting experience. I was fortunate to spend my formative years as a teacher at Thomas Tallis School in Kidbrooke, London. I would like to thank Kate Smith, with whom I taught A level, and the students at the school who made the experience particularly rewarding. I would also like to thank Jim Hodgson for his confidence in this project and Annabel Dalziel for designing the book cover.

HOW UNIFIED WAS ITALY BY 1914?

Introduction

The unification of Italy in 1871 was, in reality, Piedmontisation[1]. The constitution of that year imposed the legal structures, political institutions, foreign policy and cultural norms of Piedmont on the rest of Italy. From 1871 to the eve of the First World War, the process of government and direction of policy was to reconcile what could be termed 'real' Italy to this 'legal' Italy (as represented by the state)[2]. However, this was not necessarily a process of unification; 'legal' Italy in all its forms did little to actively integrate real Italy into the political or economic system. The limitations of social policy and its manifestations such as large scale emigration underline this point.

The process of trasformismo, which was the absorption of various political groups into the 'liberal system', was basically one of bribery and corruption. Its aim was to maintain the power of the ruling elites. It was only ever partial and went hand in hand with repression for those groups not absorbed. It is very difficult in this sense, or in any others, to claim with conviction that Italy was in truly unified by 1914. In fact it is possible to argue that the years 1871 - 1914 not only highlighted but saw the accentuation of the divisions in Italian life.

The New State

The constitution of 1871 was based on the Piedmontese model, the Statuto of 1848.

Symbolically, the King Victor Emmanuel[3] remained 'the Second' as he was of Piedmont rather than 'the First', as he was of the new state. As a constitutional monarchy, the sovereign body of the state was to be the King in Parliament. The Chamber of Deputies of the Parliament was elected on a minimal suffrage. Before 1882 electors were male, over 25, literate and paid taxes of forty lira a year or more, approximately 2% of the population in 1871. On top of this Catholics did not vote because of the papal opposition to the new state[4]. Those elected tended to be local dignitaries and usually a member of the liberal establishment. Local government was controlled by centrally appointed 'Prefects'[5] whose job it was to control the municipal councils (*communi*) and the mayors who ran them.

Transformiso

The Chamber of Deputies was managed by the Prime Minister of the day by granting them favours. There was no party system although a loosely defined 'left' (mainly associated with the South of the country) and a loosely defined 'right' (associated with the North). Governments came and went with regularity, there were 28 from 1871 - 1892, but not so ministers e.g. Agostino Depretis held the post of Prime Minister for all but two years between 1876 and 1887 despite numerous governments. As governments were essentially non ideological and lacked any coherent doctrine, policy was implemented in piecemeal fashion. The governments of the right which dominated until 1876 were characterised by public order and low expenditure policies. From 1876 - 1887 governments were dominated by the so called left and the *trasformismo* of Depretis. In 1882 the suffrage was widened to 7% of the electorate - but this was in part to favour the left. Certain reforms were undertaken such as compulsory primary education in 1877 and the abolition of the grist tax on milling in 1883. The periodic governments from 1887-96 of Francesco Crispi introduced reforms which widened the local suffrage in 1889 by 2 million and gave large councils the chance to elect their own mayor. To protect northern industrial and agricultural interests, a new tariff was imposed in 1887 on imported goods which had important consequences, discussed below.

Foreign policy

As a new state, successive governments consciously followed a cautious line abroad. In 1882, however, Italy joined the Triple Alliance with Germany and the Hapsburg Empire. In 1885 it began its own colonial expansion by the seizure of the port of Massawa and in 1890 Crispi joined up Italy's East African colonies to form Eritrea. This had been preceded in the 1880s by a vast expansion in Italy's naval capacity. None of this was to match in importance the effects of the defeat of Italian forces by the Abyssinians at the battle of Adowa[6] in 1896, the shadow of colonial failure cast itself into the next century.

Church/State relationship, 1871-1900

The early years after unification saw opposition to the state come from many quarters. Most significant was the hostility of the Catholic Church. By the '*Syllabus of Errors*' of Pope Pius IX of 1864, the Church denied the validity of the new state's claim to legitimacy. From then onwards the state often passed legislation which was anti clerical. The Law of Guarantees of 1871 gave the crown a veto over the appointment of bishops and further legislation disbanded religious orders and banned pilgrimages. The 'Roman Question' i.e. the status of Rome and the Papacy's control over it remained unresolved and hence, from March 1871, Catholics were advised not to vote in elections. In 1886, Leo XIII went further and banned Catholics from voting[7]. There was little respite in the tension between Church and State. In 1890, Prime Minister Crispi reformed the country's charity based welfare system to the exclusion of the church which was a major blow to the church's position in society. The papal response, *Rerum Novarum*, of 1891 set out the principles for a form of 'Social Catholicism' i.e. that Catholics had a role to play in intervening in the economic sphere to alleviate the effects of exploitation. This was backed up by the reorganisation from 1892-4, of the major Catholic lay movement the *Opera dei Congressi* as an organisation which could implement these ideas. The response of the government to this perceived threat was a crackdown in 1897 on Catholic associations. A year later all Catholic organisations were crushed. From then on, however, the state and Catholics were drawn closer together in informal alliances against what was seen as a far more serious threat to both.

Social Unrest

Anarchism spread rapidly in the early years of the new nation. In 1874 there was an attempted armed rising in Bologna and another failure at Matese three years later. Repression against anarchists in 1878 - 9 followed an attempt on King Humbert's[8] life in 1878. Many anarchists were forced into exile but King Humbert was assassinated by an anarchist in 1900. In the long term, the development of organised socialism was perceived as a far more serious threat to the liberal establishment. The 1880s saw repression of emerging movements such as the POI[9] (disbanded in 1886). In 1884 the revolutionary socialist PSRI[10] was founded, led by Andrea Costa. Most significantly, the workers' congress convened in Genoa in 1892 formed the intellectual basis of the Italian Socialist Party (PSI) founded in 1895 as an evolutionary Marxist party and led by Filippo Turati. In its organisation and structure it was a modern European party which attracted 216,000 votes in the 1900 election. As with other groups outside the liberal establishment, the socialist movement suffered periodic repression. In October 1894 the PSI was dissolved and its deputies arrested. The Chambers of Labour[11] which were worker self help organisations, were closed down in the repression of 1897.

In the tradition of Mazzini[12], Italian Republicanism flourished after 1871 especially through the medium of worker's aid societies. Many Republicans supported what is known as 'irredentist' claims i.e. the liberation of land such as Trieste held by the Hapsburgs. Periodically the movement was repressed such as the arrest of leaders in 1874. Italian Radicals were led by Garibaldi[13] in the 1870s but essentially absorbed into the government of the left. The 1880s saw the movement challenge imperialism and yet also challenged itself by the growth of workers' parties. In the 1890s the Radicals came to the fore with a comprehensive political programme of institutional reform, regional autonomy, civil rights and social legislation based in the 'Pact of Rome' of 1890. Fear of such ideas and the growth of parties which stood outside the establishment, prompted a constitutional debate in the 1890s based on the politician Sidney Sonnino's article in 1897 that it was time to 'return to the Statuto' i.e. to greater executive power. These ideas were discredited in the Parliamentary wrangling of 1889 -1900[14] and the election of 1900 ushered in a victory for the left, Socialists, Republicans and Radicals winning 96 seats. Periodic riots threatened the stability of the political system. Most important was the food rioting of 1898 in response to high food prices and protection on imported wheat. Rioting took place across the country, many of which turned into demonstrations for greater political liberty. The demonstrations in Milan in May ended in violent repression and maybe as many as 150 killed. The rise of the *fasci*[15] posed a further challenge to the establishment. Manifesting themselves in different guises, these groups were rurally based and loosely socialist in their ideals. Highly complex in organisation, the *fasci* were involved in rural strikes which provoked their banning in1894 by Crispi's government.

Increasing stability 1896-1914

Whilst the period 1896 -1914 saw rapid economic growth, in particular in the industrialising North, the growth was of a unique model - a balance between state subsidised and independent industry. Considering the significant boom in the economy post 1900, it is not surprising that Italy was politically far more stable. There was further integration of at least sections of groups such as the Catholics and Socialists into the liberal system. The main architect of this process on and off from 1903-14 was Giovanni Giolitti. The means by which this was done was a series of concessions to appease different political groups. In 1902 the Supreme Council of Labour was set up to advise on labour issues and legislation as a concession to the labour movement. Radicals were brought into government, first the Radical Marcora became speaker in 1904, then Sacchi and Pantano joined Sonnino's government in 1906. Despite Giolitti's attempts to reduce government intervention in trades disputes and strikes, there was still considerable public disorder as shown by the general strike called in 1904 in response to the shooting of a striking miner, in the quaintly named Buggerú. There were some improvements in social welfare e.g. 1902 legislation limiting the working day for women to eleven hours or in 1907 making a rest day in the week compulsory.

The issue of reconciliation of Catholics to the state was partially aided by the disbanding or the *Opera dei Congressi* in 1905. The replacement, lay movements, such as the *Unione Donne Cattoliche* for Catholic women continued the strong influence of the Church. There was some participation of Catholics in elections from 1909 and Catholic dominated local governments in towns throughout Italy, in particular in Lombardy and Veneto. By 1914, however , the main issues had not been resolved, that of the 'Roman Question'. For Giolitti and the 'liberal establishment', however, the emerging threat was that of Italian Nationalism. As a philosophy, Nationalism was set against the background of imperial failure pre-1900, in particular that at Adowa. It was implacably against the liberal system and *trasformismo* as institutions and practices which had failed to unite Italy. The conservatism of Giolitti and the concessions towards Socialism offended the middle classes and these grievances were aired at the first Nationalist Congress in 1910. To an extent the invasion of Libya in 1912 was an attempt to conciliate Nationalist opinion.

The Collapse of the Giolittian system

The Libyan War was victorious but became the catalyst for the collapse of the system. The Socialist PSI, on whom Giolitti had relied for support, was split by its opposition to the war. The Nationalists won support for the war and in 1913 won five seats in Parliament. Most importantly, the war had strengthened the case for universal suffrage. In 1912 all literate men over twenty one and all illiterate men over thirty were given the vote. The results of the 1913 election seemingly backed the introduction of wider suffrage - the Liberal and 'constitutional' seats i.e. all the votes Giolitti could count on fell, but only to 318 out of 511. Much more disconcerting was the rise of mass politics. Under the 'Gentiloni Pact' Liberal candidates who agreed to sign the seven points of the Catholic Electoral Union received the Catholic vote. Many, perhaps over 200 Liberal candidates signed, with the crucial result that the Liberal system relied on Catholic support. In 1913 a major strike in Turin was won by the Socialist engineering union FIOM with many industrialists blaming Giolitti and his policy of non- intervention. By the eve of the First World War, the Giolittian system had crumbled with the tension of balancing the support of such disparate groups as Radicals and Catholics.

ANALYSIS.

Introduction.

The continuation of the division between 'real' Italy and 'legal' Italy is the most obvious evidence of the failure to achieve unification. The political process essentially consisted of making Piedmontisation acceptable to political groupings which stood outside the small Liberal elite. The methods used were a combination of *trasformismo* and concessions. There were many groups which lay outside this system, either by choice e.g. the Catholics and Nationalists, or by rejection e.g. the Councils of Labour. It is more accurate to argue that the Liberal regime did not intend to integrate or unify 'real' Italy into the political system - one need look no further than the restricted suffrage or the widespread use of repression to verify this point. There is little evidence of unification becoming the catalyst for economic integration. In fact one should argue the opposite. The large numbers seeking to emigrate and the absence of any coherent or cohesive social norms or values developing as a consequence of unification reiterate the argument against unification being much more than an imposition of 'legal' Italy, even by 1914[16]. In the words of the Italian writer Gramsci[17], 'Italy' lacked 'hegemony'[18]. Perhaps the greatest proof of the narrow basis of the Liberal system was how it was undermined by mass politics and the wider suffrage from 1912.

Political unity?

From 1871, the strategy of the Liberal establishment

was to build broad coalitions in parliament which could sustain it in power. This was managed through the granting of political favours and the acceptance of some local power held by notables as mayors of the 'comuni'. This acquiescence in local power further strengthened the state, however, as it resulted in a compatibility of aims. The government of the Italian state revolved around granting favours to deputies to secure a majority and, at election time, granting favours to the electorate to gain the right deputy. Most importantly, the electorate was limited and in no sense representative as a whole. In 1870, the electorate was half a million (2.2% of adult men), in 1880 it was 622,000 (8% of adult men). In 1874 the successful candidate in any constituency would receive no more than around 500 votes. There was a geographical electoral divide, even after extended suffrage in the 1880s and 1890s by 1895, 56% of the electorate was from the North, 26 % from the South. The electorate was literate and even subsequent suffrage reforms post 1871 maintained a literacy requirement. Similarly, the electorate remained predominantly urban. Such an electorate, in the main, produced a political class which was receptive to trasformismo. The criticism of this system was that those who were 'absorbed' such as the Radicals who gave support to the 'left' governments of Depretis and Cairoli after 1876 were not representative of 'real' Italy as a whole and were estranged by their absorption. An example of this phenomenon was the low Radical vote in artisan and working class areas of Milan in 1886. Many deputies from the South were supportive of successive administrations from 1882 onwards, not because those regimes acted in the interest of the South but because of the corrupt nature of Parliamentary politics. To all intents and purposes, the Southern elite were bought off as an alternative to political integration.

Emergence of mass politics

The process of absorption was undermined by the development of mass politics. Because of its nature, absorption could not accommodate the aspirations of large groups, partly because these groups were less likely to be bought off with piecemeal concessions yet also because to accede to the demands of one group could upset another. It was a political balancing act but vulnerable at all times as a consequence. The Gentiloni Pact of 1912 and Giolitti's reliance on the Catholics thereafter offended the Radicals who were steeped in anti - clericalism. Hence they withdrew their support from the government. The process of absorption was never fully comprehensive as the extent to which Giolitti was able to absorb the Socialist movement proves. From 1900, Giolitti was able to absorb large numbers of PSI[19] deputies with social welfare policies such as the state Maternity Fund of 1910. These deputies (known as 'reformists') were generally middle class, twenty two out of twenty eight deputies in 1904 having a university education. Their class was dictated by the composition of the electorate and many deputies such as the PSI leader Turati sympathised with the aims of the Radicals and the policies of Giolitti. Yet it could never be argued that the Liberal regime managed to 'absorb' the socialist movement - too much of it lay outside the world of parliamentary politics. An example of this was the General Confederation of Labour (CGL) formed in 1906, and the Chambers of Labour which acted independently of the PSI. The latter in particular had great influence in certain areas as was shown in its control of the labour market in Emilia from 1904. There were socialist co-operatives in the countryside, by 1910 they had 218,000 members. The significance for the political system was that to a greater extent many of these groups lay outside and in opposition to the establishment, 200 people dying in strike related violence between 1900 and 1904. Such violence made full support for the establishment by even the deputies impossible. After 1912, with the rise of the left and the demise of Turati's reformist wing, absorption became even harder to achieve. Strikes and violence led to resentment against the system from employers who, particularly after the general strikes of 1904, the introduction of National Insurance in 1912 and the victory of the union FIOM in the Turin strikes of 1913, believed Giolitti to be too sympathetic to socialism. Similarly, the reliance of Giolitti on Catholic influence deputies after 1912 alienated the traditionally anti-clerical radical deputies from his coalition. The system which dominated from 1871 to 1912 was based on the manoeuvrings of an elite, a restricted and literate electorate and patronage. The Liberal establishment had no broad popular basis and this can recognised in the limitations of the Giolittian system.

Church-State division

It is in the relationship between the state and Catholic Church where the absence of reconciliation between 'legal' and 'real' Italy becomes most apparent. The institutional anti-clericalism of the state was a result of the influence of the radical movement but primarily due to the dismissal of the state in the *Syllabus of Errors*[20] which was translated into the prohibition of Catholics to vote from 1881. The result was a ' duality of influence' - Catholics organising into national groups such as the '*Opera dei Congressi*' from 1874 with the explicit aim of countering the influence of the state. Despite its rejection of national politics, Catholics became heavily involved in local government, partly to counter the growing socialist influence[21] but also to create a base from which they could exert influence of their own. This was given impetus by *Rerum Novarum*[22] in 1891. The extent of *Opera's* influence in the 1890s (3,982 rural banks, 24 newspapers and 105 periodicals in the North) reflects, conversely, on an absence of state influence. The state retaliated by introducing anti clerical measures such as Crispi's reforms of 1890 which attempted to limit the role of the church in social welfare[23], or di Rudini's dissolving of all Catholic associations in 1897. Although post 1900 such overt antipathy between church and state no longer existed, in the main because of the socialist threat, the church was not reconciled to the state. It is correct to point out that by 1909 the rule on non voting had been partially abandoned and '*Opera*' dissolved by Pope Pius X in 1905. Similarly, Catholics had increasingly become involved in local and even national politics by 1914. The aims of this were twofold, to diminish the influence of socialism as proposed by priests such as the influential Fr. Luigi Sturzo and to further the cause. The primary example of this was the 'Gentiloni Pact' of 1912 which so undermined the Giolittian system. By 1914, the Catholics had maintained an 'otherness' which underlined the limitations of so called 'unification'. From the women's *Unione Donne Cattoliche*, to the continued role in welfare, the Catholic Church continued to develop parallel institutions to those of the state. Although the start of the new century saw the beginnings of a rapprochement between Church and state, the issues which divided them were based on the legitimacy of the state itself. Therefore in this sphere it is impossible to describe Italy as unified by 1914.

Popular unrest

The persistent threat of popular disaffection is a common thread which runs through this period as is the repressive nature of the regime in dealing with that threat. This in the main stemmed from the regime's lack of a popular basis, the consequence often being over-reaction when absorption was not possible. Therefore outbreaks of unrest which had economic causes often developed into politically motivated action. A clear example of this was the unrest of 1898. What started as rioting against high bread prices in January developed into something far more serious in May because of the shooting of demonstrators by the police. The consequence of the Milan insurrection was widespread repression e.g. Turati was imprisoned for twelve years. The awarding of the Cross of Savoy to General Beccaris[24] for his role in the repression characterises the insecurity of the establishment. However, such insecurity was not limited to 1898, a 'state of siege' being declared ten times between 1861-1922 which entailed the introduction of martial law. This more than any other fact underlines the fragility of Italian unity and the precarious position of the establishment. Central government used the police, judiciary and prefects to control the regions. The extent of their usage reveals the extent to which the establishment relied on such levers of power to rule effectively. When in 1904 the local election at Bassano resulted in a Catholic administration the Prefect dissolved the council. Prefects were responsible for 'fixing' elections, which often resulted in the election of candidates who would support the status quo. In the South this resulted in the majority of deputies supporting the government despite the fact that the government did little for the South as a region. The police were given wide ranging powers to act in the interest of the state - an example being a system of internal exile which was used on over 5,000 people at any one time in the 1890s. Further police discretionary powers a state controlled judiciary and a jury system based on only 30,000 eligible jurors nation-wide very much reinforce the impression of a centralised and defensive state.

Economic division

A. Agriculture

Perhaps the greatest division within the Italian state was the economic chasm between North and South. The contrast between a capitalist North with its large farms, irrigation, technical improvements and the feudal South, blighted with malaria[25] and sub-division of land did not change as a consequence of unification. It should be argued that unification reinforced and accentuated the division. The sale of church land after 1871 (500,000 hectares between 1867and 1874) resulted in the consolidation of the economic and political power of the local elites. It is found to be the case that this class had also benefited from the decline of the feudal system and the auction of common land. Many peasants who bought plots often were forced to resell as the new state imposed increased land taxes. Therefore the process of land redistribution reflected the balance of political power and reinforced the feeling of alienation which manifested itself in the *'fasci'* of Sicily for example. The tariff of 1887 is further proof of the close relationship between political and economic elites. In 1886-7 nearly 1 million tonnes of cheap wheat were imported, in the main from the United States. Those who were hit hardest were large wheat growing landowners and the Corn Laws - raised from 14 lire/tonne in 1887 to 75 lire/tonne by 1894 - were in the interests of that class. The reciprocal tariffs imposed by France and other European countries after 1887 hit the Southern agricultural economy of wine and olives particularly hard (wine production fell by around 25% from 1886 to 1890). The 'agricultural revolution' based on machinery, innovation and capital investment was limited to the North, in particular around the Po Valley. Whilst wheat production in the North grew by 100% from 1873 to 1913, in the South the amount of land cultivating wheat actually fell by 8% between 1883 and 1913. The state heavily invested in land reclamation but again the picture is of Northern progress and Southern stagnation, of the 352,000 hectares improved by 1915, only 2,300 were in the South. The massive emigration discussed below was indicative of the imbalance of the state's intervention in the agricultural sector. Its priority in the South was to cultivate and maintain the support of local elites hence subsidy and legislation were framed in such a fashion to ensure continuity. In 1906/7 laws relating to Calabria were passed granting tax concessions on land, monies for construction projects and agricultural credit. These reforms were mainly cosmetic. Any attempt at real reform such as Sonnino's proposed land and social reforms of 1906 to create a literate land owning peasantry in the South were opposed with great hostility by the Southern establishment and were not implemented. The consequence was geographical economic division and social unrest.

b. Industry

The industrial development of Italy from 1871 onwards was heavily influenced by the nature of unification. As in agriculture, the chasm between the industries of North and South was made more pronounced. The South benefited from selective state subsidies, such as the government sponsored industrial development of Naples in 1904, but this system of subsidy was linked to political patronage. The influence of the government in shaping Italy's industrial development was as great as it was revealing of the interests of the government. There is no doubt that this period saw spectacular industrial growth, the value of manufactured goods doubling between 1896 to 1908 and national income rising by 32% between 1895 to 1915. State protection from 1887 provided the environment for the growth of particular industries such as iron and steel. The capital needed for such large scale investment was provided by banks such as the Banco Commercile Italiana which had close links with successive governments. Most instructive of all was the close relationship between the growth of the steel and shipbuilding industries and state funding. The steel industry was dominated by the firm Terni and, from 1911 by a cartel dominated by ILVA. These companies raised capital from the banks such as Bank Commercile and heavily relied on state subsidies and state orders for warships in particular from the building of the *Dandolo* (1876) and *Duilio* (1878). The state also heavily subsidised the building of the railways although much of the materials to build what was a network of 13,600 km by 1890 came from abroad. From nationalisation of the railways in 1905, the state encouraged the further growth of the engineering industry by placing orders such as for 3,000 carriages with Italian companies. The picture of industrialisation, therefore is characterised by the intervention of both government and banks. The tariff might have retarded trade with France until an agreement was made in 1898 but there is also no doubt that it protected industries such as steel and cotton from might have otherwise been fierce competition, the latter seeing a doubling of the number of spinning frames from 1900 to 1914. It is wrong to characterise all of Italy's industrial growth in this period as being reliant on state encouragement.

The motor industry, led by Fiat of Turin (which employed 6,500 and made 4,500 cars in 1914), is a classic example of industry flourishing in the atmosphere of confidence which was prevalent after 1896. The key point, however, is that Italy's industrial growth was reliant on state intervention and thereby reflected the interests of the state. Initially, unification was a disaster for the industrial South as the abolition of internal tariffs saw a collapse in some industries which found that they could not compete e.g. in Calabria there was a fall of around one third in the number of industrial workers between 1881 and 1901. The benefits of the emerging steel - ship - banks infrastructure were to be felt primarily in the North, Liguria being the centre of the shipbuilding industry, Piedmont that of engineering. The productive state capital investment was mainly in the North such as in the burgeoning hydro - electricity industry. The nature of industrial growth was as artificial and as imposed as political unity. Those areas in the North which were favoured, such as the Po valley, flourished but many areas remained backward and impoverished. It was partly the consequential and obvious economic gap which made a liberal hegemony impossible.

Social division

The litmus test of a united Italy is the extent to which the state had managed to 'make Italians' out of a geographically, linguistically and culturally divided population in 1871. It should be argued that, as with the political and economic structures, there had developed certain national institutions yet there was no social hegemony and social division predominated. The most evident manifestation of this fact was the growth of emigration from Italy in the period. In 1879 roughly 20,000 Italians emigrated to the Americas, by the turn of the century the figures had risen to roughly 150,000 p.a. Although this period also saw increasing internal migration - especially into the Northern industrial cities such as Milan whose population doubled from 1901 to 1911, much of the migration into cities was from the hinterland. In fact only 12% of the workers of the Northern provinces counted in the 1911 census were born outside their province. The figures show that the transatlantic migration was predominantly Southern {70%} which is not surprising when the crippling effects of the 1887 tariff are considered. In fact, the whole issue of emigration was one used by new writers such as the nationalist Gabrielle D' Annunzio who saw emigration as a reflection of the failure of the Liberal establishment to 'make Italians'. Although many northerners emigrated to Northern Europe to find work, this migration was more seasonal. The fact is that Italy lost over 1.5 million citizens permanently between around 1900 - '14 and most of these were from the South.

Linguistic divisions

A major obstacle to 'making Italians' was the linguistic differences of the peninsular. It was not that most Italians did not speak 'Italian' but that the vast majority spoke in dialect. It was only in Rome and parts of Tuscany, the birthplace of the modern language, that Italian was commonly spoken (i.e. by 2.5% of a population of around 26 million). This continued to be the case since the state lacked the will and resources to promote widespread education reform, and through it literacy, which would have familiarised them with their new mother tongue. Yet this was to an extent intentional, as has been seen , the illiterate were deliberately excluded from the political process by the restricted suffrage. In reality, this effectively excluded vast swathes of the population of the South. It is likely that around 70% of the population were illiterate in 1871, a figure which had fallen to just under 40% by 1911. In the province of Calabria, however, illiteracy remained at around 70% of the population in 1911, whilst in Piedmont it had fallen to 11%! To explain this astonishing difference one has to look no further than the state of primary education in Italy. Despite supposed compulsory schooling for three years from 1882, the effect of the diet of nationalism fed to students in these schools was mitigated by poor attendance rates. In the 1880s in the South it was calculated as low as 20% and seasonal at that. It is true that the state attempted to influence primary education to combat the influence of Catholicism, such as the Daneo - Credaro Law of 1911 which set up Schools Councils, with some government control, to run the primary sector. However, it did not attempt to strengthen primary education throughout Italy, whilst some Northern provinces received 568,000 lire state funding for school building between 1861 and 1911, some areas of Calabria got nothing. With regards to secondary education, the majority of the nation's technical schools and 'popular universities' (secondary education courses set up by universities) were situated in the North. This pattern of education fits in well with the developing economic structure with its accentuated North - South split.

The making of Italians linguistically was a tall order in an age of only emerging mass communication. In fact the use of dialect prevailed until after the Second World War and was only broken down by the showing of popular Hollywood movies which had been dubbed into Italian. The Italian cinema emerged in the 1900s with many films celebrating the glories of unification. By 1914, however, it had not yet quite become the mass entertainment it was to be post 1918. The press also emerged in this period and weeklies such as *Gazzetta dello Sport* (founded in 1896) had a circulation of 1.5 million by the turn of the century. When the literacy rates are taken into account, it is difficult to accept this as an indication of developing national unity. Moreover, the press was not populist but a mirror of the political attitudes of the establishment. Although such newspapers such as the influential *Corriere della Sera* criticised the Giolittian system it was from the standpoint that the system was too introvert. There is no doubt that newspapers were sold nation-wide such as *Giornale d'Italia* (set up in 1902) and yet again it is misleading to deduce that this was of a significance in terms of unifying the country culturally - in the South the readership was limited to the elite, those groups which had been absorbed.

Hostile nationalism

The failure of the Liberal establishment to unify Italy was reflected in the emergence of a hostile nationalism towards the end of the period. This nationalism should be seen as a critique of the state's failure to build a nation as defined in late nineteenth century terms. The failure of colonial policy as represented by defeat at Adowa was keenly felt by such people as Alfredo Rocco and Enrico Corradini who became the Nationalists' foremost writers. The main criticism of the Giolittian system and the Liberal state was that it had not followed a foreign policy which represented the nation's interests. Italy's lack of colonies was acutely felt and the defeat in 1896 even more of a national humiliation. The invasion and defeat of Abyssinia should be seen in this light, although Giolitti being who he was, also invaded Libya to please the Catholic lobby. Yet invading Libya was a crucial error in that it legitimised the mainly extra-parliamentary nationalist movement and destroyed the fragile balance of the compromised political parties. Even through a foreign policy which was generally successful in the security of the Triple Alliance from 1882 and a colonial policy which made some gains despite Adowa, the Liberal regime failed to unite Italians into any sense of national purpose.

Conclusion

The unification of 1871 was a unification of legal institutions. The political classes which administered this 'legal' Italy attempted to reconcile strategically important groups to the state through a policy of concessions. Those groups which it could not 'absorb' into the system it repressed. As time passed, so more groups became 'absorbed', yet the policy was never comprehensive and became contradictory. Both social and economic developments reflect the political priorities and necessities of the new state's elites. That these priorities were often at variance with the interests of swathes of the country's populace was not of import as long as control was maintained by the state apparatus and local elites. That this system eventually crashed is due to its desire to maintain a status quo which did not include a politicised population. There were cultural changes over the fifty years between 1871 and 1914 which meant the spread of spoken Italian. In precious few contexts, however, is it possible to talk of a unified Italy by 1914.

[1] Piedmont was the Northern Italian state which had most influence over the process of unification which took place up to 1871. From 1848, Piedmont had been ruled under a relatively liberal constitution - The *Statuto*, and had seen economic modernisation, in particular with the building of the railways.

[2] This distinction is clearly explained by Martin Clark in his seminal *'Modern Italy' 1871 - 1982* published by Longmans.

[3] The king was sovereign 'by grace of God' and executive power was his alone. He had extensive executive powers including that over ministers and foreign policy - the latter being Victor Emmanuel's real interest.

[4] The annexation of Rome in 1871 by the Italian state left the Pope a supposed 'prisoner in the Vatican'. Before 1871, Rome had been in the control of the papacy and protected by French troops. The defenders of the papacy left in 1871 because of the outbreak of the Franco - Prussian War.

[5] The prefects were extremely important as the means by which the state controlled the provinces.

[6] Never had a European power been comprehensively defeated by an African army. The legacy of Adowa as an unprecedented humiliation should not be underestimated.

[7] In 1881 the declaration of *non expedit* (i.e. it is not expedient) by Leo XIII was a prohibition which, if flouted, could be punished with excommunication.

[8] King Humbert I (in Italian, Umberto I) succeeded to the throne on the death of his father in 1878.

[9] The POI was the Partido Operaio Italiano -the Italian Workers' Party.

[10] The PSRI stood for the *Partido Socialista Rivoluzionario Italiano.*

[11] The Chambers were set up to act as labour exchanges and to protect workers' interests.

[12] Mazzini, who died in 1872, had been one the most influential figures in the Risorgimento or rebirth of Italy. He had taken part in the uprisings of 1848 and was a leader of the ill - fated Roman Republic of 1849. His aim was for Italy to be unified by the consent of the people as a republic.

[13] Garibaldi had led the seizure of Sicily in 1860 with his famous 'red shirt' supporters. A maverick and adventurer, he was a hero throughout Europe.

[14] This period saw a near breakdown in the Parliamentary system because of the use of procedures in Parliament which undermined its authority including the use of royal decrees.

[15] The *fasci* literally means bundles of sticks. It represents the idea that collective action is stronger than individual action.

[16] In many senses 'legal Italy' had to struggle against the host of divisions of class, culture, belief and regionalism.

[17] Gramsci was an Italian Communist who was imprisoned by the fascists from 1926 to his death in 1937. His writings in prison were prodigious and form a powerful analysis of , amongst other things, the development of Italy post 1871.

[18] Hegemony is the acceptance of the values and norms of the ruling classes by a large section of society.

[19] The PSI was the *Partido Socialista Italiano*.

[20] *The Syllabus of Errors* was issued by Pope Pius IX in 1864. It rejected the development of 'isms' such as nationalism and liberalism, placing the church's interest in the spiritual more than the temporal (day to day issues 'of this life').

[21] From the 1890s, local government was fought over by Catholics and Socialists for power and influence. Whilst the Catholics were never formed into an organised conservative party, they were the establishment's bulwark against the rise of socialism.

[22] *Rerum Novarum* was issued by Leo XIII and concentrated on the problems of society. It was a critique of capitalism and encouraged Catholics to intervene in the economic sphere to ameliorate conditions.

[23] These reforms aimed to increase lay control over charities but went to the heart of Catholic social activities.

[24] Beccaris' actions in1898 had inflamed the situation in Milan. He used cannon and cavalry charges against ordinary citizens. He also encouraged the savage sentences on Socialist and Catholic leaders, many of whom had urged restraint. His decoration by the king was considered a scandal in many quarters.

[25] Malaria had a huge effect on the Italian economy. In many Southern areas until 1900, it was the main cause of death in agricultural areas and made most low lying land uncultivatable. It was made worse by soil erosion as a consequence of deforestation and the building of the railways. The disease was curtailed from the turn of the century with the distribution of quinine.

Signor Giolitti

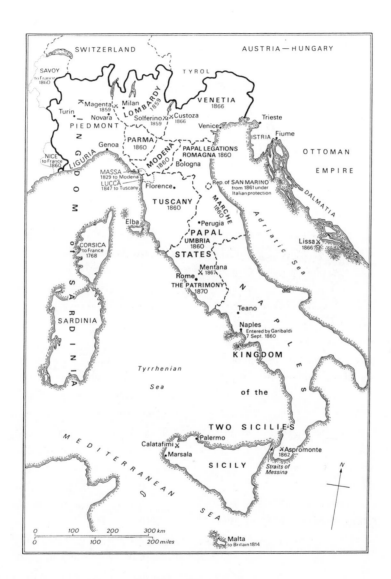

UNIFICATION OF ITALY

WHY DID MUSSOLINI GAIN POWER IN ITALY IN 1925?

Introduction.

The year 1925 marks the end of the Liberal state in Italy and the beginning of the fascist dictatorship led by Benito Mussolini. The rise of fascism in Italy was neither inevitable nor was it predictable. To answer the question of why Mussolini's fascists were able to gain power, one must look to the actions of the establishment[1] and the context in which they acted. As has been explained previously[2], the Italian establishment maintained itself in power by absorbing elements of different political groups into the power structure and thereby gaining their support. The introduction of mass politics[3] and the destabilising consequences of the First World War created conditions in which the liberal state was plunged into crisis. This was the context in which the establishment attempted its boldest and, as it subsequently turned out, its final absorption, that of Mussolini and his fascist followers. It was a move which attempted to give the establishment a mass anti socialist base which it could use to maintain power. In reality, the move legitimised Italian fascism and gave it a base from which it could exercise power independently. The war and its aftermath were the catalysts for change, yet the structural insecurity of the Liberal state and the actions of the establishment were the primary reasons for Mussolini's rise to power and the eventual establishment of a fascist dictatorship.

The 'Age of Giolitti'[4] ended with the appointment of Antonio Salandra as Prime Minister in March 1914.

A strong conservative, Salandra pledged himself to stand against the rising tide of socialism and end the democratising drift of Giolitti's governments. In June 1914 this policy was put to the test as a general strike was suppressed with the use of thousands of troops in so called 'Red Week'. The ferocity of the state's reaction embittered many working class leaders and seemed certain to accentuate the growing political and social polarisation.

The question of war

Growing social unrest was overshadowed by the rush to war which followed the assassination of Archduke Franz Ferdinand in Sarajevo on June 28th 1914. The Italian foreign minister San Giuliano and his successor Sonnino were faced with the dilemma of whether Italy should stay neutral or intervene in the war. If the latter course was chosen there was the further dilemma of on whose side should Italy intervene. By the terms of the Triple Alliance[5], Italy was bound to stay neutral if an ally i.e. Austria, or Germany, declared war on another country. There were other considerations to take into account. For many Italians, the primary enemy was the Austrian Empire which held territory they coveted, such as Trent and Trieste[6]. A fear therefore, was that an Austrian victory would extend her influence in the Balkans and leave Italy without the land she desired. Similarly, war against Britain would threaten Italy's supply of coal and other raw materials whilst leaving her coastline exposed to the attentions of the Royal Navy. On the other hand there was a strong lobby, including much of the army, which felt that Italy's interests would be better served by joining Germany and Austria. Negotiations were entered into with Austria to secure promises of territorial concessions in return for support. The Chief of Staff, General Cadorna, calculated that victory against France would be swift and might bring Italy Nice, Corsica and Tunisia. To the more conservative politicians, war against republican France was an ideologically more preferable option.

Entry into war

The decision to enter the war in March 1915 lay almost entirely with the politicians Salandra and Sonnino. Their guiding principle was that of *'sacro egoismo'* literally a sacred egoism. In practice, this meant that all decisions would be made on the basis of their potential benefits for Italy. Consequently, Italy signed the Treaty of London in April 1915 with the promise from Britain and France of Trieste, Dalmatia, Trentino, the South Tyrol and Istria[7]. These territories would be given to Italy when the war was won, and was conditional on a declaration of war against Austria[8]. In the words of the writer, Gaetano Salvemini, Italy had entered the war with 'the knife of Shylock rather than the liberating flag of Mazzini'. The treaty was signed without the knowledge of the army, parliament or the political nation. The King, Victor Emmanuel III, authorised the treaty despite the news of an Arab uprising in Libya which had chased the Italian army across the

desert, highlighting the weakness of the armed forces. The actions of the King and his ministers sparked off the so called 'interventionist crisis'. Led by Giolitti, many deputies showed support for a continuation of the state of neutrality. The political turmoil of May 1915 had important repercussions. Giolitti's opposition to the war meant that the war could be portrayed as one against the Austrian Empire and against the system and parliamentary order which Giolitti symbolised.

Military disaster

The Italian army entered the First World War completely unprepared for the type of warfare which it was to face. It lacked the necessary technology and training to fight trench warfare having only 300 working machine guns. Throughout the war the army suffered from poor morale and poor leadership. The 5 million conscript troops were mainly southerners, they were paid only 1/2 lira a day and were poorly nourished[9]. Discipline in the army was excessive with over 6% of the ranks being tried by Courts Martial, mostly for desertion. Despite the capture of Gorizia in the summer of 1916, military successes were few and far between. The defeat at Caporetto in October 1917 was a national humiliation. Most of Veneto was lost and 300,000 were taken prisoner. The failed General Cadorna was replaced by General Diaz who was a more cautious military strategist. In the last days of the war, with the Austrian Empire crumbling, Italian troops overran Trieste, Trent and Veneto[10].

Political division

Whilst it was not the prerogative of the Italian Chamber of Deputies to make war[11], the fact that there was never a pro war majority was a factor for instability. From May 1915 to June 1916, Salandra's government relied on conservative support and that of more democratic 'interventionists'[12] such as Nitti. The problem for the government was that it was effectively sidelined by General Cadorna[13] and had little influence in the running of the war e.g. the dismissal of Salandra's idea in January 1916 for a more effective war council to co-ordinate the military campaigns. The opponents of the war, who identified with Giolitti, formed themselves into the 'Parliamentary Union' in 1917 but this provoked many of the 'democratic interventionists' and 'conservative interventionists' of Orlando's post Caporetto government to form themselves into a counterbalancing 'Parliamentary Group of National Defence' in late 1917. There were other opponents of the war in Italy. The Pope Benedict XV[14], opposed the war in August 1915 as did rioting crowds in Turin in September in the same month. On the left, there was widespread support for neutralism as shown by the socialist PSI's leadership, the Directorate, and its popular paper *Avanti*. However, many PSI deputies such as Bissolati were drawn into the 'democratic interventionist' camp on the grounds of patriotic duty. The war polarised the socialist movement as it divided the political nation. This was accentuated by the publication of the Treaty of London by the Bolshevik government in Russia which showed that the Italians were fighting for land outside their proposed national borders i.e. Northern Dalmatia and the South Tyrol. This offended many 'democratic interventionists' such as the Republican Barzilia who called for a revision of war aims to preclude such territorial claims. This brought them into conflict with more conservative interventionists and nationalists who pressed for the extension of borders. By the armistice of 1918 the political nation was more deeply divided than at any time previously.

The cost of war

The economic policy followed by the state from 1915 to 1918 was growth at any cost. This is what in fact occurred. Production of munitions rose spectacularly, by 1918 6,500 planes were being produced per annum and FIAT was made over 24,000 lorries in 1918 as opposed to just over 4,000 in 1914. The state was plunged heavily in debt as a result of the war, the national debt rising from 15.7 billion lire in 1914 to 84.9 billion lire in 1918. Even more threatening to social stability was that prices rose four fold in the same period. This led to a decline in real wages of about 25% in the period of the war, frustration with which was compounded by a long working week and poor living conditions. In August 1917, serious riots in Turin broke out. Inflation also changed attitudes in the countryside, many peasants taking advantage of rising prices and fixed rents to pay off their debts. This led to an increased demand for land ownership, a fact recognised in the government propaganda of 1918 which promised 'land for the peasants'. In the same year there were examples of peasant land occupation in Emilia to the north of Italy and around Rome.

Versailles and the aftermath of war

The fact that the war had ended victoriously, coupled with the uncompromising behaviour of Orlando and Sonnino at the peace talks at Versailles raised popular expectations of significant territorial gains. Not only did the two politicians press for the terms of the Treaty of London to be implemented in full but, at Sonnino's insistence, the Italian delegation demanded the port of Fiume and the whole of Dalmatia[15]. In the end Italy received the sizeable territories of Trent, Trieste, Alto Adige and Istria yet the myth that Italy had won only a 'mutilated victory' was already widespread currency. She was denied Fiume, Dalmatia and any of Germany's colonial possessions. The consequence was unrest amongst 'interventionist' groups who felt that Italy had been betrayed. In May 1919, Orlando's government was replaced by one led by Francesco Nitti. This government introduced proportional representation on the surface to reward the soldiers, but in the main to destroy the basis of Giolitti's political system. Yet Nitti's government was completely undermined by the actions of the nationalist writer and leader, Gabrielle D'Annunzio. In September 1919, he marched into Fiume with 2,000 supporters, and declared the town annexed to Italy. This was done with the connivance of the army. Not only were his actions extremely popular, they legitimised extra-parliamentary action and, for fifteen months, stood as a symbol of the inadequacies of parliamentary government. The Treaty of Rapallo of November 1920 between Italy and Yugoslavia declared Fiume independent, thereby satisfying many nationalists who were simply interested in keeping it out of Yugoslavian hands. In December 1920, Giolitti sent the navy in and D'Annunzio surrendered. This was a decisive step on the part of Giolitti, but otherwise his government and the whole political system was in growing crisis. In 1919, the Catholics formed their own political party, the *Partido Popolare Italiano* (PPI). The consequence of this was that the liberal politicians could no longer rely on the conservative Catholic vote as they did in 1913 with the Gentiloni Pact[16]. In parliament, however, they came to increasingly rely of the PPI's support - the party winning 100 seats in the November 1919 election and 107 in May 1921 (in both occasions with around 20% of the vote). The new system of proportional representation strengthened the influence of the socialist movement (PSI), in the same elections they won 156 and 123 seats respectively.

Unrest

Outside parliament there was increasing industrial militancy due to inflation and the end of the war- the labour movement being suppressed by wartime measures. In 1919, over 1 million went on strike. In April 1920 there was a ten day 'general strike' in Piedmont. Most significant, was the 'Occupation of the Factories' of September 1920. What began as a wage strike in the engineering industry developed into the occupation of their factories by 400,000 workers. The government intervened, and promised greater worker participation in the management of industry. As a result, the occupation ended but not without great bitterness on both sides. The story was the same in the countryside, with growing numbers of land occupations and incidents of violence. The government intervened, yet it seemed to the landowners that they were automatically siding with the peasantry, an example being the decree of October 1920, which granted permanent tenure to illegal occupiers of uncultivated land. The Liberal establishment found it increasingly difficult to form governments against such a backdrop of parliamentary opposition and political instability. Both the governments of Ivanoe Bonomi (June 1921 to February 1922) and Luigi Facta (February to July 1922 and July to October 1922) failed to stem the growing crisis.

The rise of fascism

In October 1921, the *Partido Nazionale Fascista* (PNF) was founded by Benito Mussolini. The party grew quickly, by May 1922 it had 300,000 members. The movement had its base in the 'squadrismo' or squads which comprised its paramilitary section. Increasingly used by landowners and the local establishment in general as the main weapon of law and order and the most effective bulwark against socialism, the squads flourished. In 1921, they swept the 'red' provinces of Emilia and Tuscany, breaking strikes and the socialist peasant leagues. In July/August 1922, fascist volunteers helped ensure the failure of the 'Alliance of Labour'[17] strike. From then onwards the fascists held the upper hand and in October 1922, Mussolini pressed for a place in government backed by the threat of a mobilisation of the fascist militia. The Facta government requested that the King would introduce a state of martial law, but on 27th October, Victor Emmanuel III refused to sign the relevant decree, ostensibly to prevent bloodshed. Despite having only 6% of the Chamber's deputies, Mussolini was invited to be prime minister on October 29th. The following few days of celebration by the fascist blackshirts were later transformed into the myth of the 'March on Rome'[18].

Consolidation of power

In his first so called 'National Government', Mussolini included representatives of the PPI and Liberal establishment[19]. In January 1923, the squads were tamed by the creation of a new organisation, the Fascist Militia (MVSN) which was placed under the centralised control of Mussolini. To remove the problems of PSI and PPI representation, the electoral law was revised in 1923 to a system whereby the party with the largest number of votes (as long as it achieved over 25%), received 2/3 of the parliamentary seats. In April 1924, the right wing 'list' of candidates received 66.3% of the votes anyway, approximately 60% of this block being fascists. The most outspoken critic of increasing fascist domination was the leader of the PSI, Giacomo Matteotti. On 11th June 1924 he disappeared, murdered by fascists. In the furore following the assassination, the PSI walked out of the Chamber of Deputies and Mussolini's government was plunged into crisis[20]. The opposition hesitated, however, and Mussolini was able to seize the political initiative. On the 3rd January 1925, he reassured the establishment that he would reassert law and order to the country and reinstitute strong government. The Matteotti crisis was a watershed. It was the last chance to remove Mussolini from the centre of power for, it transpired, nearly twenty years but a chance which was missed.

ANALYSIS

Introduction

Mussolini came to power because the political system was in a state of crisis. He was drawn into government by the political elite which hoped that he, and his movement could be used to restore law and order against a backdrop of civil unrest. This is the most important immediate reason but it must be placed in a wider context. The extent to which the leading characters of Liberal Italy were prepared to aid the fascists in the take over of power from 1922 to 1925, indicates how far the governing class recognised their precarious position of being a ruling elite in an era of mass politics. So the attempted absorption of the fascists into government was an act of self-protection. It was an attempt to draw into the system a mass party of the right which would be supportive of the regime. This helps to explain why opportunities were not taken by either the King or politicians to remove Mussolini from power between 1922 and 1925. The price they paid was the emergence of a regime which at least partially destroyed the process through which they influenced the governing of the state.

The crisis in government was in many senses provoked and moulded by the consequences of the war. The political divisions caused by the war, the 'humiliation' of Versailles, the economic turbulence and social violence all created the climate of uncertainty on which fascism thrived. These, then, should also be seen as contributory factors which form the context to the governing class's decision and Mussolini's rise to power. Instead of attempting to crush fascism, they tried to use it as the means by which they could end uncertainty and recreate the former *status quo*.

The actions of the governing elite

The actions of the governing elite were the primary reason why Mussolini was brought into power and how he was able to consolidate his position. Fascist propaganda portrayed the take over of power in October 1922 as some kind of 'coup d'état', the so called 'March on Rome', but nothing could be further from reality. Mussolini was brought into government in an attempt to fill a power vacuum. From 1912, the advent of mass politics as a consequence of an extension of the suffrage signalled the end of the process of government by concession and absorption. By Orlando's introduction of universal suffrage in December 1918 and Nitti's introduction of proportional representation in August 1919, Liberal Italy was effectively killed off. It was impossible for the governing classes to absorb the Catholic or Socialist movements en masse without losing control of government. Yet it was similarly impossible to govern effectively without the support of a wide based party which could give government legitimacy. The creation of the PPI in 1919 as a lay Catholic party which was explicitly hostile to the Liberal state was a severe blow to the establishment as it could no longer rely on the Catholic vote as a conservative bulwark against socialism as it had in 1913. The elections of November 1919 and May 1921 reiterated the point as the PSI and PPI together made up around half the seats in the Chamber of Deputies.

This made governing effectively through the Chamber impossible for the series of prime ministers from Giolitti in the summer of 1921 to Facta who resigned in October 1922. In such a desperate situation, desperate action was taken and the inclusion on the government list of the 35 fascist deputies after the 1921 election is a case in point. This is a prime example of how the establishment, in this case Giolitti, legitimised fascism. Even after it became apparent that Mussolini had no intention of being used, the Liberal elite continued to support his government in the name of stability. The huge majorities Mussolini was given in the Chamber of Deputies and Senate[21] in late 1922 to dispense with Parliament for a year reflects the level of dissatisfaction with the process of parliamentary government from amongst the ruling class. It is also instructive to note that the reformed electoral system of 1923 which gave the winner in any election 2/3 of the seats in the Chamber, was supported by such notables as Giolitti, Orlando and Salandra. In the following election in April 1924 the latter two politicians appeared on the fascist dominated and victorious list. The fact that in that election the PPI gained only 9.1% of the vote and combined communists and socialists 14.6%, was justification for the establishment's tactics of attempting to use the fascists to defeat their enemies. It also helps to explain how Mussolini held onto power once he had been installed as prime minister.

The extent to which the establishment were responsible for the rise of Mussolini can be shown by studying the events of October 1922 and the

Matteotti crisis of 1924. In the former instance, the role of the King was vital but he represented a widely held view amongst the establishment that bringing the fascists into government was infinitely preferable to accommodating the socialists. It also would bring under control the fascist *squadristi* which had seized control of a series of provincial towns in the summer of 1922. The mass rally of 40,000 *squadristi* in Naples on the 24th October reflected the strength and implicit threat of the movement. That Mussolini was the only person who could control the actions of the *squadristi* was clear. Similarly his ability to mobilise a volunteer force to smash the 'Alliance of Labour' general strike in July 1922 was impressive to a political elite which patently failed to do the same in 1920 with the 'Occupation of the Factories'. The local fascist bosses, the *ras*, such as Balbo in Ferrera exerted significant local influence and developed links with both carabinieri and army. It is significant that orders from the governments of Bonomi and Giolitti in 1921 to local prefects to suppress the *squadristi* were ignored[22]. This places into context the decision of the king to ignore the request of Facta's cabinet in October 1922 for a state of martial law to be declared. Many politicians including Orlando and Salandra favoured absorption of the fascist movement as an opportunity to give the government the broad popular base it so patently lacked. There was widespread sympathy with the fascist amongst the army and General Diaz informed the monarch that the army, despite its loyalty, should not be pushed into confrontation with the fascists[23]. The King also fell under the influence of prominent industrialists and their representatives such as the

editor of *Corriere Della Serra*, Luigi Albertini. They urged Victor Emmanuel to install Mussolini as prime minister in preference to another period of the reforming Giolitti whose actions during the 'Occupation of the Factories' were seen as tantamount to betrayal. So the King was very much influenced by representatives of the ruling class in his decision not to declare martial law and to appoint Mussolini.

The greatest threat to Mussolini's government came during the Matteotti crisis. The outcry at the murder of the reformist socialist in June 1924 might well have led to Mussolini's resignation. The walk out of parliament by the socialist deputies was not supported by prominent liberal politicians such as Salandra or Giolitti. The establishment's views can be easily surmised by again studying the action of the King. He consistently refused to dismiss Mussolini, even in November and December 1924 when it seemed that the established politicians such as Orlando began to move against Mussolini. Even senior members of the Royal Household such as Senator di Campello spoke against the government in the Senate in December 1924. Despite this the monarch resolutely refused to accept the evidence of Mussolini's part in Matteotti's murder[24]. In fact the King very much helped Mussolini survive. In July 1924 a royal decree introduced far stricter censorship laws and Victor Emmanuel again refused to use the army against the fascists despite growing violence throughout the country by the turn of 1925. The dictatorship which Mussolini introduced on 3rd January 1925 was not an anathema to many of the establishment and was infinitely more preferable to a government of the left. That is why Mussolini survived. Despite the excesses of the *squadristi* as exemplified in the Matteotti affair, his government was infinitely more preferable to the establishment than one based on socialism. The liberal elite had no popular base with which to form a viable government. It is true that in December 1924, important politicians such as Orlando and Salandra[25] spoke out against the government but their reaction was too late. The initiative had passed to Mussolini.

The consequences of the war

a. Crisis in the political system

There is no doubt, therefore, that many members of Italy's political class capitulated to Mussolini in the hope that he could restore a stable political framework to the country. His appointment as prime minister was welcomed by politicians from across the spectrum who hoped that he would also restore some credibility to a much derided system. The social democrat Gaetano Salvemini, for example, saw in Mussolini a chance for political renewal as he personified a different style to that of the flawed democracy. One should argue that this deep crisis of the political system had its roots not only in the introduction of mass politics but in particular, in the deep divisions caused by the war and the question of intervention in the war.

To Giolitti, his followers who formed the 'Parliamentary Union' and the majority in the Chamber of Deputies, the war was folly. To the 'interventionists', such as the conservative Salandra, or the more democratic Orlando, opposition to the war was defeatist. The main point is this; the 'interventionists', from a wide political spectrum, equated defeatism with the Giolittian and the parliamentary system which produced it. They became committed to undermining both. The foundation of the pro-war Fascio of National Defence in December 1917 is a case in point. It included democrats such as Bissolati and showed that the fundamental division had become between 'interventionists' and those who opposed the war. As opposition to the existing parliamentary system became a main feature of the 'interventionist' creed, it is not surprising that after the war so many politicians were prepared to accept Mussolini and what he represented. As editor of *Popolo d'Italia*, Mussolini presented the extreme 'interventionist' cause and railed against the 'corrupt' governments of Giolitti and Nitti. The activities of the thuggish squads could be presented as fighting the 'interventionist' cause against the socialists and defeatists. For that reason they received the tacit support of the army which was to prove decisive in October 1922. The war had polarised the Italian political nation, that Mussolini was able to win over so much of the establishment to his cause is due to the fact that he was able to present himself as the champion of the 'interventionist' tradition.

This polarisation also meant that any anti - fascist front was only ever sectional i.e. it only was supported by the traditional parties of the left and they constantly squabbled amongst themselves. The opposition list which lost the April 1924 election was riven with division and hatred, for example the socialists were divided between Matteotti's reforming socialists and the PSI. There were various movements which were formed to counter the growing influence of the fascists but none of these attracted the support of conservative or former 'interventionist' politicians. Even during the Matteotti crisis, opposition to Mussolini from conservative politicians was never concerted or fully convincing. It is true that Salandra resigned as president of the budget committee on December 26th 1924 in protest over Mussolini's conduct, as did the liberals Casati and Sarrocchi resign from the Cabinet on the 30th of the same month for the same reason. Yet the walk out from the Chamber of Deputies in June 1924 was limited to one hundred opposition deputies and, despite the precarious situation for the regime in November/December 1924, it did not fall. After the collapse of parliamentary government in 1925, some of the liberal elite such as Salandra, faded into political obscurity (he took a seat in the Senate). However many politicians, Boselli being a prime example, moved to support the new regime and many were quick to profess their repugnance for parliamentary democracy. This definition of Italy as anti-democratic had became a central tenet of 'interventionist' culture. By 1918, the influence of that belief is all apparent in 1925.

b. Changing expectations

The war acted as a catalyst for change. Its main effect on Italian society was to radically alter the expectations of many of its members. That Liberal Italy was unable to fulfil these expectations became apparent and helps to explain the growth in the acceptability of the fascists. More than half the 5 million strong army had come from the peasantry and those who survived expected land redistribution[26] on their return from the trenches. This hope was reinforced by the government propaganda during the war which promised just that. The consequence was a post war upsurge in 'land occupations' of usually uncultivated land, the numbers of peasant landowners doubled between 1911-21. In other areas such as Bologna and Ferrara, land ownership was not the issue but security of employment[27], to that end the Chambers of Labour operated what amounted to a closed shop - no labourers could be employed without union membership. It is very important to stress that this was a revolution in the countryside and it threatened the rural elite and the whole power structure. The spread of the suffrage reinforced this shift in rural power by resulting in the election of PSI and Popolari municipal governments. To cap this, for many larger landowners was the seeming acquiescence of Liberal Italy e.g. the government decree of September 1919 which accepted the principle of 'land occupation' by allowing land seized to be recognised as lawfully owned. The threat these factors posed to the rural elite was clear, they undermined the principle of unchallenged land tenure and did little nothing to diminish the growing power of the peasant unions. It is the intensity of this threat which helps us understand the speed with which *squadrismo* was accepted despite the levels of violence and thuggery.

From 1919 the squads attacked local unions, socialists, labour leagues and Chambers of Labour. By removing the power of these groups, often overnight, through intimidation and destruction, the squads received widespread support from those groups which had felt threatened by the rising expectations of the landless and under employed. Many of these new supporters joined the local *fasci* and thereby formed the basis of the mass movement which was so important in bringing Mussolini to power. The link is this - as *Duce* - Mussolini could stand above the brutality of the squads whilst manipulating their violence. In both October 1922 and December 1925, the threat of *squadrismo* violence was sufficient for the establishment to give way to fascism. It was able to do that because at a local level the squads had often acted in the interests of the landowners. The domination of labour by fascist unions such as the National Confederation of Syndical Corporations, which had nearly half a million members by June 1922, was infinitely more preferable to the establishment than the Chambers of Labour or the peasant leagues. So the war created the conditions of social turmoil which allowed fascism to be both legitimised and in which it would flourish. This resulted in a mass movement which frightened the establishment but which they felt they could control through political absorption - hence the decision of October 1922.

c. Economic Turmoil

The war created similar tensions in industry which were to have important repercussions post 1918. In particular, the rising expectations of an exhausted workforce produced unrest which was perceived as a threat to industrialists and the middle class in general. The weakness of successive governments from 1918 to 1922 allowed the fascists to seize the initiative and present themselves as the most effective protectors of these interests. Wartime production had distorted the Italian economy with massive state investment, the national debt growing to from 15.7 billion lire in 1914 to 84.9 billion in 1919. There was rapid urbanisation - Turin's population growing by one fifth during the war - strict labour discipline and a long working week (often 75 hours). The significance of these conditions is that the post war economic slump unleashed a wave of industrial militancy which the government found impossible to control. Unemployment reached 2 million in November 1919. Businesses were stripped of government subsidy and collapsed, in 1920-'21 the industrial giants ILVA and Ansaldo folded. Inflation meant that prices were six times higher in 1920 than 1914 hit wages and savings and resulted in a rash of labour disputes such as the 'Occupation of the Factories'. It was the government's inability or unwillingness to side with the employers which lost it credibility in such circles. This is so crucial in understanding why there was considerable industrialist support for Mussolini in October 1922. The manner in which fascist volunteers discredited the ' Alliance of Labour' general strike in July - August 1922 simply reinforced their effectiveness in anti - labour action. The *squadrismo* was driven by a hatred of socialism which endeared it to the ruling class. This so vividly contrasted with

Giolitti's attempted settlement of the 'Occupation of the Factories' - the move towards so called 'trade union control of industries'. Even though this proposal to end the dispute (which it successfully did) eventually came to nothing, it was an implicit threat to the employers and their class. This helps to explain why a powerful group of Milanese industrialists telegraphed the King on the night of 28th October pressing him to accept Mussolini's demands. The alternative might well have been a return to the reformism and conciliation of Giolitti. The post war economic crisis had created the conditions, however, in which attempted conciliation was perceived as collusion with the unions. It had also reinforced the anti parliamentary convictions of many industrialists. Mussolini was partly brought into power as he presented himself and his movement capable of restoring law and order. This was in the interests of the middle and industrial classes who had been so threatened by the consequences of the economic turmoil caused by the war.

Versailles an its aftermath

The humiliation at Versailles and its aftermath created certain precedents which made Mussolini's rise to power possible. The refusal of President Wilson to give Italy either Fiume or Dalmatia at Versailles was to have extremely important ramifications for Italian politics. In particular it discredited the 'democratic interventionists' such as Nitti and those in the centre ground who had supported the war but wished for democratic change after it both

at home and abroad. This group had relied on Wilson's Fourteen Points which promised national self-determination, point nine defining Italy's true borders as being along 'lines of nationality'. When Wilson refused to back down over Fiume and Dalmatia the 'democratic interventionists' could do little but accept. They had gone along with Wilson's principles and they were virtually bound to his application of them, accepting all along that Dalmatia should not be annexed although Fiume was desirable. This clarified the division between those who perceived Italy's war aims to be for expansion and those who did not. The irony of the situation was that some of the areas handed over to Italy at Versailles went against this principle e.g. the town of Tarvisio was not predominantly Italian. The problem was that the majority of Fiume's citizens were. Therefore, when Nitti's government failed to press Italian nationalist claims to the city, D'Annunzio acted independently. The popularity of D'Annunzio's action did little to disguise that it was in direct defiance of the state. Although the occupation of Fiume was ended in December 1920 the episode had important political repercussions. It showed the state to be weak and the army to be ambivalent in its defence, in fact it is likely that D'Annunzio was helped by various army units. The bombardment of Fiume by Giolitti made it possible to label him, and the system he represented as being unpatriotic. The Fiume episode showed that direct action was possible and deemed acceptable in the name of Italian patriotism and the 'interventionist' cause. It is wrong to label Sonnino and Orlando's diplomacy as being 'a failure'. In objective terms Italy gained much from the treaty of Versailles; its borders were strengthened and gained significant national territory. Yet the fact that so many within Italy accepted D'Annunzio's verdict that Versailles was a 'mutilated victory' reveals much about the division caused by the war. The fall of Fiume galvanised many into support for *squadrismo* which, despite its illegality, still represented the 'interventionist' cause. The perceived failure of Versailles, therefore, was another important episode in the polarisation of Italian politics and society. The Fiume episode and its aftermath helped crystallise views. It is wrong to state that Versailles led directly to the rise of Mussolini. However, it did much to entrench attitudes and discredit the Liberal state. In that it should be seen as a vitally important contributory factor for the emergence of a fascism which was acceptable to the establishment.

Conclusion.

One should look at Mussolini's rise to power in the context of the failing Liberal state and the consequences of the war. The attempted 'absorption' of the fascist movement was a move to give the establishment the secure foundation of a mass movement in an era of mass politics. Mussolini was brought to power by the King and the country's elite as an attempt to restore some form of social stability, despite the fact that it was the *squadrismo* who had undermined the peace in many districts. Yet Mussolini could present to the political class the impression that he could control the squads and thereby maintain law and order. Fascism was a viable alternative to the emerging mass socialist movement and, to the establishment, infinitely more preferable. Its direct action against unions and labour leagues endeared it to a middle class which felt increasingly threatened.

The war and its settlement at Versailles, divided and polarised the political nation. It also caused economic dislocation and created expectations of the state that were not fulfilled. The animosity against the Liberal state by those loosely labelled as 'interventionists' i.e. those who supported the war, was to be of fundamental importance in the rise of Mussolini. Their influence at court and in Parliament provided the impetus for Mussolini's rise to prominence. The fact that he was 'one of us' gave him the necessary legitimacy in the eyes of the conservative elite and permitted them to turn a blind eye to the excesses of his supporters. This 'protection' extended as far as an unwillingness to overturn his government in 1925 as a consequence of Matteotti's murder. There is no doubt that the war created the political structure and the economic and social conditions which made the rise of Mussolini possible. It was the actions of the establishment that turned that possibility into a reality.

---

[1] The establishment in Italy at this time were the King, courtiers, army, conservative politicians and representatives of the industrial and landed classes.

[2] See the chapter on the Italian state 1870 - 1914.

[3] By the extensions of the suffrage in 1912 and 1919.

4 Giolitti had dominated politics from 1903 - 1914, being prime minister for nearly 8 years in that period. His ministries were marked by the granting of concessions to a range of groups to bring them into the political system. Such policies of conciliation and compromise were extremely unpopular with sections of the middle class and the establishment, even before the First World War.

5 Italy had been a founder member with the Triple Alliance in 1882. It was signed as a foreign defensive, conservative alliance and formed the basis of foriegn policy until 1914.

6 Known as 'irredentism', the campaign to 'liberate' Italians living within the Austrian Empire had a strong radical/republican base going back to 1871. In 1878, 'irredentists' attempted to provoke war against Austria. By the turn of the century 'irredentism' had become synonymous with nationalism and a highly emotive subject.

7 When the Bolsheviks published the Treaty of London in 1917, it showed that Sonnino had pledged Italy to war for territorial gains - in particular Dalmatia. This was not Italian speaking and therefore not ceded to Italy at Versailles under the principles of Wilson's Fourteen Points. This was to create a considerable political storm (see below).

8 War was declared against Austria in May 1915.

9 The Italians making the mistake of actually reducing the bread ration in December 1916.

10 These victories in October 1918 became representative of the interventionists' favourite depiction of Italy i.e. warlike and victorious. This stood in contrast to the pictured cowardice of the Giolittian parliament, the establishment and all others who opposed the war. The victories at the end of the war were somewhat hollow, however, the Austrian Empire being on its last legs.

11 By the *Statuto* of 1848 which formed the basis of the Italian constitution, it was within the King's power alone to declare war and make treaties.

12 'Interventionists' supported the war. The label arose as a consequence of Giolitti's opposition to the war and the myth that Italy had gone to war because a handful of politicians acted on the call of the nationalist 'interventionists'. This was not the case. There were some 'interventionists' who wished for territorial gain and to whom the war was a chance to forge a more illiberal state. One should not ignore that the war had many 'democratic' supporters who hoped that victory would open up the state.

13 Cadorna exercised his powers as Chief of Staff in the name of the King.

14 The Pope called the war 'appalling butchery'.

15 The Treaty of London had promised half of Dalmatia.

16 The Gentiloni Pact gave Catholic support to liberal politicians in return for certain assurances concerning divorce and the place of religious education in schools.

17 The 'Alliance of Labour' was formed to protect wages and cut unemployment. It was backed by the main socialist parties and consisted of some of the most important trade unions including the dockers and railwaymen. Its failure, therefore, was a significant blow to the prestige and power of the socialist movement as a whole.

18 The 'March on Rome' was the fascist myth that power was wrested from the establishment by the groups of fascists who descended on Rome at the end of October 1922. In reality, power was handed over to Mussolini, the 'March on Rome' being the drunken acknowledgement of that event by his blackshirted supporters.

19 There were four liberal ministers and three from the PPI included in the government.

20 Although there was no direct evidence linking the fascists to the murder, Matteotti's defiant speech against the rigging of the 1924 election made him an obvious target of the squads.

[21] The only political groups to vote against such a measure were the socialists and some of the Republicans. Most of Italy's ruling class voted with the measure including Orlando, Facta, Salandra and even Giolitti.

[22] It was the local nature of fascism which gave it its strength. Supporters of the 'interventionist' cause formed themselves into 'fascio' which literally means bundle although it came to mean groups. The roots of the movement were in local action and, ultimately, local control. It was this feature which gave the national movement legitimacy and Mussolini such considerable political clout.

[23] The famous phrase of Diaz to the King was reported as being: 'The army will do its duty; however, it would be well not to put it to the test'.

[24] Italy's foremost writer of the time, Benedetto Croce, supported Mussolini at the time but was later to write that he only survived because of the patronage of the monarch. Numerous politicians, including those who had supported the monarch's decision in October 1922 attempted to persuade the monarch to remove him from office. In July 1924, Bonomi, Sforza and other ex cabinet ministers gave the king detailed evidence of Mussolini's part in the murder of Matteotti. The King ignored their evidence.

[25] Salandra resigned as president of the budget committee on December 26th, thereby somewhat reducing the potential for damaging the government as all were on holiday.

[26] In the South, land ownership was held by the absentee landlord, the *latifundista*. The expectations of the peasantry were for land belonging to these landlords which lay uncultivated.

[27] In these areas, agriculture was undertaken by tenant farm owners employing wage labourers. Security of employment could keep wages higher.

D'ANNUNZIO

ITALY SINCE 1919

TO WHAT EXTENT DID FASCISM TRANSFORM ITALY IN THE PERIOD 1925-'43?

Introduction

Italian fascism was born as a child of war. Throughout its period in power, its stated objective was to transform Italy into a state and society committed to war. The means to this end was a totalitarian state which would control and indoctrinate society, political institutions and the economy. One should argue, however, that this intended transformation was at best only partial and at worst one based entirely on propaganda. The dismal performance of the Italian economy and armed forces coupled with a collapse of morale on the home front during the Second World War , somewhat dispels the view given that the fascists had succeeded in transforming Italy into a militaristic nation. Similarly, despite a transformation in some of the institutions of state e.g. the destruction of Parliament and civil liberties, many of those of the Liberal state survived. Hence it is difficult to accept that the new state was anything approaching totalitarian.

Italian fascism influenced certain patterns of social behaviour, in particular with regards to leisure and the intelligentsia[1], but it did not transform society. As with economic policy, much of what was implemented was based on propaganda. Despite its outward appearance, the fascist regime was based on an element of consensus[2]. It relied on the conservative support of those groups which had brought it to, and supported it in power[3]. Indeed when an explicitly radical transformation was attempted in the late 1930's, it brought the regime an unpopularity from which it failed to recover. The complete collapse of

fascism and the lack of support it commanded in 1943, show the extent to which the regime lacked hegemony. It was a regime which had, in some periods, commanded acceptance but it never enacted a real transformation of Italy.

Consolidation of power.

The period from 1925 - '28 saw the foundations laid of the new fascist state. A series of statutes were passed by the monarch with little discussion in the Chamber of Deputies. Through this legislation of 1925 - the *Legge Fascistissime* - the work of repression was extended. The control over the press was tightened, all journalists were to be registered and every newspaper to have a director appointed by the government. All freemasonry[4] and similar secret society activities were banned in May of that year to be followed by the establishment of government control of local government through the appointed *podestas*[5]. In December 1925 a further Press Law was introduced which brought the press even more into line with the regime. Only state registered journalists could write and their registration could be removed for criticism of the regime. Another law of the same month stated that no law could be presented to parliament without Mussolini's consent and that cabinet ministers would be responsible to him and not to Parliament. The monarch's powers were reduced and consisted chiefly of the power to appoint and dismiss the prime minister. In January 1926 the prime minister was authorised to govern by decree[6] when he believed necessary. This was to form the basis of fascist rule - over 100,000 decrees being passed by 1943. The year saw a further increase of repressive legislation. After three assassination attempts on his life[7], a law was passed in November 1926 which provided the death penalty for any actions undertaken against king or the head of state i.e. Mussolini. In the same month, a 'Special Tribunal for the Defence of the State' was set up to try opponents of the regime, the so called 'political trials', all opposition parties were banned and the police were allowed to banish 'enemies of the state' to remote parts of the land (this punishment was known as *confino*)[8]. Those deputies who had walked out of the Chamber of Deputies in June 1925 in disgust, were barred entry on return. A new electoral law of May 1928 ended any charade of democracy by abolishing universal suffrage and restricting the vote to men over 21 who paid syndicate rates or taxes of over 100 lire p.a.. In any election the 400 candidates were to be submitted to the electorate by the Fascist Grand Council and voted for or rejected en bloc.

Fascism restrained

Whilst altering the institutions of state, Mussolini simultaneously dealt with the more radical elements of the fascist movement. In October 1925 he ordered the squads to be dissolved and dismissed the powerful PNF secretary Roberto Farinacci[9]. In 1926 the party's nature was altered by an influx of new members, 338,000 in one year. The local structure of the Fascist party was abolished in October 1926 and the PNF given a new organisation. This consisted of all appointments being made from above and an ending of the party's political role. In February 1928 the Fascist militia was incorporated into the regular army, thereby reducing its independence of action. The Fascist Grand Council was made an important organ of state, in theory at least, and given widespread constitutional powers[10]. This was the climax of the fusion of state and party.

Economic and social change

The economy was to be organised along the lines of a Corporate State which entailed creating institutions and structures which would incorporate the interests of both employers and unions. The strengthening of fascist unions or syndicates was a main aim of the new regime. However, it was of importance that this was at the expense of other unions and not in relation to the interests which had been so influential in bringing Mussolini to power. In April 1926, a law introduced by Alfredo Rocco, the Minister of Justice recognised a number of labour syndicates and established compulsory arbitration in industrial disputes. The syndicates were not given a role in government, however and were forbidden to become involved in strikes or lockouts. As part of the 'corporatist' ideology, a Ministry of Corporations was set up in 1926 to be followed in 1929 by a National Council of Corporations. This latter body was created to arbitrate in disputes in the interests of national production. Economic policy itself was dominated by the creation of the '*quota novanta'* in 1926. This revalued the lire from 150 to 90 to the pound, thereby creating a new course in policy by encouraging the turn away from exports to an economy dominated by subsidised heavy industry[11]. To counter the impact of the world-wide depression of the early 1930s, the government lowered money wages and, in November 1934, encouraged a forty hour working week. This kept unemployment down to perhaps 2.0 million in 1933 and 900,000 in 1936 but at the cost of a reduction in real wages by 10%. An important innovation in capital finance took place in 1931 with the creation of the state backed *Istituto Mobilare Italiano* (IMI) and in 1933, the Institute for Industrial Reconstruction (IRI) which gave industry long term protection from bankruptcy. The latter organisation became the means through which the state intervened in the management of industry. By 1939 the state had an interest in a range of large industrial concerns such as ILVA (steel) or Ansaldo (shipbuilding).

In agriculture the state intervened, mainly for ideological reasons, Mussolini stating his desire to 'ruralise Italy'. The aim to be self sufficient in wheat in times of war was the rationale for the 'Battle for Wheat' embarked upon in 1925. Through the use of high tariffs (by 1933 it was 750 lire/tonne) and improved farming techniques such as the introduction of modern farm machinery, the production of wheat grew by around 50% between 1925 -'35. Consequently the importation of foreign wheat fell by 75%. The government also intervened to encourage land reclamation. Agriculture in the previous century had been blighted by malaria, the spread of which was encouraged by marshy land. Accordingly, the Liberal state had encouraged reclamation as part of the improvement of the countryside. The 'Mussolini Law' of 1928 furthered this process by offering huge sums of state capital to finance suitable projects. In some areas this policy bore impressive results, such as the Pontine Marshes[12] near Rome which were reclaimed for cultivation. The economic problems of the predominantly agricultural Southern economy remained. In the 1920s the quota of Italian immigrants was cut by the US, with the consequence that by the 1930s the yearly migration was only 5% of its 1910s figure. This meant overpopulation and internal migration, the population of Rome doubling between 1921 -'40. Such urbanisation was in part due to the damaging effects of the 'Battle for Wheat' yet contradicted the aim to 'ruralize' Italy. Closely linked to agricultural policy and this supposed 'ruralization' was the regime's attempt to boost the birth rate. By a series of measures the state attempted to improve fecundity. A bachelor tax, 'marriage loans', family allowances and employment preferment to the productively married were some of the measures introduced in the so-called 'Battle for Births'.

Relations with the Church

A long standing problem for the Italian state had been the hostility to it from the Catholic Church[13]. This was tackled by the regime through the negotiation and signing of the Lateran Treaties in 1929. This series of measures included the creation of the Vatican and its recognition as an independent state of 108.7 acres. A concordat regulated the activities of the Catholic Church, ensuring the survival of lay groups and accepting religious education in secondary schools[14]. The papacy received an indemnity payment of 750 million lire and 1 milliard lire in state bonds as compensation for land lost before 1870. This led to a less tense relationship between church and state although there was still to be friction. In 1931 'Catholic Action' a Church youth organisation was set up and consequently partially suppressed as it offered pastimes such as sports which closely matched the activities of fascist youth groups. The Catholic student organisation (FUCI) managed to prosper in these years and stood, again, as a rival to the fascist regime. The popularity of Church education grew as state reforms altered the nature of Italian secondary education. The sum result of the 1923 reforms of the Minister of Education, Giovanni Gentile, was a reduction in technical education and an increased stress on literature, philosophy and history. It probably was the introduction of a compulsory examination sat the end of secondary schooling which helped boost the numbers of students in Catholic secondary schools to around 100,000 in 1940 from approximately 30,000 in 1927.

Social behaviour

The regime attempted to promote its values through propaganda and leisure activities and until 1936 this was relatively benign. In 1925 the *Opera Nazionale Dopolavoro* (OND) was set up to co-ordinate leisure activities. Known as the *Dopolavoro*, its membership grew to 4 million by 1939, attracted in the main by the cheap holidays and the wide variety of recreation on offer[15]. The fascists created the *Opera Nazionale Balilla* in 1926 to indoctrinate the young. Formed primarily as a militaristic organisation, it catered for all ages from six to twenty one. Again, membership became the norm as was conformity in most of society. Only 11 out of 1,200 professors refused swear an oath to the fascist regime and state dominated broadcasting was generally popular. In 1934 and 1938, the regime basked in the glory of successive World Cup victories. The cinema was generally popular despite being censored and, from 1934, it was funded by the state. From 1937 all aspects of the media were controlled by the Ministry of Popular Culture. The late 1930s saw a change in the emphasis of the regime's social policy. In 1938 the 'reform of customs' was introduced. This included an insistence on the use of the fascist salute, the widespread wearing of uniform and the Italianisation of English phrases which had crept into common usage e.g. cocktail became *coda di gallo*. More sinister was the introduction of anti - Semitic legislation despite a previously sympathetic attitude to Italy's 45,000 Jews. Following a press campaign and the issuing of a 'Manifesto of Racial Scholars' by the Ministry of Popular Culture, anti - Semitic legislation was introduced on August 3rd. By this, all Jews who had taken up residence in Italy since 1919 were to leave within six months, Jewish teachers and students were barred from universities and schools, marriage was banned between Jews and non- Jews and Jews were forbidden to own substantial business interests or land. The measures resulted in the emigration of 6,000 Jews but alienated the establishment, Church and business who all found such an application of fascist ideology repugnant.

Foreign Policy

In 1924 Mussolini managed to persuade Yugoslavia to recognise Fiume as Italian which was an important symbolic triumph[16]. In 1925 he then managed to present himself as a diplomat of stature by signing the Treaty of Locarno in person and by attending the Stresa Conference a decade later[17]. Of greater significance was the invasion of Ethiopia in October 1935 which took place to fulfil Mussolini's colonial ambitions and partly to avenge Adowa. Defeat for the Ethiopians was relatively swift as over half a million men were thrown into the conflict. Despite the application of sanctions voted by the League of Nations in November 1935, the Italian armies commanded by General Badoglio had seized Addis Ababa by May 1936. The triumph for Mussolini was complete but it was won at a considerable financial and diplomatic cost, the estrangement from Britain and France having important long term implications. In 1937, Italian forces became heavily involved in the Spanish Civil War on the grounds that Italy could not 'permit' the establishment of a 'communist' government on the Mediterranean. Italian forces contributed little to the Nationalist war effort despite comprising of 75,000 troops and 1,400 pilots. In March 1937 they suffered the ultimate humiliation of defeat at the Battle of Guadalajara at the hand of an army with a heavy

presence of Italian anti-fascist volunteers. Such involvement further estranged Italy from Britain and France and pushed her closer to alliance with Nazi Germany. In October 1936 the two fascist countries had signed an agreement about Austrian independence and in November 1937 Italy joined into an anti-communist pact with Germany and Japan. The following month she withdrew from the League of Nations. Despite the threat that *Anschluss* posed in 1938 and despite a mending of relations with Britain which culminated in an Anglo-Italian Pact of November of that year, Italy concluded a close military alliance, the 'Pact of Steel'[18], with Germany in May 1939.

Italy was unprepared for war and the regime was horrified by the news of the German invasion of Poland in September 1939. To avoid humiliation, Italy remained neutral or 'no-belligerent'[19]. By May 1940, however, the prospect of easy pickings with the imminent collapse of France plus the fact that the regime's whole rationale was based on war led to a declaration of hostilities against the allies[20]. Italian military involvement in the war was constituted of a series of disasters. In October 1940 Mussolini's army invaded Greece only to suffer a series of reversals which resulted in the resignation of Marshal Badoglio in December. The Italian army were driven out of East Africa by the spring of 1941 and had to be rescued by German forces after being defeated in the North African campaign by the British. Strategic errors and problems of supply simply lowered morale further amongst the armed forces and on the home front. This growing crisis was

reflected in Mussolini's dismissal of eleven cabinet
members in February 1943. The following month
saw a series of strikes in industrial centres such as
Turin which reflected the weakness of the regime.
There is no doubt that the establishment which had
brought Mussolini to power was actively conspiring
to depose him from spring of that year. On 9/10th
July, Sicily was invaded by the Allies and, far more
significantly, Rome was bombed for two hours on
19th July. The fascist Grand Council, which had not
met since 1939 was convened and criticised
Mussolini. On July 24th the King dismissed
Mussolini and had him arrested. The government
which replaced him was led by General Badoglio.
Although Mussolini was restored to power in the
North as leader of the ill-fated Republic of Salo, it
was only as a puppet of the Germans. In April 1945
he was strung up in the Piazzale Loreto in Milan by
the partisans.

ANALYSIS.

Introduction.

The Fascist regime remained in power for eighteen
years. Its explicit aim, as presented in its propaganda,
was to transform Italy into a militaristic nation. All
social and economic policies were designed with this
end in mind. Similarly, institutional structures were
altered and political life changed to facilitate and
reflect this process. However, much of the supposed
transformation of Italy in this period was superficial.
The weight of evidence points to a failure of fascism
to radically transform Italy. There was change, in
particular of institutions and institutional
relationships, but this was often only partially
successful. The military and economic performance
in the Second World War, and the obvious lack of
support it engendered, are the most striking
indicators of the failure to effect a transformation.
Yet there are other pointers which lead to the same
conclusion; the hostility to fascist ideology, the failure
of social and economic policies, the continuity in
power of much of the establishment and the blatant
gap between the myth of the regime as portrayed
in its propaganda and reality.

A militaristic nation?

It is most obvious that Italy was not transformed into
a nation which had adopted the regime's slogans of
'believe, obey, fight'. War was at the centre of fascist
ideology, whether it be real warfare or preparation
for it such as the 'Battles' for wheat or births. Yet when

drawn into the Second World War in 1940, the regime's insistence that it was ready to fight such a war, e.g. Mussolini's 'eight million bayonets', was exposed as pure invention. Italy performed so disastrously in the war for the single reason that the economy had not been transformed into one capable of sustaining a major war. In 1940 Mussolini had expected a rapid peace, but the fact that Italy did not join the war in 1939 reflected the concern that the armed forces were woefully under prepared. The army in particular lacked the means to fight a mechanised war, production of tanks peaking at 185 a month in June 1942 which was totally inadequate. Similarly, the army received too few vehicles for transportation of men and materials, only around 80,000 between 1940-'3. This constrained the tactical options of the army whose planned strategies were already extremely limited, as can be seen by the dismal failures in Greece and Africa in 1940-'1. To make matters worse, production of armaments and war essentials actually fell during the war e.g. in 1941 Fiat produced approximately half the number of vehicles it produced in 1938! The 227,000 soldiers on the Eastern Front were very badly equipped to fight any type of war. The reason for this was a shortage of fuel which reduced Italy's productive capacity to a fraction of her enemies. Whilst Italian steel production fell to 1.9 million tonnes in 1941, Russia was producing 25 million tonnes and the UK 14 million tonnes. The fascist regime failed to transform the Italian economy into one which was self sufficient and could provide in times of war, in fact the opposite was true. As the war progressed Italy became totally reliant on imports of oil from

Romania and coal from Germany and these were both woefully insufficient. In practical terms it made all armed forces uncompetitive. The air force was expected to undertake the main burden of war in the Mediterranean as the Italian navy had no aircraft carriers. This was hampered by lack of aviation fuel. There was no co-ordination of the armed forces with often tragic results, in 1940 during the battle of Punta Stilo, Italian ships were bombed by their own air force. What is remarkable is that Italian economic policy before the war was geared to rearmament and *autarky*[21], by 1939 the state had built up a crippling debt of 12.7 milliard lire in the main trying to reach this end. This policy was a failure on a grand scale, despite 15 billion lire a year being spent on the military.

The efforts of the regime to transform the economy to support a war failed. The bureaucracy which developed as a result of the state interference of the 1930s placed a constraint on enterprise and development. The nature of economic development under the fascists resulted in cartels and mergers which produced monopolies such as Fiat, Olivetti or Pirelli. This limited the scope for innovation which was essential for a war economy, e.g. Italian aircraft such as the Fiat CR 42 were consistently outperformed by the Spitfire or Hurricane. Too much money was wasted on the colonisation of Ethiopia which brought Italy little tangible gain.

An ideological transformation?

Despite all the propaganda, the fascist regime failed

to transform Italian society into one which would actively support and participate in war. Quite the opposite is true, in fact, which underlines the superficial effect that fascism had even after fifteen years in power. The *Dopolavoro* was harmless in itself, and popular for that, but beneath the message of sport and recreation lay a more sinister aim. The youth groups such as the *'Balilla'* were created and run with the explicit aim of producing a generation imbued with militarism and nationalism. In schools, students were indoctrinated by the fascists into accepting their view of the past and of the value of warfare as a means to satisfy the nation's honour. The popularity of the Ethiopian war as shown by the 250,000 wedding rings donated to the war effort (including those of the king and queen) and the huge celebrations after the fall of Addis Ababa in 1936 it might be accepted that the regime had, in fact, effected a transformation. This was not the case, however, and the lack of support for the war from 1940-'43 contrasts with the response in Germany or Britain to state propaganda. It is true that the fascist war aims were unclear and the early defeats in the war reduced morale. This was compounded by bombing, which led to mass de-urbanisation - half a million had left Milan by 1942. The strikes in Turin and elsewhere in 1943 were symptoms of a far wider malaise. The Catholic Church maintained its independence and Pius XII's condemnation of aspects of the war in 1942 further undermined the regime. This was not an isolated incident, however. Throughout the war the church's newspaper *Osservatore Romano* criticised the war and attracted a growing readership. In reality not only had fascism

failed to transform society but the Fascist party itself was not prepared for war and crumbled in the face of public criticism and derision.

It is valid to argue that the regime was accepted without significant opposition until the late 1930s. In the main can be explained by the fact that fascist policy was conservative, stressing traditional values and preaching a message of social stability and economic harmony. Behind this was the failure of radicalism and the defeat of ideology early in the dictatorship. Despite the propaganda, radical fascism was undermined in the early years of the regime with the absorption of the militia into the army in 1924, the purging of *squadristi* from the PNF in 1925 and the change in PNF membership from 1926 - '28. The fascist regime relied on the support of the establishment and it ruled in such a manner not to clash with these interests. The central reason, therefore, for the lack of a transformation of Italian society was the new fascist regime shared many of the interests of the state that preceded it. With the introduction of policies which owed their origins to radical ideology, e.g. the 'reform of customs' or the anti-Semitic laws of 1938 came widespread criticism and alienation from the regime. The contradiction is apparent when one considers that perhaps 5,000 or 10% of the Jews in Italy were members of the PNF. However, perhaps the most startling evidence to prove the widespread rejection of fascist ideology was the non participation in and often active subversion of the Final Solution from 1941-43. It is the fact that until September 1943, no Jew under the jurisdiction of the Italian armed forces was ever surrendered to the Nazis. This is not to deny that there were not Italian anti Semites, in fact Mussolini encouraged the careers of fanatics such as Telesio Interlandi, editor of *La Difesa della Razza* (the defence of the race). There is substantial evidence of anti Jewish atrocities in the Republic of Salo from 1943-4. The trial of Eichmann and the numerous documentaries made since the war, however, have recounted the widespread kindness shown to Jews throughout Italy from 1938 -'45. There are many examples of when Italian soldiers and civilians risked their lives helping Jews find shelter. In March 1943 the German ambassador visited Mussolini to protest against the protection the Italian army had afforded the Jews of Croatia. It is too simplistic to explain this simply in terms of the Italian 'national character'. In fact it is far more appropriate to ascribe such actions to a rejection of fascist values and the failure of a fascist hegemony. It also is evidence of the limitations to the power of the fascist, or any other state, to affect an ideological transformation of its citizens.

A totalitarian regime?

It should be argued that the fascist state was never totalitarian in that it never prevented the existence of rival loyalties to institutions other than those of the state. Therefore there was always a significant alternative to fascist ideology. This was apparent in the form of the church and, still to an extent, Liberalism. The Lateran Treaties assured the position of the Church within a fascist state but it also ensured that fascism would not be unchallenged. Therefore, Catholic Action and Catholic youth movements flourished as alternatives to the Balilla, membership standing at 1 million and just under 400,000 respectively by 1939. The Catholic student movement FUCI formed another rival to the official organisations. It is true that the church sanctioned the regime and that the Lateran Treaties gave the fascist government enhanced legitimacy, yet they also made impossible totalitarian rule. It should be pointed out that by 1940 one in every six secondary school students were being educated by the Church and not the state and these were often the children of the middle classes. As education forms the basis of indoctrination so these figures reveal the extent to which the regime fell short. Even during the war the Vatican radio and *Osservatore Romano* continued to present an alternative interpretation to that of the regime with important consequences for morale. It was this alternative which might explain the longevity of the regime and the lack of a coherent opposition. For the failure of the fascists to create a totalitarian regime made overt opposition unnecessary when non fascism as represented by the Catholic organisations was possible.

An institutional transformation?

The fascist years in Italy saw a transformation in the institutions of state and in the machinery of government. In particular, the loss of freedoms associated with the Liberal State, were a radical departure. The abolition of a Parliamentary democracy was begun with the suspension of provincial elections in June 1926 and continued by the electoral law of May 1928. This new departure was confirmed by King, Senate and plebiscite in 1929. It overturned the *Statuto* which had formed the cornerstone of Piedmontese and Italian constitutions since 1848. The final act in the destruction of the democratic state occurred in 1939 with the 'abolition' of Parliament i.e. the replacing of the Chamber of Deputies with a 'chamber of fasci and corporations'. The change to a system of non democratic rule was perhaps the most significant transformation brought about by the fascists. Yet even this must be qualified by the fact that the transformation was accomplished in the interests of the establishment and old elites. The fact that the *Statuto* was overturned did not mean that the establishment which had ruled by it, lost power. In fact, the opposite is true. When the fascist state is studied in depth it is valid to point out that there was much continuity. This does not deny that the fascists introduced change and that there was a new political elite ruling through new political institutions such as the Grand Council. The point is that all of this institutional change should be placed in the context of a continuity of power. The monarchy maintained its power and influence despite the fact that Victor Emmanuel seemingly accepted fascist policy without question, himself signing decrees ranging from the anti - Semitic legislation of 1938 to the abolition of the Chamber of Deputies a year later. Despite this seeming subservience and that the monarchy lost powers of choice over ministers and even the royal succession to the Grand Council in November 1928, it should be pointed out that Mussolini was sacked by the King in 1943. As the monarchy, in consultation with the establishment brought Mussolini into power, so it removed him.

That is very clear evidence as to the limitations of any fascist take over of power. The fascists set up a police state and the introduction of *confino* against individuals suspected of opposition was widespread. However the police remained in traditional hands, the chief of police from 1926 - '40 was a career Prefect, Arturo Bocchini. There was no Gestapo, and apart from the new 'Special Tribunal' set up in 1926 to try political crimes the courts remained independent to the same extent they had been under the Liberal state. In local government, elections were abolished in 1926, but to many of the local elites this was greatly welcomed. Similarly the suppression of the squads in 1925 followed by the reform of the PNF weakened the influence of the *ras*. In fact, the fascist state relied on the traditional ruling elites acting as Prefects, to govern the localities effectively. In the main, the Prefects were still chosen from the same class, in 1940 still only 1/3 being political appointees. The municipalities were controlled by the *Podesta* whose appointment was in the hands of the Prefect. Therefore, destruction of democracy consolidated the old elites. When they came into rare conflict with Mussolini such as over the anti -Semitic laws of 1938, it was the regime which suffered. The Senate retained a non fascist influence, there were still forty senators in 1939 who were not members of the PNF. More importantly, the nature of fascist rule meant that the civil service, which was still dominated by the old elite, had greater influence than pre 1925. Although new institutions were created and the state 'transformed', in reality there was no great shift in power from 1925 - '43, in fact these years saw a retrenchment of power.

Economic policy - propaganda or reality?

Most of the economic and policies of fascism were based on propaganda. It was extremely important to the regime that it convinced its supporters and the wider world of its radical nature. That was the basis of its claim to power: to rule Italy in an alternative fashion to the Liberal state. Yet for the fascist leadership it was not so simple, for important business interests had to be appeased and served. This contradiction of aims explains the substance of economic policy in particular. The ideological element of fascist economic policy such as the corporate state remained more propaganda than reality. It is true that the fascist unions -syndicates- did play a role in the economy but it was different to that envisaged by fascist ideologues. State intervention to help business, however, was an important development. However, as has already been shown, it fell far short of fulfilling its aim of creating an economy geared for war.

A key element of fascist ideology was the role of syndicates in the economic system and the state. Essentially the argument was that in a corporate state which presented a 'third way' to capitalism and socialism, labour as represented by the syndicates should become a central institution of the state when joined with employers in corporations. To placate those interests which had put him in power, however, Mussolini sanctioned Rocco's 1926 legislation which explicitly prohibited syndicates taking a role in government. Although a Ministry of Corporations was founded to be followed by a National Council of Corporations in April 1929, the effect of these bodies was minimal. They failed to create corporations in important industries where employers and employees would make important planning decisions, in fact the 'corporate state' was very much propaganda. The syndicates played a traditional union role e.g. they pressured the state to introduce the 40 hour week in 1934 to cushion against unemployment. Importantly they pressured the state to introduce welfare provisions, some of which were forthcoming such as family allowances. The syndicates were popular - by 1940 - in Milan alone their membership stood at over half a million. Perhaps the real significance of the syndicates was that they were less likely to engage in strikes, although disputes did periodically occur. In the sense that labour had been tamed through the syndicates there was a significant change, but much of the credit for that might go to the fact that the Depression weakened the hand of labour everywhere. The leading planning role that fascist propaganda and ideology ascribed to corporations and the syndicates did not materialise. In most cases the employers maintained their power and syndicates failed to prevent a falling the standard of living of over 10% between 1925 -'38.

A real change within the economic sphere was in the creation of institutions to support business and the banks in the Depression. These institutions were the instruments by which Italian capital really could dominate the economy unlike during the years of the Liberal State. The IRI, which was ran by a non-fascist Alberto Beneduce, helped cushion the effects of depression by supporting ailing industries and developed into an important investor. It was instrumental in projects such as the development of the hydro-electricity industry which produced nearly 15 billion kilowatt hours in 1937. Most of this was produced in the North and electricity was the twice the price in the South. By 1939 the IRI owned a share in many of Italy's largest companies including Ansaldo and ILVA. This was a departure from previous practice, in particular the shift to a reliance on state capital. However, this change should be put into the context of the main aim of economic policy, to build a structure capable of sustaining a war. To that end, many of the pressing problems of the Italian economy were ignored. The South continued to stagnate and policies such as the 'quota novanta' or autarky simply made matters worse. It is true that manufacturing production rose by 3.9% p.a. in the 1930s but this was mainly concentrated in the select heavy industries such as chemicals, steel and ships which were northern based. These were the same concerns which had benefited from government policy and protection pre-1914. The only industry in the South lay in ships and steel near Naples. The vast majority of industry and industrial workers were based in Piedmont, Liguria and Lombardy. Also as with pre-1925, there was little stimulation of export industries and Italy still trailed the leading industrial powers in terms of output, in 1940 its production of 1 million tons of pig iron placing it at the same level as Luxembourg. As pointed out above, the cartelisation of industry which was a product of state policy had serious implications for innovation and production in wartime. So state policy did not fundamentally alter the Italian economic structure. There were some important innovations, in particular the IRI, but there was much continuity of interests. The worsening regional economic disparity in the period serves to show the limited extent of real change.

The famed drive for self sufficiency and autarky was again as much to do with propaganda as reality. Land reclamation was a much heralded policy but the figures of only around a quarter of a million hectares improved at a cost of 8 million lire put the policy's achievements into perspective. Similarly the 'Battle for Wheat' was not the triumph for Italian agriculture it was proclaimed to be. In 1933, Italy still imported 504 million lire of wheat. The figures for increased wheat production given above can be countered by a decline in other areas of agriculture, e.g. pasture, fruit and olives all declined by up to 20% in the period of fascist rule with serious consequences for the South in particular. The expressed policy was to 'ruralize' Italy but the drive for increased wheat production hastened urbanisation as it discriminated in favour of the larger landowners and those who farmed more fertile soil. Yet this was the dilemma of fascist agricultural policy: it promised to transform peasant life, but the basis of fascist support had been the large landowners. In reality, agricultural policy was formed in their interest. The regime attempted to prevent the drift to the cities with a series of powers given to prefects and decrees such as that in 1938 which stated that one could only register as unemployed in the municipality of one's residence. This, as with all other attempts, failed.

The point should again be made that the failure of the regime to impact change reflects the non totalitarian nature of the state and the chasm between intent and action. The population policy, the so called 'Battle for Births' had little effect on the birth rate which declined up until 1936. In fact the birth rate in 1936 was only 2/3 of its 1911 figure and this despite all the inducements to procreate. Despite the fact that a bachelor paid double income tax, in 1939 over 1 million Italians paid for the privilege. Late marriage (at around 28 for men from 1936 -'40) was still the norm although vast amounts of cash were handed out by the regime in 'marriage loans', in 1939 this cost the state 89 million lire. The state's pronatalist policy was a grand failure.

Conclusion.

A judgement has been made on the ability of the fascists to transform Italy - since that was their stated intention. They failed to turn Italy into a military state just as they failed to militarise its population. Similarly, whilst it is clear that the fascist regime was tolerated for much of its period in power, it was because of minimal radical reform. In reality, economic policy was geared to cushioning against the worst ravages of the Depression and protecting industry from foreign competition. Although institutional structures were altered, the power structure which they reflected was not. Perhaps the most significant transformation came about as a consequence of its failure to translate propaganda into deed. The collapse of the fascist state in 1943 came directly as a consequence of Italy's disastrous performance, both militarily and economically, from 1940 -'43. Its eventual replacement, the Italian Republic proclaimed in June 1946 ushered in an era of government which in many senses was the converse of the fascist state. Italy was to be democratic, republican, non imperialist and anti nationalist. Under the new constitution civil liberties, the rights of labour were enshrined and the state weak. This was the most enduring transformation of the fascist years, its legacy of a state and society run on lines which were its ideological opposite.

[1] Until 1938 the regime was accepted by a cross section of the intelligentsia which was subsidised and flattered by Mussolini. This did not mean that they automatically accepted the party line as many did not e.g. Croce or Morandi. They were tolerated by the regime, however, as it reflected Mussolini's personal intellectual pretensions.

[2] This is a word associated with the fascist regime until 1938 and is used to convey the social stability and lack of opposition to the regime up unto this point.

[3] These groups, the monarchy, landowners, business had turned to fascism as a mass movement in an era of mass politics which would protect their interests despite its radical elements.

[4] The purge of freemasons form the civil service was a cornerstone of fascist ideology. It did little to reduce the power or character of the civil service, however, most civil servants in 1938 being career bureaucrats.

[5] Appointed by the Prefects, the *podestas* had considerable power. Most often they would be chosen from the traditional ruling elites.

[6] A decree being an order which has the force of law.

[7] The first attempt on April 7th was undertaken by a deranged Irish noblewoman, Violet Gibson. She only managed to injure his nose.

[8] Despite its fearsome name the tribunal passed only nine death penalties up until 1940. *Confino* was a traditional form of punishment, the feeling being that for a northener to be sent to the South of Italy was punishment indeed. The most celebrated victim of confino was Antonio Gramsci, the communist leader and writer, who was left in peace to write his influential collected works.

[9] Farinacci was the most extreme and outspoken of the fascist local bosses, the *ras*. His behaviour as PNF party secretary, encouraging squad violence and purging the party played into Mussolini's hands as it gave him the excuse to reduce the influence of the ras nationwide.

[10] These constitutional powers included relations with the papacy and the monarchical succession.

[11] The policy damaged those industries which had boomed pre war, in particular cars and textile firms which had to diversify to survive.

[12] The marshes were close to Rome and the site of many a propaganda film.

[13] This stemmed from the incorporation of Rome into the new Italian state in 1871 against the wishes of the papacy.

[14] These were considerable points for the church when one considers the anti clerical nature of legislation in the 1890s in particular.

[15] The *Dopolavoro* was authentically popular, its activities taking in not only leisure but welfare.

[16] This was of particular importance because of the attempted takeover of Fiume by nationalist Gabrielle d'Annunzio. Its failure in 1920 and the compromise of making Fiume an independent city by the Treaty of Rapallo left the nationalist cause

undiminished. Mussolini's success in 1924 underlined his nationalist credentials and boosted his personal standing.

[17] His commitment to Austrian independence in 1935 at Stresa, shows how, even at this time, Mussolini was very much in tune with Britain and France against German expansionism.

[18] This pact was never ratified by the King, Victor Emmanuel, and therefore was technically invalid.

[19] Neutrality was widely welcomed in Italy, especially as the Germans had only recently signed a pact with Stalin. It was highly ironic considering that many of those who had initially supported fascism did so to oppose the 'neutralists' of the First World War.

[20] The King gave his consent to the declaration despite widespread opposition amongst armed forces, establishment and the populace at large. Mussolini was very much the driving force for war.

[21] *Autarky* was the policy of economic self sufficiency which had been the inspiration for initiatves such as the 'Battle for Wheat'. It became all important with the introduction of League of Nations sanctions against Italy after the invasion of Ethiopia.

BENITO MUSSOLINI

Chapter 3

HOW STABLE WERE THE 'STRESEMANN YEARS' OF THE WEIMAR REPUBLIC, 1924-'9?

Introduction

It has been assumed that the years 1924-'29 were ones of relative stability in Weimar Germany after the upheavals caused by revolution and hyper-inflation in the years immediately following the First World War. However, such an analysis is far too simplistic. These so called 'Stresemann[1] Years' saw a failure to rectify the structural political defects of the Weimar state. In reality, the weaknesses which were to lead to a breakdown of democracy can largely traced to the middle years of the 1920's - the stress on the fact that these years were ones of political stability is misleading. Similarly, this period saw the beginnings of economic depression and social discord which were to be accentuated by the collapse of 1929. It was only in diplomacy, in which Stresemann excelled, that Germany's position was structurally improved. The view that stability was reflected in the cultural flowering of the Weimar period is also misleading. The opposite is true, the modernism of 'Weimar culture' stood in stark contrast to the conservatism of large sections of a disapproving society. One should argue that these years were ones of cultural polarisation which was to be reflected in the events of the early 1930's and beyond. Any stability of these years is relative to the periods which immediately preceded and followed them. In actual fact, the Stresemann years were anything but stable.

Background 1918-'24

Defeat in the First World War resulted in the collapse of the Imperial Regime[2]. The last months of 1918 and early ones of 1919 saw the spread of revolution which threatened the established order. In November 1918 a Bavarian Socialist Republic was set up against the background of mutiny in the armed forces such as that at Kiel[3]. The abdication of the Kaiser Wilhelm II confirmed on November 28th was followed by a struggle between the extreme left, the Spartacists[4], and the Social Democrats to fill the vacuum. The former opposed a plan to set up a National Assembly and staged a revolt in January 1919 which was crushed. The National Assembly was elected in January and met at Weimar the following month with the Socialists comprising the largest group. The most important issue facing the new state was the peace treaty drawn up by the victorious powers at Versailles. In June 1919 the cabinet under Gustav Baüer accepted unconditionally the Allies' proposals despite the fact that the Weimar Assembly had voted for a conditional acceptance only[5]. The constitution adopted in July set up the Reich as a parliamentary democracy with the Chancellor and cabinet needing majority support in the Reichstag. There were constraints on the democracy, however, and the constitution provided for a strong executive in the form of a President elected on a seven year cycle and with strong counterbalancing powers. The President could dissolve the Reichstag and counter legislation by calling a referendum. Most importantly, by Article 48 the President could suspend the Reichstag and rule by decree in the case of 'national emergency'.

The constitution also introduced proportional representation voting which had a strong influence on the nature of politics in the years ahead. The background to the constitution's formation was bitter social conflict which was reflected in events such as the creation and suppression of a Soviet republic in Bavaria in April-May 1919. This unrest continued into the following year with an attempted monarchist coup - the Kapp Putsch in March and another Spartacist revolt, this time in the Ruhr, which was put down by troops in April.

The pressure continued on the new Republic to adhere to the terms of the Versailles treaty. The treaty had been based on Article 231 by which Germany was made responsible for the war and thereby liable to pay reparations to the Allies. On 1st May 1921 the victorious powers finally set reparations at 20,000 billion gold marks[6]. This plan was accepted by the Weimar government which feared further occupations such as the Allied occupation of Duisburg, Düsseldorf and Ruhrort in March 1921 in response to a German rejection of earlier terms. The main problem for the German state was that the currency had already become de-stabilised as a consequence of the war, reparations simply made matters worse. All German politicians hoped for a revision of these terms as well as the terms of the treaty. Chancellor Wirth and Foreign Minister Rathenau[7] who accepted the reparations plan hoped that by doing so they could influence the Allies into changes. In July, 1922, however the government asked for a moratorium to suspend payments, the Allies refused and in January 1923 they occupied the Ruhr. The denial of vital revenue from this area and all the other financial pressures resulted in hyper inflation. In December 1922 the exchange rate stood at 8,000 marks to the dollar, by November 1923 it had reached 4.2 billion. The currency collapsed[8] as did the stance of 'passive resistance' the government had taken over the occupation. The new government under Stresemann began to take measures to stabilise the situation. In September 1923 payments of reparations were resumed and the French agreed to set up a commission to study the problem of the German economy. In November 1923 the Rentenmark was established by the Finance Minister Hans Luther to replace the old mark . This new currency was covered by mortgage bonds on industrial and agricultural assets and the printing of it was strictly limited[9]. There was still unrest on the extremes of politics, in October 1923 a KPD[10] inspired uprising was crushed in Hamburg. The following month a NSDAP[11] *putsch* in Munich led by a certain Adolf Hitler was contained by the police.

Political manoeuvrings 1924-'9

Stresemann's government collapsed in late November 1923 to be replaced by one led by Wilhelm Marx of the Centre Party[12]. The Republic was in a state of emergency which was only lifted in early 1924. In the Reichstag elections of May of that year the Nationalist and Communist parties made significant gains at the expense of the more moderate parties of the centre[13]. This made much more difficult the passage through the Reichstag of the Dawes Plan[14]. The collapse of the SPD[15] vote in the election, down from 171 to 100 seats, and their ideological divisions over whether they should take part in 'bourgeois coalitions', made the task of pushing through the agreement on a two thirds majority even harder. There were many aspects of the Dawes Plan which were unpalatable to many parties within the Reichstag in particular the acceptance of the continuation of reparation payments. Born out of the financial chaos of 1923, the plan suggested that the French leave the Ruhr and that further sanctions be harder to apply. Reparations would be paid over a longer period and credit would be advanced to help rebuild the German economy. The Plan was approved in the Reichstag on 29th August 1924 with the necessary support coming from members of the DNVP[16].

In December 1925, a new election brought a revival in the fortunes of the SPD, gaining 31 seats (mainly at the expense of the KPD who lost 17). The new coalition of January 1925 led by Hans Luther excluded the socialists but included members of the nationalist DNVP for the first time. This was to prove the undoing of this government as the DNVP objected to the terms of the Locarno treaties negotiated by Stresemann and only passed with support from the SPD in November 1925. A new coalition was sought but the SPD still objected to joining a coalition with 'bourgeois parties' (i.e. the DDP, Centre or DVP). This stalemate was reinforced by the new President Hindenburg[17] who was elected to office in April 1925 and made it clear that he would not accept SPD participation in coalition government. Instead, in January 1926, Luther formed

a minority coalition involving the Centre Party, DVP[18] and DNP but this cabinet was not to last for long, foundering on the instructions it gave to the country's diplomatic corps to use the old imperial flag[19]. The Reichstag passed a vote of no confidence in May 1926 and Luther was replaced by Wilhelm Marx as Chancellor. On June 20th 1926 a referendum took place on the confiscation of royal property, the vote failing to reach the required majority. The Marx cabinet relied on the support of the same parties as its predecessor and until late 1926, had the tacit support of the SPD. That support was removed in late 1926 and the cabinet fell. It was replaced in January 1927 by another Marx government which this time included the nationalist DNVP. There was always a strain on the cabinet, the interests of these 'bourgeois' parties being divergent. Nevertheless some important social legislation was passed including a comprehensive reform of unemployment insurance passed in July 1927. The coalition collapsed in February 1928 over the issue of religion in education.

The election of May 1928 was an important turning point for the Weimar Republic. The left made important gains, the SPD increasing its share of the seats by 22 to 152 and the KPD showing a rise of 9 seats to 54. More significantly, as the parties of the centre and right saw their share of the vote drop, so there was a rise in the vote of splinter parties such as the *Bauernbund* (23 seats and 4.5% of the vote) which represented farmers interests. The sharp fall in the DNVP vote (down from 20.5% of the vote in 1924 to 14.2% in 1928) was to cause convulsions within the party. The publishing of what became known as the Lambach Article in 1928 was the trigger for a shift in the party's policy. Written by Walter Lambach, the piece urged DNVP members to renounce their nostalgic monarchism and become reconciled to the permanence of the Republic. Such was the backlash amongst party members that Alfred Hugenberg was elected leader of the DNVP in October 1928 on an unavowedly anti-democratic platform and promptly brought the party into alliance with the NSDAP. Similarly the Centre Party saw a drift to the right which resulted in the election of Monsignor Kass as party leader in December 1928. In June 1928 a ministry dominated by socialists was formed led by Hermann Müller and including members of the DDP, DVP, Centre and BVP[20]. This so called 'grand coalition's' main task was to steer through the Reichstag the Young Plan of 1929. Linking the French evacuation of the Rhineland to the issue of reparations, the passage of the plan was temporarily halted by a petition from the right (the so called 'Reich Committee') which contained some four million signatures[21]. Demanding a repudiation of Article 231 of the treaty and an immediate evacuation of areas occupied by allied powers, the number of signatures was enough to demand a referendum on the issue (on what became known as the Freedom Law) which was duly held on December 22nd 1929 and resulted in a defeat for the right. This was despite the support for their campaign from the President of the Reichsbank Schacht. Although the Reichstag eventually passed the relevant Young Plan legislation in March 1930, events were increasingly becoming overshadowed by the collapse of the New York Stock Exchange in October 1929.

Foreign Policy - The work of Stresemann 1924-'9

After the antagonism in relations between Germany and the Allied powers, 1924 saw a significant change in attitudes on all sides. The election of a Labour government under Ramsay MacDonald in Britain in January 1924 produced a more conciliatory line to Germany and this was maintained by subsequent governments. For the German foreign minister Stresemann[22] this created opportunities to achieve some revision of reparations and Versailles through constructive diplomacy. This was further strengthened by a change in French attitudes in the wake of the Ruhr occupation[23] of 1923. Although the primary aim of the French was to maintain security, the international backlash against the perceived aggression of the French resulted in a more conciliatory policy towards Germany, in particular in the wake of a victory for the left in the elections of May 1924. The acceptance of the Dawes Plan in 1924 was the first step in the move towards all interested parties acting collectively. By it, the London Plan of reparations was put on hold until 1929 and Germany was to receive foreign aid of 800 million marks.

The change in emphasis could be seen in the diplomatic events of 1925. There was a very real possibility at the end of 1924 that an Anglo-French agreement would be brokered to address the issue of French security. Stresemann saw this possibly leading to the prolonging of the occupation of the Rhineland and therefore proposed a settling of the security issue. This was made more urgent by the statement issued by the Allies in January 1925 that they would not vacate Cologne by the due date of the 10th of that month. Months of negotiations followed which culminated in the meetings at Locarno in October 1925. The Locarno treaties which were the outcome, guaranteed Germany's western borders and all parties agreed not to use force to alter these frontiers[24]. A series of arbitration treaties were signed at Locarno between Germany and France, Poland, Czechoslovakia and Belgium. Stresemann held out against a Locarno style settlement for Germany's eastern borders hoping for revision of them at a later date. Not only was he successful, but he managed to secure guarantees from France that it would not attack Germany in the event of a war with Poland in which Germany was not the aggressor. Soon after the treaties, the first evacuation from the Rhineland took place in 1925. However, despite further talks on the subject between Stresemann and the French foreign minister Aristide Briand in September 1926, there was no more movement on the issue until 1929.

As part of the Locarno agreements, Germany was admitted to the League of Nations on 8th September 1926. It was agreed at the talks that although she was granted a permanent seat on the Council, she was free from the military obligations as laid out in Article 16. This was part of the process of calming the doubts expressed by the Soviet Union over Germany's admittance. To this end, in April 1926,

the Treaty of Berlin was signed between the two countries which reaffirmed the Treaty of Rapallo of 1922 and stressed each country's neutrality in the event of attack by a third power. Despite these overtures, or perhaps because of them, relations between Germany and the Western Powers continued to improve. In late 1926, occupation forces were cut by a further 60,000 and in January 1927 the Allies finally withdrew the IMCC[25] from Germany. There were also economic side effects, a commercial treaty being signed between France and Germany in August 1927. However, some tensions did remain which were heightened by Hindenburg's speech on 18th September of the same year in which he denied Germany's war guilt and repudiated Article 231.

The Young Plan of 1929 was Stresemann's last major diplomatic achievement. Most importantly, it linked the evacuation of the Rhineland[26] to the successful revision of the reparations programme. There were considerable other benefits to Germany, including a rescheduling of the debt to 2,000 million Reichmarks to be paid yearly until 1988. Stresemann did not see the treaty ratified, his death coming in October 1929.

Weimar culture

The trends in German culture of modernity and liberation had their roots in pre-war Germany. The years 1924-'9 saw the development of a style which was unique to Weimar, that of *Neue Sachlichkiet*. This was essentially a stress on objectivity and a matter-of-factness and manifested itself in variety of media. Architecture and consequently many other art forms were dominated by the *Bauhaus* movement associated with Walter Gropius. He stressed the relationship between art and technology, the functionality of design and the freedom from the past. The influence of the *Bauhaus* should not be underestimated, providing the inspiration for creativity as diverse as the painting of Kandinsky to the architects and urban planners who built the new towns in the mid '20s and in particular Weissenhof near Stuttgart in 1927. To mirror the departure from tradition was the music of Schönberg and the ironic literature of the *Neue Sachlichkiet* writers such as Thomas Doblin or the satirist Kurt Tucholsky. The theatre and cinema in the mid 20's was dominated by plays which reflected social issues with a seriousness which also permeated much of literature. In particular, in this period there were numerous works published based on the Great War, of special note being the pacifist *All Quiet on the Western Front* by Erich Maria Remarque published in 1928.

ANALYSIS.

Introduction.

Any stability which existed in the Weimar Republic between 1924-'9 was relative to the chaos of the post war years and the collapse of democracy which followed. The weaknesses created by the constitution and the underlying fragility of the political system remained, only to be masked by a temporary improvement in the economy and lessening of the extremist threat. In particular, this period saw the development of executive power and influence which was to be used with such a damaging effect on democracy from 1929-'33. To counter this there was no parallel development of parliamentary democracy, to some extent quite the opposite, it being stunted by weak coalition government and the tactics of the SPD. Towards the end of the 20's there is a discernible shift in attitudes to the right and political extremes and away from the established centre and democratic parties. It is in these years, therefore, that the seeds were sown for the collapse of democracy and with that in mind it is difficult to speak of this period being one of real political stability.

The same conclusion should be drawn about the economy and society in these years. Although there was economic improvement and a greater degree of social harmony than in the previous five years, recovery was still precarious and there were signs of deepening problems before the collapse of 1929-'30. It is in the area of foreign affairs more than any other that there was significant structural improvement, in that the policies of Stresemann effected real change. Yet even in this field it is difficult to talk of stability, such were the structural problems that remained. One can argue that the structural instability of the Weimar Republic was reflected in the conflict of cultural expression between what has been termed 'Weimar culture' and the conservatism of large sections of society. Therefore, any stability in this period of the Weimar Republic was relative, the inherent tensions and the negative dynamic which were inherent in political, economic and cultural life being clearly apparent.

Political tension and instability?

The middle years of the Weimar Republic were marked by an absence of the attempts at extra Parliamentary action typified in the 1918-'23 period by the Spartacist uprising, Kapp Putsch, 'German October' or Munich Putsch. That said, it is still inaccurate to describe these years as ones of political stability as the parliamentary system failed to mature and develop, despite the reduction in threat from the extreme left and right. There are many reasons for this, primary amongst which was the failure of the coalition system to produce governments which had sufficient support to tackle the problems which faced the new democracy. Previous to 1914, political parties did not have responsibility for forming governments or compromising to create viable governments. This naiveté and cultural deficiency became highly apparent during the Weimar years when the parties still acted more as interest groups representing their own sectional interests rather than national parties of government. The most glaring example of this was the behaviour of the SPD although it was a trait common to all the leading parties. Between 1924 and June 1928 it resisted becoming involved in forming viable coalition governments despite its position as the Reichstag's largest party. The main reason for this course of action was a belief that coalition with the 'bourgeois' parties would lead to a compromise of the party's ideals. This was if anything strengthened by the adoption of a Marxist (Communist) based series of policies by the Heidelburg programme of 1925. The consequence of such action was to reduce the influence of the socialists in the Reichstag, although their tacit support for governments such as that of Wilhelm Marx was often the key to that government's survival. Such rejection of political responsibility also weakened the whole process of democracy as it contradicted the concept of representation and accountability. In that the actions played in to the hands of the opponents of the Republic and weakened its political legitimacy. A further example can be seen in the actions of the SPD members in March 1930 in bringing down the Müller government by vetoing any short term agreements with the coalition partners the DVP and Centre Parties over unemployment insurance. Such action was essentially suicidal.

By the time the SPD were prepared to form a coalition after the May election victory of 1928, the political polarisation which was a developing feature of the period, meant that forming a stable majority government had become nigh on impossible. This was not only the responsibility of the SPD. From his election as President in 1926, Hindenburg worked tirelessly to create coalitions which would exclude the SPD.[27] Therefore the Müller government formed in June 1928 was beset with problems from the start, many of the DVP and Centre parties reflecting Hindenburg's reluctance to accept SPD dominance of a government despite the fact that they were by far the largest party in the Reichstag. Responsibility for such behaviour has also to be shared amongst all the parties whose actions throughout the period in question were often at best counter productive. Even though the 1928-'30 coalition was able to steer the Young Plan through the Reichstag there was no consensus on how to deal with the country's growing economic and social problems. In fact, such a consensus was absent for most of the 1920's within governmental coalitions and was often the main cause of their downfall, e.g. the collapse of the Luther cabinet in late 1925 after the withdrawal of the DNVP over the Locarno treaties. The consequence was minority coalition governments under Luther and Marx, based on the support of Centre, DVP and DNP deputies, but which were largely ineffectual to stem the tide of growing unemployment. Yet whenever the coalitions were broadened as discussed above, or in the case of the fourth Luther government from January 1927-May 1928, they were hamstrung by the tensions of the differing aims of the parties, in this case disagreements over education. The narrowing of interests of the mainstream parties was eventually a cause of their decline, voters looking increasingly to parties of the extreme. This sectionalism was already apparent, however, between 1924-'29 e.g the DVP's ever increasing association with the interests of business causing it to refuse coalition with the SPD in 1926.

Presidential interference

Such undoubted instability as explained above, implicitly undermined the democratic process. As parliamentary government failed to fulfil its potential, so there was increasing scope for the interference of the President. This, of course, was a vicious circle with executive interference undermining the legitimacy of the Reichstag as the most important element within the constitution. The blame for this must be placed with the constitution itself which reflected an unease with democracy as shown in the powers extended to the President in Article 48 or the ability to dissolve the Reichstag. It is assumed that Hindenburg acted to undermine the democracy in his use of Article 48 and political manoeuvrings after the economic crisis of 1929. This is correct, but what is often ignored is the level of Presidential interference in the political system before that date. It has already been shown that Hindenburg attempted to exclude the SPD from office, and when they formed a coalition government in 1928, insisted that they gave it as wide a base as possible. There is little doubt that the fourth Marx government formed in 1927, included the DNVP on the insistence of Hindenburg thereby ruling out the possibility of a 'grand coalition'. In blocking the attempt of the Ministry of the Interior in 1926 to formalise the use of Article 48, Hindenburg gave significant notice of the importance he already gave to extra parliamentary rule. He most definitely was not alone in this period in that view, the election of Hugenburg to the leadership of the DNVP in October 1928 clearly showing the anti democratic sentiments of a majority of the party's membership. The results of the 1928 election also highlight a subtle but real shift away from the established parties to those on the fringes of political life, the protest interest parties such as the *Bauernbund* or the *Deutsche Landvolk* which gained 10 seats. It is true that the vote for the NSDAP in this election fell to 2.6% but the KPD vote rose to 10.6%. What this election shows is that the drift away from the centre ground parties began before the 1929 crash and that growing popular disillusion with the Republic was increasingly manifesting itself at the ballot box.

Economic and monetary stability

Between 1924-'29 there was significant monetary stability which was particularly important to those classes who had suffered because of the hyper-inflation of 1923. This was due mainly to the establishment of the Rentenmark and the consequences of the Dawes Plan. In the wake of the Plan, there was a significant influx of foreign capital to the tune of 25.5 billion marks between 1924-'30. The vast majority of this capital came from the USA and it enabled the reconstruction of German industry to take place. This was also due to the delaying of payments at the highest rate stipulated by the Dawes Plan[28], thereby stimulating some inward capital investment. As a consequence, national income was 12% higher in 1928 than in 1913 and industry experienced spectacular growth rates. The collapse of the economy in 1929 is seen as the catalyst for increasing economic discord and polarisation of employers and labour. This is too simplistic an analysis. Whilst the period 1924-'9 saw currency stability and economic growth, it did not experience peace in industrial relations but quite the opposite. Whilst there was monetary stability in this period other areas of the economy suffered continuing change and unrest. The main problem for both sides was to adjust to a period of relative normality in comparison with the recent years of turbulence. Yet that turbulence left a legacy which made industrial peace virtually impossible.

This legacy also had serious social and political repercussions. The main issue for employers from 1923-'29 was to claw back the initiative which they felt they had lost to labour from 1918-'23. Although all sides had temporarily accepted the spirit of co-operation expressed in the constitution of 1919, the mid 20's saw a increasingly concerted attack by employers on the rights of labour. In 1923, the legislation of 1918 which enforced an eight hour day was altered to allow employers to institute a ten hour day in some circumstances. The union demands for higher wages in this period were resisted by employers to the extent that between 1924-'32 around 76,000 cases were brought to arbitration. There is little doubt that employers increasingly resented having to use such a procedure and in late 1928 over 210,000 workers in the Ruhr were locked out rather than the ironworks owners accept the findings of arbitration. The fight by the DVP on behalf of industrialists who opposed increasing unemployment insurance contributions in 1929-'30 was symptomatic of a growing economic polarisation. This manifested itself in the refusal of the DVP to collaborate constructively with the SPD from the mid 1920's. In fact the growing antagonism between the parties which made coalition government nigh on impossible, had its roots in increasing conflict between those groups the parties represented. It is correct therefore to see the period in question as one of economic growth, yet the term 'stability' is an inappropriate one to apply, in particular with industrial relations in mind. There is also little evidence in the voting figures of a return of confidence in the mainstream parties of the Republic, in fact as has been shown, quite the opposite is true[29]. Unemployment figures also tend to bear out the view that many of the economic problems may have had their roots in the supposed years of stability, e.g in late 1928 the figure of those without work stood at 3 million or 15% of the workforce.

Foreign policy success?

The naming of this period the 'Stresemann Years' is indicative of the fact that it was in the sphere of foreign relations that it has been felt the Weimar Republic succeeded most. It is true that significant progress was made towards the revision of some of the articles of the Versailles treaty which so dominated the foreign policy of the period. This was done by Stresemann through the policy of 'fulfilment' i.e. by fulfilling the terms of the treaty, Germany could

show how unjust and unworkable they were. Simultaneously, Germany worked towards agreement with the Soviet Union as shown by the Treaty of Berlin of 1926, which prompted the Western Powers into a more sympathetic approach to Germany. The achievements of German diplomacy in the Stresemann era are considerable and in particular the greater understanding with France as reflected in the Locarno Treaties of 1925. This contrasts with the attitude of the French government to the German moratorium on repayment of loans in 1923 and the consequential invasion of the Ruhr. Yet one must not exaggerate the extent of the French change in attitude towards Germany. The meeting between Stresemann and Briand at Thiory in September 1926 failed to find a solution of the contentious issue in Germany of France's continued occupation of the Rhineland as there was not sufficient political willpower in France to withdraw. However, the fact that a solution to the problem of the Rhineland was linked to reparations repayments by the Young Plan in 1929-'30 was testimony to both the desire of all parties to find a collective solution to the problems facing them and the success of Stresemann's tactics to effect a revision of Versailles. This was not the only success of this policy. Most importantly, Stresemann's policies resulted in Germany regaining diplomatic influence and the ability to influence the Allies. The absence of a Locarno style settlement of Germany's eastern borders in 1925 is a case in point as is her acceptance into the League of Nations in 1926 with a permanent seat on the Council. Perhaps most important were the two plans to reorganise reparations, Dawes and Young, which gave Germany some breathing space to develop her economy. The removal of the IMCC in 1927 or the French withdrawal from the Ruhr all point to the success of the policy of fulfilment in achieving positive outcomes for German interests.

However, the success Stresemann enjoyed was not recognised universally in Germany where there was no consensus apparent on the best tactics to force a revision of Versailles. In this sense, therefore, it is difficult to assess Stresemann's diplomacy as resulting in domestic political stability for this was not the case. There is little doubt that the Dawes Plan was fundamental in strengthening the German industrial base and better relations with the USA in particular, improving trade. Yet the main issue of Versailles, Article 231, reparations and the 'stab in the back' continued to undermine the Weimar Republic. Whilst 'fulfilment' brought some relief, the policy did not alter the humiliation felt in large sections of German society. There are numerous examples of this, not least the referendum of December 1929 on the Freedom Law which opposed the signing of the Young Plan. The fact that 5.8 million Germans were prepared to vote for a law which rejected Stresemann's policy and labelled him a traitor is suggestive of the perceived limitations of the success of the 'fulfilment' policy. The issue of Versailles plagued politics and was the main cause of disagreements between the DNVP and the DVP/DDP, e.g. their coalition in 1925 collapsing over Locarno. There is little doubting Stresemann's achievements, in particular with regard to Locarno. Through the lack of military means at his disposal, there were precious few options available than to follow the peaceful policy he did. Although his policy did lead to greater economic stability, the gradual approach to the restoration of German power meant that those who proposed more radical action to end Versailles were still able to act as a de-stabilising influence on German politics. It was not the policy of Stresemann which was responsible but the existence of the Versailles treaty.

Cultural divisions?

What is popularly described as 'Weimar Culture' was only one manifestation of cultural expression in the mid 1920s. The objectivity of the *Neue Sachlichkeit* contrasted with the nostalgia, romanticism and escapism of popular literature, the modernity of *Bauhaus* with the traditional taste of the majority of the population and so on. There is little doubt that cultural divisions ran deep which very much reflected the political and social polarisation of the period. Therefore, the cultural developments of the period did little to help stabilise the Republic but became part of the process by which it was undermined. The development of *Neue Sachlichkeit* is a case in point as its matter-of-fact style was used to expose the weaknesses and injustices of Weimar society as it had developed by the mid 1920s. In the theatre, the works of writers such as Friedrich Wolf and Peter Lampel became the dominant force of the mid-20's, concentrating on a range of social issues. An excellent example was Lampel's *Revolte in Erziehungshaus* performed first in 1928 which led to a prolonged debate on education reform. That the movement summed up the public mood is a debatable issue, for as will be seen, the public mood was very much divided. What it did reveal was a disenchantment with Weimar and a scepticism about its ability to reform. This is very clear in the writing of authors such as Alfred Doblin who in the 1929 novel *Berlin Alexanderplatz*, castigates the decline of the Weimar years. Alienation from the Weimar Republic was a common feature of writing on the left and right but it was also prevalent amongst an artistic community which attacked its failure to construct a viable new political culture. This is best represented in Ernst Toller's *Hoppla wir leben* (1928) in which a revolutionary is released from an asylum after many years incarceration, only to find that society and politics have stagnated and gone into an ethical decline.

As shown with the Versailles treaty, the war's legacy was to create division within Germany and this was reflected in culture. Whilst those of the right such as Arthur Moller and Oswald Spengler preached an anti-democratic German 'destiny', literature which glorified the experiences of the trenches became highly popular through the work of authors such as Ernst Jünger and Werner Beumemelberg. This was countered by the anti war offerings of Remarque and Renn. It was not only in its treatment of war that literature was divided. Whilst the *Neue Sachlichkeit* author described social issues so in the cinema films such as *Die freudlose Gasse* (1925) by G.W. Pabst, discussed the topical in a rational manner. Yet there was a parallel culture at this time which very much rejected the objectivity if *Neue Sachlichkeit* and found

refuge in escapism. This was reflected in the increased sales of authors such as Hans Grimm or Lons Flex. In the cinema it found its expression in the films of Charlie Chaplin. The significance of their popularity was that their works of comedy, fantasy, nostalgia and mythology were in direct contrast to the modernity of *Neue Sachlichkeit*. The important point is this, neither of these two poles of cultural expression gave support to the regime or the values which underpinned it. Instead they stood as opposites yet both in antipathy to the Republic. So whilst the Weimar Republic became identified with cultural change and liberation, these forces did not act as a foundation for stability. In reality quite the opposite is true for those who felt left behind or alienated by the changes blamed the new democracy for such 'decadence' and in particular the freer attitude towards women and morals. What 'Weimar Culture' and such movements as the *Bauhaus* represent is the opposite of stability. The onus on experimentation, a rejection of the past and of traditional values mirrored a socio-economic and political system in flux.

Conclusion

Therefore, it is with great care that one should use the term 'stability' to describe the years 1924-'9 in Germany. Whilst recognising that there was a return to comparative normalcy after the turbulence of the immediate post war years, stabilisation was only very relative. The work of Stresemann in foreign policy, the consequential re-stabilising of the currency, economic growth and the decline of the extremist threat to political stability are the much used indicators to prove a return to stability. However, it should be argued that these indicators are essentially superficial ones. The structural weaknesses of the political system remained and were to become apparent in this period. In the failure of the political system to assert its primacy and the development of Presidential influence one sees that the causes of collapse of Weimar democracy in the 1930's have their roots in the mid 1920's. Similarly, monetary stability disguised worsening industrial relations and growing unemployment. These factors were to worsen after 1929 but, again, one sees signs of instability in the mid 1920's. When judged against the yardstick of diplomatic achievement, Stresemann was highly successful. The policy of fulfilment won breathing space for the Republic in terms of reparations and a return to international respectability. Yet, Stresemann aside, Versailles in itself continued to be a fundamental factor of instability of Weimar. It was the democracy's 'Achilles heel' and Stresemann's German contemporaries often judged his diplomacy in a far more negative light without the historian's hindsight. This underlying instability was mirrored in the cultural diversity and conflict of the mid 1920's which acted not to legitimise the Republic but further undermine it.

[1] The Stresemann Years were named after the politician Gustav Stresemann who was Reich Chancellor in 1923 and Foreign Minister from 1924-'9. In the latter role he was highly successful, hence the period's title.

[2] The Imperial regime is defined as that which came into being as the German Empire declared on 18th January 1871.

[3] The mutiny of the sailors at Kiel began on October 28th, 1918 and was caused by the order to set sail and face the British navy. The refusal of the sailors to do just that resulted in a rebellion which spread to other ports.

[4] The Spartacists were led by Rosa Luxemburg and Karl Liebknecht. Their aim was to enact a revolution and form an alliance with Soviet Russia.

[5] The tactic of a conditional acceptance only was used to avoid invasion. The majority of delegates could not bring themselves to vote for a treaty which was near universally despised in Germany.

[6] This agreement was known as the London payments plan and stipulated a payment of 2,000 million gold marks a year plus 26% of the value of Germany's exports.

[7] Rathenau was shot by a member of a far right organisation, Consul, in June 1922.

[8] The collapse in the currency had a hugely damaging effect on whole swathes of society making savings, pensions and many salaries worthless. The middle classes suffered terribly as did German labour, by the end of 1923 only 29.3% of trade unions members worked full time.

[9] The mortgage on all industry and land was placed at 3,200 million gold marks. Luther took further measures to balance the budget including the sacking of 700,000 state employees.

[10] The *Kommunistische Partei Deutschlands* (KPD) were the German Communist Party. The threat they posed between 1919-'23 was very real but with the defeat of the 'German October' in 1923 their influence began to wane.

[11] The *Nationalsozialistische Deutsche Arbeiterpartei* or Nazis was at this stage a party very much on the fringes of politics.

[12] The Centre Party was predominantly Catholic but relatively flexible on economic issues. It therefore played a role in all coalitions between 1919-'32.

[13] The far right nationalist party, the DNVP gained 105 seats. Up until 1928 it was prepared to take part in Weimar politics, being twice a member of coalitions between 1925-'8. The KPD increased its share of the vote in this election, winning 62 seats.

[14] The Dawes Plan was put together by a committee of economists and other experts with the expressed aim of finding a solution to the reparations problem.

[15] The Sozialdemokratische Partei Deutschlands (SPD) was the main socialist party in Germany and the largest party in the Reichstag from 1919-'30.

[16] The Deutschenationale Volkspartei (DNVP) was the largest party of the right throughout the period in question. As a large party it was a broad church including former members of groups as diverse as the pre-1914 Conservative Party, the National Liberals and Christian Social groups. Although many within the party opposed both Versailles and the democratic republic, there were others who were prepared to work within the system as this vote shows, to improve the lot of their constituency.

[17] Hindenburg's election was to have serious consequences for the survival of the Republic, in particular when one takes into account the powers invested in the Presidency by the constitution. As the victor of the Battle of Tannenberg in 1914 he was much respected. He won the election because of the split in the anti right vote, gaining 14.6 million votes in comparison to 13.7 million votes for Marx of the Centre party and 1.9 million for Thalmann of the KPD.

[18] The Deutsche Volkspartei (DVP) were formed in December 1918 as an offshoot of the old National Liberal Party. Led by Stresemann it increasingly became dominated by business and industrialists. The Deutsche Demokratische Partei (DDP) was the main inheritor of the liberal tradition.

[19] The old Imperial flag being the black, red and white tricolour.

[20] The *Bayerische Volkspartei* was a Catholic party based in Bavaria. In the 1928 election it gained 3.1% of the vote.

[21] The campaign was particularly important for the fact that it included, on the invitation of Hugenburg, Adolf Hitler. In being associated with respectable figures such as the industrialist Fritz Thyssen or the leader of the Pan-German League, Heinrich Class, Hitler's stature amongst those of the right grew considerably.

[22] Stresemann's aims in foreign policy were revisionist in that he desired to see an alteration to the terms of Versailles. He differed from many of his contemporaries in his methods of working towards achieving that end.

[23] At this point the French under Poincaré were extremely belligerent towards Germany and hoped for a withdrawal of the German frontier to the Rhine. On the basis that Germany had defaulted on payments, Poincaré ordered the occupation of the economically important Ruhr.

[24] The parties involved were Germany, France and Belgium with Britain and Italy guaranteeing the agreement.

[25] The Inter-Allied Military Commission (IMCC), was set up to oversee German disarmament as demanded by the Versailles treaty.

[26] By the terms of the Plan, this was to be undertaken by the Allies by June 1930 which was five years ahead of the schedule laid out by Versailles.

[27] The coalition option which spread from the SPD to the DVP is known as the 'broad coalition', the best example being that of Muller between June 1928 to March 1930.

[28] The Dawes Plan allowed the Germans to pay at the rate of only 1 million marks a year until 1929 when the rate would be increased to 2.5 million marks.

[29] Whilst the vote of the Centre Party held up from 1920-'29, it and the DDP saw a considerable drop from the election of 1919. Similarly, the number of votes won by the DVP fell from 3.9 million in 1920 to 2.7 million in 1928.

STRESEMANN

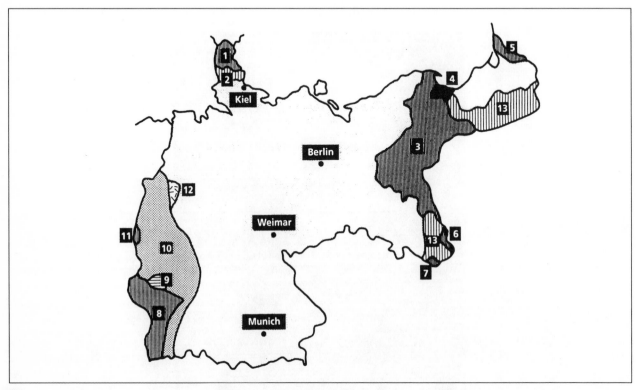

1 Northern Schleswig ceded by Germany to Denmark

2 Holstein remained part of the German Empire after a plebiscite.

3 Posen and West Prussia were ceded to Poland.

4 Danzig was made a free port

5 The Memel region was ceded to Lithuania.

6 Eastern Upper Silesia was ceded to Poland.

7 Hüttschin territories were ceded to Czechoslovakia.

8 Alsace-Lorraine was ceded to France.

9 Saarland.

10 The Rhineland was occupied by Allied troops and became a demilitarisied zone for Germany.

11 Eupen - Malmedy was ceded to Belgium

12 The Ruhr district belonged to Germany but was occupied by France and Belgium in 1923.

13 Plebiscite areas.

GERMANY: FIRST WORLD WAR LOSSES

WHY DID THE NAZI PARTY RISE FROM OBSCURITY TO OFFICE IN JANUARY 1933?

Introduction.

The administering of the oath of office to the new Chancellor Hitler[1] on January 1933 did not constitute the immediate creation of a dictatorship. Power was seized by the Nazis in stages throughout 1933/34 yet the coming into office at the start of 1933 marked the crucial point in the transition from Presidential government to fascist dictatorship. The explanation for the rise of the Nazi party should be divided into three factors. One should place the emergence of a previously marginalised organisation into the context of the growing crisis of the Weimar state as explained in the previous chapter. The turning point or catalyst which translated this crisis into widespread lack of confidence in the established political system was the economic collapse of 1929. That the Nazi Party was to become the beneficiary of this discontent was due to its organisational and ideological flexibility which enabled it to become the natural repository for the hopes of the millions of disenchanted Germans. Yet this on its own does not explain why the Nazi Party was on the verge of seizing power in 1933. The answer lies in the destruction of the Weimar democracy by the establishment[2] between 1930-'33. Led by Hindenburg[3], the aim behind such a policy was the restoration of authoritarian[4] government and it was as part of this process Hitler was appointed Chancellor and in this political environment that the Nazi party flourished. It was from this base that Hitler indeed restored authoritarian rule within Germany, but not in the manner his sponsors had anticipated. The rise of the Nazi Party

was neither inevitable or inexorable but essentially reliant on the conditions of the establishment's making.

The Origins of the Nazi Party 1919-'24.

The Nazi Party was born of humble origins. Founded in January 1919 as the German Workers' Party by Anton Drexler[5] it developed against a background of political turmoil. It assumed its new name, the National Socialist German Workers' Party (NSDAP) and a 25 point programme at the Hofbrauhaus meeting in Munich in February 1920. Included in this manifesto, written by Drexler and Hitler, were themes which remained constant throughout the 1920s and beyond; the revision of the Treaty of Versailles[6], the destruction of the establishment and anti-Semitism. Through the work of Hitler and other new members including Ernst Röhm[7], Alfred Rosenburg and Dietrich Eckhart[8], the new party became one of the more noticeable amongst the many splinter groups of the right. In December 1920, the party increased its membership and was able to buy a local newspaper which renamed the *Volkischer Beobachter*[9]. In the following three years, Hitler consolidated his leadership of and influence on the party becoming chairman of the party in July 1921. This was followed by the creation of the SA[10] which was to become the paramilitary wing of the party. As Germany was in political turmoil, so the SA was involved in widespread political violence and thuggery. On 4th

November 1921 it engaged in a running battle with socialists at a political meeting in Munich and in street violence against the same foe in Coberg in October 1922. By mid 1923 the party had some 55,000 members[11], many of whom were attracted by the 'catch all' manifesto and the radical nationalism of the movement. Throughout the Ruhr crisis of 1923[12], Hitler and the Nazi press kept up its barrage against the Weimar Republic. After an abortive attempt at direct action on May 1st, the Nazis attempted a further coup on 8th/9th November. Known as the Munich Putsch[13], it resulted in seventeen dead and the arrest of Hitler. His trial for high treason in February/March 1924 was transformed into a propaganda coup by giving him a nationwide platform for his beliefs. The sympathy of the judges ensured he received the minimum term of five years imprisonment[14].

Reorganisation 1924-28

Incarcerated in Lansberg Castle in 1924, Hitler embarked on the writing of *Mein Kampf*[15] which was to become his enduring political testament. In what is a generally incoherent and rambling text, Hitler developed his *Weltanschauung* (world view or outlook). The main points were the elimination of Jewry from German life and the provision of *Lebensraum (living space) in the east for the* Germanic peoples. In May 1924, the Nazis in alliance with other parties of the right won an impressive 1.9 million votes (6.5%) in elections to the Reichstag. By the December elections of the same year, that figure had fallen to around 907,000 votes (3.0%). Two months

after Hitler's release from prison on 27th February, the NSDAP was refounded. Throughout the year the party was reorganised into a centralised, bureaucratic entity. An index of all members was created and, at the party conference at Bamberg in February 1926[16], a new autocratic and centralised structure was discussed which stressed complete obedience to Hitler and adherence to the 'Programme of 1920'. This was formally accepted at a membership meeting of the party in May 1926. Also important was the failure of the challenge of Gregor Strasser to the insistence of Hitler that all action had to be dictated by the policy of 'legality'[17]. As part of this drive, Hitler attempted to quell the SA. The staged march past many of its members at Weimar in July 1926 was intended to show the public at large the extent of party control over its paramilitary arm. In the summer of 1926, Captain Franz von Pfeffer was appointed leader of the SA[18] to implement guidelines on the movement's role. There were other administrative and organisational reforms undertaken in these years. In 1926 the Hitler Youth and the Nazi Students' Association were founded. At the Nuremberg Party Congress in 1927, further reorganisation took place with unsuitable *Gauleiters* being replaced and the central bureaucracy further reorganised. Despite such changes, the performance of the party in the election of May 1928 was dismal, it registering only around 800,000 votes (2.6%) and gaining only 12 seats in the new Reichstag.

Growing electoral success 1929-30

Such a poor overall result masks the fact that when

campaigning on specific regional issues, the Nazis were able to attract a significantly higher proportion of the vote - in 1928 in the agricultural North West. The disappointment at the ballot box acted as a stimulus to further reorganisation and October 1928 saw the creation of the first Nazi professional body, the Association of National Socialist Jurists. This was to be followed in 1929 by similar bodies for doctors, teachers and students. Of far greater significance to the fortunes of the party was the opportunity presented by the campaign against the Young Plan[19] from the summer of 1929. Formed by the leader of the DNVP, Alfred Hugenburg, the Reich Committee for a Referendum to oppose the Young Plan included respected national political figures of the right including Franz Seldte of the *Stadhelm*[20] movement. Hugenberg also invited the NSDAP to join the coalition which Hitler accepted but only after prolonged negotiations on finance and guarantees of Nazi independence. The subsequent referendum in December 1929 on the so call 'Freedom Law'[21] resulted in humiliation for the coalition, only 13.8% voting in favour. The campaign, though, had given the considerable national exposure of both Hitler and the spectacular Nazi rallies such as that of 200,000 party members and supporters at Nuremberg in August 1929. The impact at the ballot box was immediate, local council elections in November 1929 saw a significant rise in the Nazi vote and in the state election in Thuringia in December they polled 11.3%.

The Wall Street crash[22] and the rise in unemployment had an important effect in further polarising German politics. In March 1930, the Müller cabinet broke up after the strains of the coalition became all to apparent over the issue of unemployment insurance. The new cabinet was formed on 30th March under the leadership of the Heinrich Brüning of the Centre party, yet it was heavily influenced by President Hindenberg. Although commanding only minority support in the Reichstag, Hindenberg made it clear that if the government was brought down by a vote of no confidence he would use Article 48 of the constitution to rule by decree. The rejection of the cabinet's financial bill[23] in July led to it being reintroduced by decree. A motion was immediately passed in the Reichstag condemning this tactic and demanding the withdrawal of the decree as it had a right to do in the constitution. The President's response was to dissolve the Reichstag and call an election for September 1930 (the finance bill finally being introduced again by decree). This period of turmoil in national politics also saw significant changes at local level. In June 1930, the Nazis won 14.4% of the vote in elections for the Saxony Landtag which was over 9% higher than the previous year. The previous spring, Joseph Göbbels had been appointed to lead the party's propaganda unit and was instrumental in the planning and execution of the comprehensive electioneering programme not only in Saxony but in the nationwide polls. The result in the September election was a triumph for the Nazis. Not only did their representation in the Reichstag increase from 12 to 107 seats, but the vote they captured increased from 800,000 in 1928 to 6.4 million in 1930. In consequence the reformed Brüning cabinet governed with even less support and had to rely on the 'toleration' of the SPD[24] and ever increasingly, the use of Article 48.

Opportunity and expansion 1930-31

The election victory of 1930 acted as an important stimulus for the party membership. Between September and the end of the year nearly 100,000 new members joined up and the period saw spectacular growth in sectional party organisations. Of particular note was the expansion of the NS *Agrarpolitische Apparat* (AA) founded by Walther Darré in 1930. Created with the expressed aims of extending Nazi influence in the countryside, creating a vibrant rural organisation and infiltrating existing farmers' organisations, the organisation was highly successful. Similar campaign tactics to those used at national level meant that the momentum of election success was maintained, throughout 1931 the Nazis averaging around 40% in local elections. However the debate over 'legality' within the party and in particular the SA persisted. In March 1931 the leader of the Berlin SA, Stennes, and some of his members rebelled against the orders of Hitler to obey the law. The revolt failed to win the support of the majority of SA troopers although it highlighted the inherent tensions within the movement. This should also be placed in the context of the crack down in 1931 on the SA in Prussia on the orders of the Prussian Prime Minister, Otto Brann[25]. It was the economic collapse in the summer of 1931 which again gave the Nazis opportunities and turned attention away from their tactics and excesses. The primary aim of Brüning's economic and financial policy had been to remove the burden of reparations. A combination of an impending freeze on payments[26] and the possibility of an Austro-German customs union prompted a flight of foreign capital out of Germany. The result in July 1931 was the collapse of the Austrian Creditanstalt bank to be followed by financial panic and the closure of all German banks for a three week period. The resultant political confusion and the rise in unemployment (which in September stood at 4.3 million) prompted Hugenburg to attempt to re-form a 'National Opposition' of the right with the aim of bringing down Brüning's government. The so called 'Harzberg Front' of Stadhelm, DNVP and Nazis met in October 1931 but collapsed after internal wrangling.

Elections, Tension and Turmoil 1932-33

The presidential election of March/April 1932, saw Hindenberg returned to office but the significance was in the vote registered for Hitler. Despite saturation electioneering, the Nazi leader managed to poll only 30.1% on the first ballot and 36.8% on the second as opposed to Hindenberg's 49.6% and 53%[27]. Yet the Nazis still managed to present such a defeat as a success as their vote had more than doubled from the Reichstag election. Defeat, however, resulted in the emergency decree of April 1932 which banned the SA and SS - mainly in response to the growing street violence and evidence that the Nazis had been formulating plans to stage a coup if Hitler had won the election. Such was move was taken against the background of intrigue amongst the President's ministers and advisers. The Minister of the Interior, General Groener, who had introduced the ban, was undermined by a whispering campaign led by General von Schleicher but with the full backing of the Nazis[28]. As the means by which Schleicher could influence the removal of Brüning and help institute a more right wing government, it was successful, Groener resigning from the cabinet after being shouted down by Nazi deputies in the Reichstag on May 10th. Soon after on May 29th Hindenberg demanded Brüning's resignation which he received the next day. A new cabinet was former with von Papen as Chancellor and Schleicher the new Minister of Defence. The date for new elections to the Reichstag was set for the end of July and the ban on the SA lifted on June 16th. The subsequent street violence in the run up to the election left over 100 dead. It was the perfect excuse for the removal of the SPD dominated Prussian government which was overthrown by von Papen on July 20th 1932. The SPD failed to react and the unions were weakened by the division on the left between KPD and SPD. The elections to the Reichstag eleven days later saw the Nazis their percentage of the vote increase to 37.3% which translated into 230 seats making them the largest party in the Reichstag. Despite such apparent success, the election did not give the Nazis an outright majority or automatic power, von Papen refusing to hand over the Chancellorship to Hitler. In consequence, on the first day of the newly elected Reichstag (September 12th) it was immediately dissolved after the government lost a vote of no confidence by 512 votes to 42. The new election in November saw a fall in the Nazi vote of some 4% (34 seats) but they were still the largest party. Such a result simply reinforced the political stalemate, Hindenberg wishing to continue Presidential government but refusing to appoint Hitler as

Chancellor without his having first achieved a majority in the Reichstag. The Nazi leader having the ability (in coalition with the Centre party for example) to vote down a government at will, the only perceived alternative for the establishment was to rule without the Reichstag and suppress all opposition. In attempting a way out, Hindenberg sacked von Papen and appointed General von Schleicher as Chancellor on December 3rd. His first act was to attempt to draw the Nazis into a coalition by offering the vice-Chancellorship to Gregor Strasser. The leading Nazi's instinct was to accept such an offer as the only way the party was going to gain power but he was forced to back down and resign after a fierce battle with Hitler. Without Nazi support, the von Schleicher government lacked a popular base, a fact which soon became apparent with the strong opposition to his economic policy presented on December 15th[29].

Into Power

From January 4th 1933, von Papen and Hitler held talks about the composition of a future government based on a broad nationalist coalition very similar to the Harzberg Front. Support for such a coalition came from a variety of sources including the Agrarian League and industrialist organisations. This had an impact on Hindenberg who turned to von Papen to form a viable government, particularly as it was clear that von Scheicher could command little support in the Reichstag. As negotiations between von Papen and Hitler progressed, the former conceded the role of Chancellor to the latter but in a cabinet that would be a coalition of the right[30]. It was this factor and the acceptability of the prospective minister of Defence, General von Blomberg[31], which persuaded Hindenberg to accept von Schleicher's resignation on January 27th and to install Hitler as Chancellor on the 30th. Those who believed that they had 'tamed' Hitler and his movement were to be proved very much mistaken. Although his 'Appeal to the German People' broadcast on February 1st was conservative in nature, the SA began to wreak revenge on the enemies of National Socialism. Twenty one days later a decree in Prussia (which had fallen under the jurisdiction of Reich Commissioner Göring) resulted in the police being reinforced by 'volunteers' i.e. the SA. On the 27th of the same month, the Reichstag in Berlin was gutted by fire. A young communist, Marinus van der Lubbe took the blame and the following days saw a clamp down on the left (including the arrest of KPD politicians) and the issuing of a decree ending civil liberties[32]. Despite irregularities and intimidation, the Nazis failed to win an absolute majority in the March election, polling 43.9% nationally. As all KPD deputies were barred from the Reichstag (despite gaining 4.8 million votes), the result gave Hitler a distinct advantage in executing his next move. The opening of the new Reichstag on March 23rd was marked by the presentation of an Enabling Act. By the terms of the Act, the government gave the power to pass laws to the cabinet and allowed the government to alter the constitution as it saw fit. It was passed by an overwhelming vote of 441 to 94, only the much harassed SDP deputies voting against. No more did the government have to rely on the Reichstag or emergency powers to legislate. The Weimar constitution was dead.

ANALYSIS

Introduction

The rise of the Nazi party must be placed into the context of economic crisis, in particular in the aftermath of the collapse of 1929. As the effects were felt across Germany, so the electorate became more receptive to the message of those who offered a radical solution. Added to this factor was the organisational and ideological flexibility of the NSDAP. Its appeal was reinforced by the apparent 'legality' of the Nazi assault on power in the late 1920s and early 30s in contrast to the attempted *putsch* of 1923. Yet none of this is sufficient to explain why the Nazis were brought into and then reinforced in power. The answer lies in the ideological and political aspirations of the German establishment which not only destroyed the foundations of democracy by the use of presidential government but attempted to use the NSDAP as the tool by which authoritarian rule could be re-established. The economic crisis was the pretext for the decline in the power of the Reichstag, but as has been shown in the previous chapter, the expansion of executive power very much began before 1929. Without doubt the Nazi party's message and tactics brought it to the brink of power. That it was achieved, however, was due to the misjudgement of an elite rather than the misplaced votes of a desperate electorate.

The Nazis brought to power

The Nazis were brought into power in 1933 by a class which believed that it could use their organisation to perpetuate its rule. That Hindenberg, von Papen and others had come to rely on the Nazis was due in the main to the disintegration of the democratic system which they had engineered from 1930 onwards. The aim of this elite was the destruction of the hated Weimar and the isolation of the equally despised SPD. That this was achieved should be put down to complex mixture of reasons. Firstly there was considerable cynicism attached to the traditional democratic parties as a result of economic collapse of 1929 and the inability of the system to tackle the root causes of depression. This manifested itself at the ballot box, the DVP[33] vote for example falling to 1.2% of the vote in July 1932 as opposed to 10.1% eight years earlier. Secondly and most importantly, the Presidential powers built into the constitution and in particular Article 48[345] gave Hindenberg the constitutional framework to undermine the constitution. What led to Hitler becoming Chancellor in 1933 was the belief that once this had been achieved, a new regime could be installed peacefully only if it had a basis of popular support and it was this which only the NSDAP on the right of the political spectrum could provide. Therefore, one should conclude that the main reason for the Nazis coming to power was that the destruction of the democracy by the establishment left a political vacuum it could not itself fill. In attempting to use Hitler and his party as the means to confer legitimacy for a new authoritarianism it in fact achieved only to legitimise Nazism.

A key moment in the process in the Nazi rise to

power was the establishment of the Brüning government in March 1930 after the collapse of the 'grand coalition'. This government was the first to be based on presidential and not parliamentary power. The Reichspresident Hindenberg made it very clear from the start that if the minority government was defeated or suffered votes of no confidence at the hands of the Reichstag, then there would be a dissolution of that institution and the nation would be governed by decree. Brüning's first cabinet had minority support from the centre parties but was defeated comprehensively in July 1930 over part of its financial bill. In attempting to pass the legislation by decree, the government was defeated again by 236 to 221 votes. This was within the rights of the Reichstag as defined by a subsection of Article 48. The subsequent dissolution of legislature is fundamental in explaining the Nazi rise to power. It is the most obvious point at which the President and his advisors openly showed their contempt for not only the constitution but the Reichstag and the Weimar democracy. It also marks the shift from parliamentary government to presidential government. It was the latter which created Hitler's path to power as it gave the Nazis a 'legal' route to success which Hitler so craved. At no point did the Nazis achieve an electoral majority, even in March 1933 they gained only 43.9% of the popular vote. It has been often rightly pointed out that the Nazi vote fell in 1932, from 37.3% in July to 33.1% in November, and that the appointment of Hitler as Chancellor was at a stage when the Nazis were declining electorally. Yet this misses the point, for by 1932 elections were not the means by which power was gained, such was the extent of the undermining of the Reichstag.

The appointment of Hitler as Chancellor and the subsequent endorsement of the Enabling Act was part of an acceptance amongst the establishment that a return to a more authoritarian form of rule was desirable at any cost. Actions were therefore undertaken which contravened the spirit and letter of the constitution. However, as these actions were the government's, they were given a kind of 'legality'. Therefore the Nazi rise to power should not be seen as the last gamble of a failing establishment but part of a wider trend. Evidence of this can be seen in Von Papen's coup d'etat against the Prussian government in July 1932. Although the action to depose the government was done in the name of the constitution (Article 48) its legality was highly questionable. That such a take over of power in what had been the cradle of social democracy was met with so little resistance was fatal. As neither the Prussian government, SPD or trades unions resisted the take over of power, so a precedent was set.

The weakening of democracy

The new regime was created as an authoritarian one with a political police which no longer served the Weimar state but obeyed the orders of von Papen and his appointees. This paved the way for the actions of Göring who, as Reich Commissioner of Prussia from January 1933, embarked on an immediate programme of arrests, purges and intimidation which had only a flimsy basis in law. The point is this, the actions of von Papen the previous July had ensured that these actions could be undertaken under a pretence of 'legality' because any legality as defined by the republic's constitution had effectively been destroyed. It was therefore possible for Göring to use the political police to arrest Communists and even, in February 1922, order by decree the recruitment of SA and SS members into that police force. By 1933 the emergency powers of the constitution had been used to effectively destroy that constitution. The Nazi inspired decrees of 1933 which destroyed the foundations of the republic, such as that of the 28th February which enabled interference in local government and suspended basic rights, was possible since this had been the trend of policy for at least three years. Therefore, from February to March 1933 the Nazis were able to arbitrarily seize power in all German states such as Bavaria, Hamberg or Hesse onwards by means which were fundamentally unconstitutional but had the semblance of legality. A typical example was the appointment in March of NSDAP Reich Commissar Karl Krogmann in Hamburg after the SA/SS had taken over the town hall and central government had placed pressure on the democratic government to resign.

The extent to which the democracy had been mortally weakened was reflected in the support given by a cross section of parties including the Centre and DNVP to the Enabling Act of March 1933. By this the Nazis seized power and destroyed the constitution including presidential rule. Support for the Nazi proposal from a wide cross section of the country's political elite, symbolises the alienation that elite felt towards the Weimar democracy and the crucial part they played in its downfall. The misjudgement of von Papen and Hindenberg in believing that they could control and use the Nazi movement is crucial in explaining the Nazi seizure of power but it has to be put into the context of the time. From 1930 onwards, government was conducted by intrigue and deals e.g. the removal of Groener and Brüning from office in May 1932. As a reaction to von Schleicher's economic policy of late 1932 which was seen as far too conciliatory to the left, initiatives were undertaken to create a government of the right which included the NSDAP. These initiatives were centred around von Papen who resented his treatment at the hands of von Schleicher the previous year. Yet he was not acting alone, there were elements of the business community which disliked von Schleicher's reforms of September 1932 and were determined to see a return to a more authoritarian rule whether it be under the Chancellorship of von Papen or Hitler. Whilst their role should not be exaggerated, industrialists such as Reusch and financiers such as Schröder[36] helped pave the way for a Nazi take-over of power through their influence and obvious preference for authoritarian rule. Influential individuals, therefore, had an important role to play in creating the political circumstances in which it became desirable on their part to bring the Nazis into power.

Electoral support

That the Nazis came to power, therefore, was because

they were seen by the elite as the means by which the republic could be destroyed, yet the left also disempowered. There is little doubt that Hitler's insistence on 'legal' means rather than those which failed so dismally in 1923 gave the NSDAP movement a legitimacy which it lacked in the 1920's. This legitimacy was enhanced by von Schleicher and von Papen who were prepared to ignore the violence and illegality of Nazism as its movement was a bulwark against the left. What made the NSDAP such an attractive ally was its nature as a mass movement and the broad base of its electoral support. This was unique in a party system where the other parties represented their own sectional interests. The established view is that the Nazi vote was primarily that of the middle class, the *Mittelstand* of civil servants, officials and those of their ilk damaged by the economic instability of the republic. Although the Nazis picked up a significant number of votes from those who had previously voted for the middle class parties such as the DVP or DNP, it is wrong to assume that it lacked a broad social base. It is correct to assume that the Nazis failed to attract significant votes from the industrial working class, but the DNVP had gained over 2 million worker votes in the 1924 election and it is to be assumed that the Nazis attracted these as voters at the turn of the decade. The Nazi vote was weakest in urban areas, in Berlin in November 1932 the left (KPD and SPD) cornering 54.3% of the vote. Despite this they were by the early 1930's the only party which could present itself as a national one which cut across class and interest lines. This was due to the attractions of the Nazis as a party of protest with lofty but ill defined ideals such as *Volkgemeinschaft*.[36] As with many a successful electoral party, policy was vague but deliberately so, style being more important than substance. Yet it was this which made the Nazis successful electorally and, thereby, so attractive to the ruling establishment which shared their critique of Weimar and the desire to destroy democracy.

Party organisation

A crucial factor in the rise of Nazism was the ability of the party to expand and provide a political home for those discontented with their lot, in particular after the crash of 1929. This should be put down to the flexibility of the party structure as created or developed in the 1920's. It was this structure which enabled the party to rapidly transform into a mass movement and to spread propaganda at elections. Most importantly, the existence of groups to represent specific sections of the community gave the party the wide base which was at the root of its appeal to the establishment which wished to use that base for its own brand of authoritarian rule. There are many examples of these organisations, among the most important being the *Agrarpolitischer Apparat* (AA) founded in 1930 to draw a largely discontented peasantry into the movement. Not only did it achieve its aims within a relatively short space of time but it managed to infiltrate and dominate other important agrarian based organisations such as the *Reichslandbund* which was important in pressing for Hitler's appointment in 1932/3. Part of the work of the AA as envisaged by its founder Walther Darré was to create a network of party members to undertake propaganda activities. This local activity effectively complemented the 'saturation' propaganda tactics devised by Göbbels. The use of rallies, speeches, lectures and 'aeroplane campaigns' in certain areas were effective in raising the profile of the party and increasing the vote at elections. In particular, the tactics of identifying and then targeting certain groups within regions brought rich electoral rewards such as in the local election in Saxony in 1929 in which the poorer farmers were targeted and 14.4% of the votes received which was a significant improvement on the 1929 election. Similarly the Nazis were successful at attracting the support of the young and particularly students - in 1930 over two thirds of members being under 40 years old. Without electoral success in the early 1930s the Nazis would not have been in a position to challenge for power nor would that power haved been offered to them.

The successful electioneering and propaganda combined with a dedicated and growing party membership was underpinned by the organisational reforms undertaken on Hitler's instructions between 1926-'8. Of particular note was the imposition at Bamberg in 1926 of a centralised command structure and the understanding that Hitler's authority was supreme. Equally important was the discipline which Hitler imposed on the SA, first with the appointment of Captain von Pfeffer in 1926 but continuing throughout until the seizure of power. This is despite numerous instances when local SA leaders rebelled against central control and the policy of 'legality' and had to be brought back within party

discipline. A clear example was in March 1931 when Hitler accepted a decree requiring police permission for rallies, thereby angering SA leaders such as Walther Stennes into open revolt. The fact that the leadership was seen to be dealing effectively with the revolts of the more radical party members such as Strasser or Stennes was important in securing confidence in Hitler's leadership and his commitment to 'legal' means of gaining power. Such organisation and discipline meant that the party was able to take advantage of the opportunity presented by the campaign against the Young Plan. With the extra resources provided by the Reich Committee for a German Referendum and the national exposure via Hugenberg's newspapers, the Nazis were able to stage impressive rallies including that at Nuremberg which attracted 200,000 supporters. Despite the failure of the Freedom Law campaign, the Nazi party was able to take greater advantage of the increasing polarisation of German politics because of the institutional and organisational reforms.

1929 - the economic catalyst

The depression and economic crisis did not in itself bring the Nazis to power. What it did was create the possibility, the opportunity and the context in which Nazi propaganda would not fall on deaf ears. It also acted as the trigger for the destruction of the republic. One should not underestimate the psychological effects of the wholesale collapse of the German economy from 1929 onwards, especially with the problems of 1918-'23 so fresh in the mind[37]. It was unemployment and the consequential insecurity which so undermined confidence in the present structures. By 1933 one in three German workers were unemployed, yet it was not these who formed the bedrock of growing Nazi support but those who believed that without political change then they too might well suffer a collapse in living standards. Such groups are detailed above, the *Alte Mittelstand*, a peasantry threatened with worsening economic conditions and so on. What the depression did is polarise opinion, and increase the popularity of those who offered radical solutions to the economic problems. This is why the intended authoritarianism of Hindenberg was widely accepted, why the vote for the KPD rose from 1928 onwards[38], why there was so little resistance to the coup in Prussia in 1932- the SPD and unions being significantly weakened by unemployment. It also helps to explain why Brüning embarked on an economic policy which did little to alleviate the depression and was more concerned with the removal of the reparations 'burden'. Such was the depth of contempt for existing structures, that the economic crisis was undoubtedly used by the establishment to dismantle the political system. Such, therefore, was the political restriction on Brüning which prevented the introduction of means to artificially stimulate economic growth such as labour schemes. Instead the economy lurched into a crisis which resulted in the banking collapse of 1931 and the subsequent flight of capital. It was true that the worsening conditions helped to further provoke the subsequent Hoover moratorium and the suspension of payments in 1932. The point should be underlined, however, that such a policy created the conditions in which the Nazis flourished with their condemnation of the present and their promises of a utopian future. There is a strong correlation between the years of Brüning's economic stewardship and the rising fortunes of the Nazis in elections. So whilst the economic conditions were not created by the establishment, their role in perpetuating the crisis for their own political ends was to have a real influence on the rise of Nazi popularity. The economic crisis crystallised the fears of those who feared social collapse and disorder. This again benefited the Nazis despite the fact that the actions of the SA were often the cause of that disorder. A prime example was the street violence in Berlin in June/July 1932 between the SA and KPD in which around 100 were killed. That such a threat simply strengthened Hitler's position as the leader who could control the SA and thereby prevent anarchy.

Conclusion

The Nazi rise to power in 1933 was the consequence of the actions of an establishment which desired and attempted to manipulate a return to authoritarian rule. It was this overriding ambition which led to the appointment of Hitler as Chancellor in 1933 and the passage of the Enabling Act soon after. Yet this would not have occurred without the electoral success of the Nazis which was due to their organisational advantages, tactical skill and the context of an economy in crisis. The Nazi movement and its popular base was coopted by an elite which believed that it could use it to its own ends. As hindsight showed, this was a mistake of monumental proportions.

[1] Adolf Hitler was the leader of the NSDAP or Nazi party. Born in Austria in 1889 he had served in the German Army as a corporal from 1914-'18. His skills as an orator and political manipulator gave him the undisputed leadership of his party.

[2] The German establishment should be defined as the conservative, mainly Prussian elite, which had held political power pre 1914. Added to that were the industrial and business elites, army and judiciary. None of these groups at any time showed any particular attachment to the Weimar Republic.

[3] Field Marshal Paul von Hindenberg was the hero of the Battle of Tannenberg in 1914 and was elected Reich President in 1925 as a candidate to inspire unity, despite his lack of sympathy for its founding ideals.

[4] Authoritarian government would end democracy and govern via dictatorship.

[5] Drexler was a locksmith at the Munich railway works. He founded the German Workers' Party as a nationalist and anti-Semitic organisation.

[6] By revision of the treaty they meant the scrapping of Article 231 by which Germany accepted guilt for the war and the ending of reparations.

[7] Ernst Röhm was the first sponsor of Hitler. Influential amongst Freikorps - groups of nationalist soldiers, he helped to ease Hitler's introduction into politics and created the Nazi stormtroopers, the SA. Although estranged from Hitler from 1925-'30, he returned to run the SA until he was killed on the order of Hitler in the 'Night of the Long Knives' purge in 1934.

[8] Both Eckhart and Rosenberg helped to shape the Nazi *Weltanschauung* (world view) throughout the 1920s and '30s. Eckhart published the first Nazi paper, the *Volkischer Beobachter*, until his death in 1923. Rosenberg continued to be the leading Nazi ideologue helping to formulate the destructive pseudo-scientific philosophy with which much the party's anti-semitism was justified. He was tried at Nuremberg in 1946 and hanged by the Allies.

[9] *Volkischer Beobachter* is translated as the 'Peoples' Observer'.

[10] The initials SA were eventually to stand for *Sturmabteilung* or stormtroopers.

[11] Up until 1923 the majority of party members were drawn from the lower middle classes, the so called *Mittelstand*.

[12] The Ruhr crisis was prompted by the French invasion of the Ruhr as punishment for a halt to the payment of reparations.

[13] The attempted take over was precipitated by tension between the Reich or central government and that in Bavaria over the refusal of the latter to arrest nationalists. The uprising aim was to create a dictatorship with General Ludendorff as President. Subsequent events turned out to be a shambles.

[14] Hitler's co-defendants also received remarkably lenient terms, Frick, Röhm and General Ludendorff being aquitted.

[15] *Mein Kampf* or 'My Struggle' was written in two volumes, the first in prison in 1924 (published in 1925) and the second written and published after his release in 1926.

[16] This conference was held as some of the party's regional leaders or *Gauleiters* were beginning to suggest policies independent of Hitler. Based in the North West of the country, they followed the more radical anti capitalism of Gregor Strasser.

[17] The policy of 'legality' was based on Hitler's insistence that power could not be achieved through a putsch as was attempted in 1923. Instead, legal means would be used, foremost being elections.

[18] From now on the SA was to undertake more mundane roles such as training and the stewarding of rallies. This did not prevent SA streetfighting in cities such as Berlin and Munich, a fact which was to cause considerable tension within the movement.

[19] The Young Plan set a time limit of 59 years for the repayment of reparations and cut the annual amount Germany was obliged to pay. Agreement to the plan was linked to a withdrawal of Allied troops from the Rhineland five years earlier than previously planned.

[20] The *Stadhelm* was founded by Seldte in 1918 and grew into the foremost nationalist ex-servicemen's organisation.

[21] Proposed in the 'Law' was a repudiation of the 'war guilt' Article 231 of the Versailles treaty, immediate withdrawal of allied troops from German soil and any politician who signed compromising treaties with foreign powers to be deemed a traitor!

[22] The crash in share prices in New York in October 1929 was followed by worldwide bankruptcies and the closure of business. This hit German industry hard, in part due to the fact that its growth in the 1920s had in part been funded by American capital which was now withdrawn.

[23] The bill proposed increasing taxes which upset the DNVP on the right whilst failing to cut military expenditure which angered the SPD socialists on the left.

[24] This was highly ironic as one of Hindenberg's aims was to remove the SPD from a position of influence.

[25] As part of this crackdown, Nazis were banned from office, the civil service and from wearing their uniforms in public.

[26] The issue of reparations was taken seriously by US President Hoover who proposed a suspension of payments for a year. The international commission formed to further investigate the problem recommended the ending of payments which was agreed at the Lausanne Conference in the summer 1932. By this time Brüning had long since left office.

[27] Hindenberg's victory was due, ironically, to the support of the SPD and Centre parties.

[28] Schleicher met with Hitler on 8th May 1932. As a result of the meeting, Hitler agreed to accept a new Presidential cabinet in return for the removal of Brüning and the lifting of the ban on the SA/SS.

[29] Von Schleicher's economic policy of work creation, tariffs and minimal land caused a negative reaction on the right from landowner and industrialist interests.

[30] The new cabinet in fact only included three Nazis, Hitler as Chancellor, Frick as Minister for the Interior and Göring as Minister without Portfolio. The vice-Chancellor was to be von Papen and other parties of the right were well represented, Hugenberg of the DNVP was put in charge of the Economics Ministry and Seldte of the *Stadthelm* was made Minister of Labour.

[31] Although sympathetic to Nazism, von Blomberg's credentials as former head of the informal Chief of Staff until 1929 made him the perfect candidate.

[32] The decree entitled 'For the Protection of People and State: to guard against Communists' acts of violence endangering the state' allowed for imprisonment without trial, the ending of press freedom, right of assembly and so forth. It also allowed the central government to take over local state government (the Lander) and introduced the death penalty for certain offences.

[33] The *Deutsche Volkspartei* (German People's Party) was founded in 1918 as a successor to the pre war National Liberals.

[34] Under Article 48 the President of the republic could proclaim a state of emergency and govern by decree to protect the public interest.

[35] It was at Schröder's house in Cologne in January 1933 that Hitler and von Papen met and entered into negotiations which resulted in Hitler becoming Chancellor.

[36] *Volksgemeinschaft* was the concept of national community in whose interest policy would be implemented. It was used by the Nazis as a vote winner through a comparison with class politics.

[37] In this period, hyper inflation acted to wipe out savings and the values of pensions.

[38] The KPD vote rose from 3.2 million in 1928 to 5.9 million in November 1933.

HITLER, THE NAZI CHIEF, MADE GERMAN CHANCELLOR: HIS FERVID ORATORY THROUGH THE MICROPHONE.

HERR ADOLF HITLER, appointed Chancellor of Germany on January 30, first became prominent in 1923, through his leadership, along with General Ludendorff, of the Munich rising, after which Hitler was sentenced to five years' imprisonment in a fortress, though released after a few months. He is now only forty-three. By birth he is an Austrian, but his birth-place, Braunau, is close to the frontier of Bavaria, his father was of Bavarian stock, and he has always considered himself a German. In youth he was poor, and worked by turns as builder's painter, labourer, and draughtsman. In August 1914 he joined a Bavarian regiment, and served through the war, winning the [Continued opposite.]

[Continued] Iron Cross, but only reached the rank of corporal. He was seriously wounded and gassed. In 1920, happening to attend a small meeting of the new National Socialist Workers' Party, he decided to join, and next year became its president and leader of the growing Fascist movement. Since 1923, his Nazis have moved from strength to strength until they became the most powerful party, mainly through his forceful leadership and violent, perfervid oratory. His Brown Army appealed strongly to German youth, and Monarchists look to him to found a new Hohenzollern régime. It is, perhaps, significant that his first Ministry contains a Monarchist element.

THE NEW CHANCELLOR OF THE GERMAN REPUBLIC: HERR ADOLF HITLER, LEADER OF THE NAZIS (NATIONAL SOCIALIST WORKERS' PARTY), WHOSE MINISTRY INCLUDES SEVERAL MONARCHISTS.

Adolf Hitler

CHAPTER 5

Reich Election Results 1919–33

	National Assembly 19. 1. 1919	1st Reichstag 6. 6. 1920[c]	2nd Reichstag 4. 5. 1924	3rd Reichstag 7. 12. 1924	4th Reichstag 20. 5. 1928	5th Reichstag 14. 9. 1930	6th Reichstag 31. 7. 1932	7th Reichstag 6. 11. 1932	8th Reichstag 5. 3. 1933
Number entitled to vote (in millions)	36·766	35·949	38·375	38·987	41·224	42·957	44·226	44·374	44·685
Votes cast (in millions)	30·524	28·463	29·709	30·704	31·165	35·225	37·162	35·758	39·654
Size of poll (%)	83·0	79·2	77·4	78·8	75·6	82·0	84·1	80·6	88·8
Total no. of seats[a]	421 (423)[b]	459	472	493	491	577	608	584	647
DNVP	3·121, 10·3%, **44**	4·249, 15·1%, **71**	5·696, 19·5%, **95**	6·206, 20·5%, **103**	4·381, 14·2%, **73**	2·458, 7·0%, **41**	2·177, 5·9%, **37**	2·959, 8·3%, **52**	3·136, 8·0%, **52**
NSDAP (in 1924: NS-Freiheitsbewegung)	—	—	1·918, 6·5%, **32**	0·907, 3·0%, **14**	0·810, 2·6%, **12**	6·409, 18·3%, **107**	13·745, 37·3%, **230**	11·737, 33·1%, **196**	17·277, 43·9%, **288**
Wirtschaftspartei/ Bayer. Bauernbund	0·275, 0·9%, **4**	0·218, 0·8%, **4**	0·694, 2·4%, **10**	1·005, 3·3%, **17**	1·397, 4·5%, **23**	1·362, 3·9%, **23**	0·146, 0·4%, **2**	0·110, 0·3%, **1**	—
Deutsch-Hannoversche Partei	0·077, 0·2%, **1**	0·319, 1·1%, **5**	0·320, 1·1%, **5**	0·263, 0·9%, **4**	0·195, 0·6%, **3**	0·144, 0·4%, **3**	0·047, 0·1%, **—**	0·064, 0·2%, **1**	0·048, 0·1%, **—**
Landbund	—	—	0·574, 2·0%, **10**	0·499, 1·6%, **8**	0·199, 0·6%, **3**	0·194, 0·6%, **3**	0·097, 0·3%, **2**	0·105, 0·3%, **2**	0·084, 0·2%, **1**
Deutsches Landvolk	—	—	—	—	0·581, 1·9%, **10**	1·108, 3·2%, **19**	0·091, 0·2%, **1**	0·046, 0·1%, **—**	—
Deutsche Bauernpartei	—	—	—	—	0·481, 1·6%, **8**	0·339, 1·0%, **6**	0·137, 0·4%, **2**	0·149, 0·4%, **3**	0·114, 0·3%, **2**
Christlich-sozialer Volksdienst	—	—	—	—	—	0·870, 2·5%, **14**	0·364, 1·0%, **3**	0·403, 1·2%, **5**	0·383, 1·0%, **4**
DVP	1·345, 4·4%, **19**	3·919, 13·9%, **65**	2·694, 9·2%, **45**	3·049, 10·1%, **51**	2·679, 8·7%, **45**	1·578, 4·5%, **30**	0·436, 1·2%, **7**	0·661, 1·9%, **11**	0·432, 1·1%, **2**
Zentrum (Centre) (in 1919: Christliche Volkspartei)	5·980, 19·7%, **91**	3·845, 13·6%, **64**	3·914, 13·4%, **65**	4·119, 13·6%, **69**	3·712, 12·1%, **62**	4·127, 11·8%, **68**	4·589, 12·5%, **75**	4·230, 11·9%, **70**	4·425, 11·2%, **74**
BVP	—	1·238, 4·4%, **21**	0·946, 3·2%, **16**	1·134, 3·7%, **19**	0·945, 3·1%, **16**	1·005, 3·0%, **19**	1·192, 3·2%, **22**	1·095, 3·1%, **20**	1·074, 2·7%, **18**
DDP (from 1930: Deutsche Staatspartei)	5·641, 18·5%, **75**	2·333, 8·3%, **39**	1·655, 5·7%, **28**	1·920, 6·3%, **32**	1·505, 4·9%, **25**	1·322, 3·8%, **20**	0·371, 1·0%, **4**	0·336, 1·0%, **2**	0·334, 0·9%, **5**
SPD	11·509, 37·9%, **163 (165)[b]**	6·104, 21·7%, **102**	6·009, 20·5%, **100**	7·881, 26·0%, **131**	9·153, 29·8%, **153**	8·577, 24·5%, **143**	7·959, 21·6%, **133**	7·248, 20·4%, **121**	7·181, 18·3%, **120**
USPD	2·317, 7·6%, **22**	5·046, 17·9%, **84**	0·235, 0·8%, **—**	0·099, 0·3%, **—**	0·021, 0·1%, **—**	—	—	—	—
KPD	—	0·589, 2·1%, **4**	3·693, 12·6%, **62**	2·709, 9·0%, **45**	3·264, 10·6%, **54**	4·592, 13·1%, **77**	5·283, 14·3%, **89**	5·980, 16·9%, **100**	4·848, 12·3%, **81**
Others	0·131, 0·5%, **2**	0·332, 1·1%	0·930, 3·1%, **4[d]**	0·598, 2·0%, **—**	1·445, 5·5%, **4[e]**	0·804, 2·3%, **4[f]**	0·244, 0·7%, **1[g]**	0·299, 0·8%	0·005, —

Source: Statistisches Jahrbuch für das Deutsche Reich, vol. 52 (Berlin, 1933), p. 539.

Note: The figures against each party indicate, first, the number of votes obtained (in millions), then its percentage of the poll, then (in bold type) the number of seats it held at the beginning of the session.

[a] The total number of seats varied from one Parliament to another, as it depended on the number of votes cast: see Bibliography, no. 337, pp. 145 ff., 361 ff.

[b] Two additional SPD members were elected by the Eastern Army on 2 February 1919, bringing the total to 423 and the strength of the SPD to 165.

[c] Results of the election on 6 June 1920, together with those of 20 February 1921 in constituency no. 1 (East Prussia) and no. 14 (Schleswig-Holstein) and 19 November 1922 in constituency no. 10 (Oppeln).

[d] Deutschsoziale Partei.

[e] Sächsisches Landvolk 2, Volksrechtspartei 2.

[f] Konservative Volkspartei.

[g] Volksrechtspartei.

WHAT WERE THE OUTSTANDING FEATURES OF THE GERMAN ECONOMY - 1939-'45?

Introduction

The outstanding features of the German wartime economy are highly controversial[1]. The orthodox explanation for the failure of the German economy to adapt to a situation of total war is that economic decisions were structured by a Blitzkreig[2] strategy until 1942. Despite challenges to this assumption, it is still the most appropriate line of argument.

Other questions have revolved around the extent to which Nazi ideology clouded, and the chaotic Nazi state prevented, rational economic judgement. This is particularly relevant to the issue of the mobilisation of women and the use of forced labour. It should be argued that neither ideology nor the irrationality of Nazism are the primary factors in the failure of the economy to significantly increase production. More important were the shortage of labour and raw materials. However, there is little doubt that Nazism with its absurd and inhumane prejudices - which add up to an irrational creed - led to actions which also countered economic logic. The monument to Nazi inhumanity and irrationality was the Final Solution which ran counter to both economic and war aims.

Blitzkreig Economy 1939-42

The outbreak of war in September 1939 saw the responsibility for the planning of the German war economy shared among competing agencies. At the Ministry of War, General Thomas led the economics section in charge of the armaments programme. Yet such was the overlap in the Nazi state that he had rivals for administrative supremacy of the war economy, chiefly the Ministry of Economics led by Walter Funk and the office of the Four Year Plan[3]. In March 1940, however a Ministry of Munitions was created under Fritz Todt[4] which went some way to ending the confusion in this area of production. In June 1940, France surrendered and plans were made to utilise the resources of the already significant Nazi empire[5]. The invasion of the Soviet Union a year later aimed to extend that empire - but the prospect of a prolonged struggle on the eastern front led to the rethinking of economic policy[6]. In December 1941, Hitler called for the rationalisation of the armaments industry to be effected by Todt[7]. Thereafter there was a significant change in priorities, industry accepting responsibility for raising levels of production with central direction coming from Todt's ministry. In February 1942, further change was apparent with the appointment of Albert Speer to be Todt's successor in the post of Minister for Weapons and Munitions. This marked the beginning of the campaign for a total war which was so markedly different to the official attitude in the early days of the war. In particular, Speer developed Todt's plans for rationalisation of industry and the more efficient control of raw material distribution.

This is not to suggest that the economy had not already undergone a significant readjustment from 1939-'42, military expenditure alone rising from 17.2 billion to 55.9 billion marks[8]. The demands of war resulted in a shift of labour, investment and priorities towards munitions e.g. the numbers working in aircraft manufacturing doubling between 1939-'41. However, such were the demands of war that a shortage of labour became apparent in the early days of the war. By May 1940 there were 3.5 million less workers in the workforce than one year before. This shortfall was partly made up by the use of French prisoners of war, some 800,000 by October 1940 and other nationals[9] which made a total of around 2 million foreign workers in Germany by the end of the year. This was not enough to meet the growing demand with 1.7 million workers drafted into the armed forces in 1941 and a further 1.4 million called up between May 1941 and May 1942. Such a shortage produced urgent measures. In February 1941, General Thomas had called for the use of more rational measures of production to increase efficiency. Yet even this would not be enough. Following on from a decree in the Netherlands in February 1942, the so called Plenipotentiary General for Labour, F. Saukel[10], issued a compulsory labour decree for all occupied countries in August of the same year. In September, the Vichy government in France established compulsory labour for men and women between the ages of 18-65 respectively. Such measures brought in around 2.5 million new workers and by the end of 1942 there were some 6.4 million foreigners working in the Reich.

Speer and 'Total War'

Despite a reluctance to conscript women, the pressures on the economy led to a gradual rethink. In January 1943, women between the ages of 17 and 45 were obliged to sign up for work although out of this only some 400,000 were finally recruited. The preference of employers and the Nazi hierarchy was still for foreigners to be employed. However, the percentage of women in the labour force as a whole was 41.5 % by 1944. Their inclusion was made necessary by the turn in fortunes of the army: in January 1943 the German Army surrendered at Stalingrad and losses in the army were running at 150,000 month. Against this background, a campaign of total war was launched by the regime. It was initiated by a speech by Göbbels at the Berlin Sportsplatz in February 1943 in which he called for universal labour service and the closure of all non-essential business. Such a move to improve production and productivity was reinforced by the appointment of Speer as Reich Minister for Armaments and Production in September 1943. This post gave Speer responsibility for all industrial output and raw materials and into these areas of the economy he introduced reorganisation and rationalisation such as the Armaments Commission set up in 1943[11]. It was due to these processes that the economy became more productive as the war continued, rather than the ever greater numbers of forced labourers. By 1944, 29.2% of all industrial workers were foreign, in all areas of work a total of over 9.3 million by the summer of that year. By 1943, up to one third of all miners were from occupied countries, in particular the East. Despite the fact that foreign worker productivity was as much as 50% lower, changes in work methods, increased mechanisation, better distribution of materials, a more equitable wage structure for German workers and the introduction of mass production techniques[12] resulted in increased productivity. In munitions, output per worker rose by 60% from 1939-'44 despite the disruption caused by Allied bombing. Although the numbers in the industrial work force increased by only 11% between 1941-'43, the production of all weapons grew by 130% in the same period.

Towards economic collapse

In 1944 the war deteriorated considerably for the Nazis on all fronts. In the east by the summer months the Red Army had pushed the German Army back to the Polish border. In Italy, the Allies continued to make slow progress and in France, forces were landed on the Normandy coast in June. The following month, an attempted assassination plot against Hitler resulted in the appointment of the trusted Goebbels to the post of Reich Plenipotentiary for Total War, thereby giving him even greater control over production

and allowing Speer more scope for change[13]. As the Allies crossed the borders of Germany in early 1945, the demands of Hitler for a policy of 'scorched earth', the destruction of all industry, was resisted by Speer. It was apparent that defeat was inevitable and Hitler ordered the evacuation of all in the path of the advancing armies. From January 1945 the German economy was in a state of collapse, partly as a consequence of invasion but also due to exhaustion and the effects of the Allied bombing programme. Indeed the bombing campaign had reduced production of essential war materials by anything up to 40% in 1944. The use of foreign labour was of even greater importance as all able bodied German men were called to the front. In an attempt to increase their productivity, marginal improvements were made in the living conditions of the foreign labour force on the insistence of Fritz Sauckel, General Plenipotentiary for Labour. From 1943 to the end of the war, 2.5 million extra foreign workers were employed and these, as with the others who had survived the brutality of their working conditions, were categorised by race. In an attempt to increase production, however, Sauckel attempted to improve the situation of all workers with regards to pay and overtime. In March 1944, all eastern workers were given the same pay and benefits as other foreign labourers. This was all comparative since conditions for the vast majority of foreigners working for the Nazis were generally unspeakable and deteriorated even further during 1945.

ANALYSIS

Introduction

The concept of a *Blitzkreig* war economy supposes that Hitler and his generals planned a series of short wars as the means by which a more expansionist war might take place. The reason why this strategy was adopted was the that Germany lacked sufficient raw materials to fight a wider war of conquest. Such materials, therefore, could only be acquired through short, rapid conquests. Similarly, because of labour shortages, an expansionist policy was necessary to enslave Europe's *untermenschen*[14]. This vast pool of labour would then be utilised to transform the Nazi economy into one which would have no problems in providing for world conquest. This was central to Hitler's life long view of the desirability of *lebensraum*[15]. The Nazi war effort from 1939-'42 was restrained by other factors, primary amongst which was the desire to avoid imposing a reduction in living standards on a population which was unlikely to accept such burdens after the traumas of the late 1920's and early 30's. It was the failure of the Blitzkreig military campaign in the Soviet Union in 1942 which led to an alteration of policy and attempts to fully mobilise the economy. That these were only partly successful was due to the shortcomings in raw materials and labour which put a ceiling on any intended mobilisation.

Consumption

When one discusses the appropriate use of the *Blitzkreig* concept in analysing the German economy from 1939-'41, the issue of consumption becomes of central importance. It was argued in the 1950's by Burton Klein that more resources were not diverted into war industries and production from 1939-'42 because Hitler wished to prevent a decline in civilian living standards. The Nazi hierarchy believed that *Blitzkreig* warfare could be undertaken without running down consumer industries - and that their political credibility relied on this. Such a theory has had much support but came under attack from Richard Overy who believed that as military expenditure grew so fast from 1939-'42, it could only have done so with a reduction in civilian consumption. Indeed, the figures seem to prove this point. The production of cars, which Overy believes to be an important indicator of consumption, fell from 276,592 in 1938 to 35,195 in 1941[16]. Similarly, the construction of houses fell from 303,000 to 80,000 in the same period. On top of this, Overy has argued that those areas associated with consumer production which did see a rise in the early years of the war did so because of increased demands from the armed forces, e.g. textiles or leather. However, these figures are somewhat misleading. The decline in housing between 1939-'42 reflects not so much a shift in resources but falling demand. Despite the success of German arms in this period, it is correct to assume that the outbreak of war (with the precedent of civilian bombing) put the dampners on the housing market. Similarly, it is wrong to use cars as a main indicator of consumption in this period, the use of the motor vehicle being limited to the upper and middle classes. However, it is correct to point out that some areas of civilian consumption were limited by the war, especially where interests clashed with the military - a clear example being that by early 1941 some 80% of chemicals production was taken by the military.

Much more important indicators of consumption are those of basic goods and wage levels. There is little doubt that the Nazi leadership intended to avoid a repetition of the scarcities in basic foodstuffs and clothing which caused such widespread unrest during the 1914-'18 war. It has been maintained by Overy that the state's policy was to deliberately reduce consumption in all goods from 1939 by the use of strict rationing. This would have thereby encouraging saving. However, it is clear that despite rationing, considerable sacrifices were not made by the consumer until 1942. The rationing system introduced in September/October 1939 was generally equitable and sufficient although the quality of the products declined. This was less a product of a shift in resources, however, than the curtailment of vitally important imports. Indeed, for a meat eating nation, the ration of 500 grammes a week was perceived as difficult but as the Wehrmacht conquered vast tracts of Europe, so there was an improvement in the supply of general foodstuffs as a whole. This was especially the case after the defeat of France in the summer of 1940 (although the German people showed little liking for such foreign foods as artichokes or aubergines). Although, the meat ration had declined to 300 grammes in 1942 it was raised by 50 grammes in October of that year. There was flexibility in rationing in Germany - greater than in Britain - with extra rations for those undertaking strenuous occupations. There were also Christmas bonuses such as that in 1942 when every citizen received extra rations including 200 grammes of meat. Of course these were propaganda stunts which masked difficulties, but the ability of the regime to undertake them reflects the importance the regime placed on maintaining adequate supplies. Whilst clothing became scarce, particularly during 1941, this can in part be put down to the panic buying in the early months of the war which reduced stocks considerably. That there were shortages thereafter was partly due to supply problems but also inefficiency in distribution - the economy suffering a lack of the rationalisation which became such a feature later on. It is incorrect to assert that there were no difficulties or shortages - there were many, but neither was there hardship as seen in the 1914-'18 war.

The main aim of the Nazi leadership was to maintain consumer confidence in the early years of the war. Therefore, despite difficulties, production of such items as stockings or cigarettes continued on the orders of Hitler[17]. This confidence was bolstered by the absence of significant inflation, the cost of living index rising from 116.2 in 1939 to 125.0 in 1942 (1913 = 100). Indeed, real wages rose slightly during the war, from 111.1 in 1939 to 114.2 in 1942 (1913 = 100). The fact that savings rose considerably was the result of a reduction in consumer expenditure. As Overy has pointed out, the surplus between the population's net income and its expenditure increased from between 14 billion marks in 1939 to 31 billion marks in 1941. Yet this is not as significant a figure as it seems, especially when one takes into account that the same period saw a far greater increase in 'military expenditure'. In fact, such an increase in savings is remarkable within the context of recent German history and the collapse of confidence in the early 1920's and 1930's. This bears out a confidence in the regime which was a product of victory in the West and the absence of significant sacrifice. It is correct to assert that consumption was curtailed, but not that resources were shifted overwhelmingly into providing for the war effort - until the war began to turn on the eastern front in late 1942. Where confusion has existed is that consumer production was maintained in the early years of the war, but that in some cases a large proportion of that production was shifted to the armed forces e.g. by 1940, 50% of textile production went to the armed forces and state and party organisations. Yet when one studies armaments output before 1942, there was obviously not a significant transfer of resources from consumer goods industries. There was an increase in the number of tanks produced from 2,159 in 1940 to 5,138 in 1941. Yet this was not enough and the figure of 9,287 produced in 1942 proves that the economy was not working at anything approaching full capacity in the preceding years. It should therefore be argued that whilst there was some readjustment for consumers from 1939-'41, it was not the radical one which might mark an immediate shift to full scale wartime production.

Raw materials

Germany lacked the natural resources - iron, coal, oil and the other materials it needed for a sustained war effort. It was this factor which more than any other, shaped Nazi war aims and plans. It is right to assume that Hitler was planning for an eventual long war. Before such a long war was viable, there had to be a series of conquests which would secure supplies of natural resources. That this was of such importance can be seen in the policy of *autarky* undertaken from 1936 onwards. From 1936 the Nazi state became closely involved in industrial production, the steel works *Reichswerke-Hermann-Göring* which was opened in 1937, being the most obvious example. The aim of such involvement by the state was to boost the re-armament process. This acted to accentuate the demands for the raw materials which Germany lacked and was a key factor in shaping foreign and military strategy. A clear example is that of iron ore, the high quality varieties of which Germany lacked. The attempt to compensate for this led to the attempts at the *Reichswerke* to develop the production of low grade ore for manufacturing purposes. Yet this could never meet the demands of the expanding military needs, thereby making Germany in part dependent on imports, in particular from Sweden. During the war the amount of ore imported from neutral Sweden remained constant, in 1940 it was 5.4 million tons in 1943 it was 5.6 million tons. However, the annexations of Austria, Bohemia, Poland and Alsace Lorraine by 1940 brought with them huge quantities of high quality iron ore. In 1943 these areas alone produced 6.7 million tons for the Nazi war effort. Overall, the supplies of iron ore to the German war economy increased from 13.4 million to 20.2 million tons between 1940-'43. Other areas of conquered Europe yielded raw materials which were vital for the war effort: manganese ore from the Soviet Union, nickel from Norway or bauxite from France to give examples.

The important point to note is this - Germany needed to annex or have control over the natural resources of other nations in order to fight a major war. That this policy failed was due to the failure of the military *Blitzkreig* from 1942. The invasion of the Soviet Union had ideological causes, the destruction of Bolshevism being a central theme of *Mein Kampf*. Yet there were very strong economic considerations, not least the desire to control the oil fields in the Caucuses. German access to oil supplies was limited, the main supplier being Romania which exported nearly 3 million tons to her ally in 1943. However, this was not enough to supply an economy and armed forces which from 1942 were engaged in total war. Even conquest did not ensure increased supply of needed materials. Despite the increase in ore and the acquisition of the steel industries of the Low Countries and France, there was a chronic shortage of steel throughout the war and particularly before 1942. In 1941 it was calculated that demand for steel exceeded supply by 30%. This was mostly due to a shortage of coal despite Germany's large natural reserves and the acquisition of large mining reserves in the Soviet Union and Belgium. As with other industries, however, the Soviets destroyed virtually all they had to leave behind. The extent of this destruction is clear when one considers that in 1942, the Donets Basin - which was rich in coal - only produced one twentieth of its pre war output. The production of German coal remained static throughout the war -output of hard coal increasing by 1.5 million tons or around 1%. This was a fact which was crucial in limiting the growth of steel production. Coal from other areas such as Belgium was used to fuel indigenous industry. The failure of the Nazis to fully exploit the raw materials of the countries they occupied was crucial in preventing the necessary expansion of the German economy, necessary to fight a major war.

The problems of labour -

a. Women.

The needs of the German economy for more labour

were not solved by the conscription of women, as was the case in Britain. It is incorrect to assert that this was solely the consequence of ideology although there is no doubt that the Nazi attitude towards women influenced the numbers of women working. Between 1939-'44 only 200,000 extra women entered the workforce despite the chronic lack of labour[18]. The refusal of Hitler to allow conscription of women was ideologically based, the Nazi view of the role of women revolving around '*Kinder, Küche, Kirche*'[19]. Even with the move towards 'total war', the registration of women to work in January 1943 had little effect - in all only some 400,000 women were recruited for work. The failure to mobilise more women created significant ideological tensions within the Nazi leadership. There was a shortfall of some 4 million workers in the economy by 1944, but still over 1,360,000 women were in domestic service. Attempts by Speer to rectify this glaring anomaly in September of that year had little effect due to the number of exemptions allowed and the fact that Hitler still refused to countenance full scale mobilisation. Yet what prevented a greater proportion of women entering war work were the social consequences of that Nazi ideology which had been espoused since 1933. As women had been very much encouraged to marry and raise families, so the numbers of women in such a situation had risen dramatically, nearly 1 million more children being born in Germany in 1939 than six years previous. Similarly a far higher proportion of women were married by the eve of the war, between the ages of 25-30 the

difference between 1933-'39 was 9.2%. A great disincentive to work were the benefits paid to wives of soldiers which meant that they could resist the temptation to supplement their husband's pay. All of this made the conscription of women harder and further complicated the labour crisis.

However, the issue of women's labour is a far more complex one than has been assumed. Ideology played a role in the state's attitude towards women but it was not the primary determining factor in limiting the increase in women in the wartime labour market. What is often ignored is that the proportion of women in the workforce at the start of the war was relatively high despite Nazi ideology. More to the point, it was significantly higher than that in Britain - in May 1939 37.3% of German women went out to work as opposed to 26.4% of their British counterparts. Of those between the ages of 15-60, 52% of women were working and an astonishingly high 88.7 % of single women were in employment. This meant that there was not the slack in the employment market which was found elsewhere, especially as Germany had been approaching full employment as a consequence of the rearmament programme started in the mid-30's. The nature of women's employment also made harder redistribution into essential war industry. This was particularly the case in that large numbers of women worked in agriculture - in 1939 they comprised 36.6% of the workforce- and their importance grew with conscription of men into the army. By 1944, 65.5%

of the agricultural workforce were women[20]. Similarly, the high proportion of women employed in textiles in 1939 - 58.2% - could not be spared to other areas of war work such as munitions given the demands on the industry and the effects of male conscription. Therefore it is inaccurate to point to ideology as being the sole reason why women were not fully mobilised into essential war work from 1939. The fact was that the proportion of women already in the workforce was significantly high is a factor to bear in mind, in particular when one remembers the relatively insignificant numbers produced by the 1943 drive to register.

b. Foreign labour

As with raw material, the key point to remember is that despite widespread conquest and the acquisition of a large pool of labour - the Nazis were unable to effectively use such booty as a means of compensating for economic deficiencies. Hitler's prognosis that a *Blitzkreig* war of conquest was necessary for the German economy to develop sufficiently so as to be able to undertake war of conquest was an accurate one. The proof of Hitler's view lay in the failure of the economy to adapt to the demands of such a war. Most obvious amongst Germany's economic problems was the labour shortfall, especially in the light of the demands of the military which was 9.5 million strong by 1943[21]. The only answer was in the use of foreign labour - by 1944 35% of armaments workers were from abroad and in total

as many as 9-10 million were employed. There was no alternative to the use of foreign labour given the constraints in supply of domestic labour. Yet foreign labour was comparatively unproductive and generally unwilling. This is not surprising considering the appalling conditions in which many workers were kept. As with the employment of women, there was an ideological element which prevented a full mobilisation of foreign labour resources. In particular, this applies to the 5.7 million Soviet citizens captured by the Nazis during the war. Treated as *untermenschen*[22] over 3.3 million of them died in desperate conditions whilst the economy suffered the problems of a chronic lack of labour. Despite this, it was on Hitler's insistence in November 1941 that Soviet prisoners should not be released to be used as labour. Here is the contradiction between the 'rationality' of Nazi economic planning and the irrationality and prejudice of its ideology. Whilst *Blitzkreig* was developed to maximise the economic potential of the materials and labour of the conquered territories, so Nazi ideology prevented that happening. Workers from the east in particular were treated with a contempt which acted to lower their productivity[23]. Although this was recognised by Saukel and Speer, their attempts to improve conditions so as to improve the motivation of the enslaved workforce was far too little, too late. Thousands died on numerous projects for want of basic food, shelter and sanitary provision. Such a project was at Peenemunde in the Harz Mountains where the V2 rocket was produced[24]. The relevance of this is that the productivity of foreign labour was from 60-80% of that of German workers and so it did not solve the basic problem of labour shortage.

c. Rationalisation

As stated above, the demand for labour and skilled labour was acute - by 1941 over 800,000 skilled metalworkers had been conscripted into the army. What is more, the ever increasing demands of war threatened to squeeze industrial output to the point whereby consumer supply was reduced. This was politically unacceptable to a leadership which attempted to resist civilian sacrifice as much as was possible. The answer was a rationalisation programme which began in earnest after the Führer Order of December 1941. What this Order did was make official the process of better work practices and centralised direction of materials and labour which had begun in 1941. The switch to a total war policy was caused by the failure of *Blitzkreig* warfare. At the start of 1942, the evidence was very clear that German industrial production was still working significantly below its potential. Many firms still were not working double shifts and production was dispersed. The aims of Speer, to whom the rationalisation process was entrusted, was to introduce labour, time and space saving measures - thereby boosting production. The results of his work were impressive indeed. The promotion of better use of floor space led to production of the Me109 at Messerschmitt increasing from 180 per month from seven factories to 1,000 per month

in three factories. The Armaments Commission created by Speer worked to standardise production thereby allowing greater mass production. Again, what was achieved was impressive, in 1944 the numbers of tank models being reduced from 18 to 7, types of different vehicles coming down from 55 to 14. The result was a greater productivity which was missing from the *Blitzkreig* economy. In the arms industry, output per head fell from 1939-'40 by 12.5% - mainly because of the effects of conscription and the concentration on consumer industries which in the same period saw output increase by nearly 16%. Central control of raw materials, the reduction of hand working practices and more realistic contracts saw a rise in output per head in armaments so by 1943 the figure was 32% higher than that in 1939. It must also be remembered that this was in the period when the workforce was in itself becoming less productive. Better processes cut the amount of precious raw materials used, e.g. each gun saw a reduction of 93% in the aluminium used after rationalisation had taken place. In all the last years of the war saw a significant improvement in industrial production[25], despite Allied bombing. Indeed this growth was an important feature in an economy so hamstrung by labour and raw material problems.[26]

Economic colonisation and the Final Solution

It is false to portray German economic performance during the war as being planned - the Nazi state was too chaotic with too many competing agencies/power blocks for any consistent policy to be formulated. Often when clear direction was given from the centre, it countered economic logic. But much of Nazism as an ideology was both irrational and illogical. Until the ideology was undermined by military failure, however, its aims were supported at least implicitly by large sections of the financial and industrial world. The looting of conquered countries was undertaken in a systematic way by sections of German business which identified itself very clearly with the expansionism of *Blitzkreig*. The most obvious was the expansion of IG Farben which used its influence with Nazi officialdom to create a position as largest chemical producer in Europe by 1942[27]. Other companies such as the state run *Reichswerke* acquired ownership of large sections of conquered enterprise, in Reichwerke's case, in steel, mining and related industry[28]. All acquisition of businesses in occupied lands was regulated by the state which limited private involvement because of the desire to avoid direct competition with the state.

However, this is not to suggest that German business did not benefit from Nazi expansionism, just as it did from the Final Solution. It has been suggested that the murdering of Europe's Jews was an economic irrationality, that it used up precious resources in their transportation and destroyed what might have been a useful source of labour. Indeed, there were conflicting views amongst the Nazi hierarchy and specifically amongst the ranks of the SS. As the network of concentration camps spread, there were those within the SS such as Oswald Pohl[29] who wished to fully exploit the labour resource at hand. Similarly, those with the responsibility for the administration of the territories in the east such as Gauleiter Wilhelm Kube, argued that the export of labour to the fatherland had left them with a labour shortage of their own which could only be filled with the Jews. A compromise was for the SS to employ Jewish labour in and around the concentration camps - but to work them to death. However, whatever the economic considerations, of primary importance - the rationale of war and *lebensraum* - was the destruction of the Jews of Europe[30]. The technical arrangements arranged at the Wannsee Conference in January 1942 for the eradication of the Jews included the detailed planning by Adolf Eichmann[31] of the use of trains so desperately needed by industry. But industry became involved with the process, companies including IG Farben using labour at the huge Monowitz-Buna complex near Auschwitz. The figures for the transportation and systematic annihilation are vast. At the largest extermination camp, Auschwitz, over a million were murdered. The camp of Treblinka - which was also in Poland - was the site for the death of 800,000, and at Sobibor 300,000 died. What is clear is that even as late as July 1944, when resources were hard pressed, Eichmann had clear priority to use the railways to transport Jews to their death, in this case from Hungary. The pursuing of the Final

Solution against economic logic puts into perspective any study of the German wartime economy. It clarifies the priority of ideological considerations against the demands of the economy for labour and materials. There is little doubt that conquest in search for the latter was the means, the tool by which the Nazi *Weltanschauung*[32] could be enforced.

Conclusion.

The German economy did not expand sufficiently to meet the demands of 'total war'. This was due to many factors, primary amongst which were the shortage of raw materials and labour. The key to economic failure was the fact that conquest did not make up the shortfall in these two essential components of any economy. Yet economic development was also influenced by factors which had a negative effect on its overall productivity. In the early years of the war, the consumer goods sector of the economy shifted production to meet the demands of the military but not wholly so. The slow growth in armaments and lack of restructuring of industry reflects the continuity with the pre war period. This was dictated by the political priorities of a regime brought to power on the back of socio-economic turmoil and wishing to avoid its repetition at all cost. As has been shown, there was a conflict between the impulses of an ideologically destructive regime and one in need of economic growth to survive. So from 1942 the economy and industry in particular underwent a rationalisation process

which made it more productive. As this was happening, however, millions of people were being transported to their death whilst workers perished for lack of basic necessities.

[1] The main controversy surrounds the state of the German war economy between 1939-'41. Based on documents from the United States Strategic Bombing Survey, an orthodox line of argument emerged. The central point of this line as espoused by Burton Klein and later Alan Milward was that Germany was not fully prepared for total war in 1939 and hence undertook a *Blitzkreig* military and economic strategy. This limited war strategy made less demands on the civilian population and helps to explain Germany's reluctance to call up women. This school has been attacked by revisionists who dismiss the *Blitzkreig* interpretation as imaginative but fictional. Led by Lundolf Herbst in Germany, this counter-attack has been partly based on the inappropriate nature of models superimposed on a Nazi state which was unlike any other. In his seminal War and the Economy in the Third Reich (1994), Richard Overy has challenged the orthodox line with many points - the primary one being that the concept of the *Blitzkreig* economy is a false one because the figures show that the economy switched rapidly away from a peacetime model in 1939 and that civilian consumption was limited almost immediately. Overy also argues that Hitler aimed for a long war and that failures to fully mobilise the economy in the early years of the war are due to the fact that it began before the German economy was ready to sustain it.

[2] Blitzkreig means 'lightning war' i.e one of rapid mobility and conquest. From 1939-'42, the Wehrmacht swept all before it using this strategy.

[3] The Four Year Plan was the vehicle through which central

planning was undertaken, similar to the Soviet Union's five year model.

4 Todt also led the Organisation Todt which was responsible for building works across the expanding Reich.

5 By June 1940, the Nazis had already conquered Poland, Denmark, Norway, the Netherlands, Belgium and France.

6 The invasion of the Soviet Union, operation Barbarossa, began on June 22nd 1941. By the end of October the Axis forces had swept to the outskirts of Moscow. As winter drew in, however, it became apparent that the momentum was temporarily lost.

7 This was via the Führer Order on the 'Simplification and Increased Efficiency in Armaments Production' of December 3rd.

8 One has to take great care with this figure. Of the rise in military expenditure, perhaps as much as 75% was due to the increase in military personnel not armaments. Therefore, they are somewhat misleading.

9 Within these other nationals was around half a million Polish prisoners, and another 700,000 from the occupied east.

10 Saukel was an important figure from 1942 until the end of the war in the effort to import foreign labour. A party animal, Saukel had been *Gauleiter* of Thuringia and was the choice for the job of the equally vile Martin Bormann.

11 The Armaments Commission was set up to improve the co-operation and co-ordination between the design and manufacturing processes in munitions.

12 The use of production line assembly in the manufacturing of the Panzer III tank in 1943, cut by 50% the man hours needed in its assembly.

13 This was because in the permanent in-fighting which characterised the Nazi state, Speer was a close ally of Göbbels. Speer's methods of rationalisation and his seemingly non-ideological approach won him many enemies. Based mainly at the Ministry of Economics, Nazis such as Franz Heyler who was State Secretary at the Ministry, and his deputy Otto Ohlendorf represented the more radical wing of the party led by Himmler or Martin Bormann.

14 The term used by the Nazis to denote those they considered to be sub-human.

15 *Lebensraum* was the 'living space' to the east which Hitler and other leading Nazis believed was the rightful inheritance of the 'Germanic' people.

16 Of this 1941 figure, military demands accounted for some 77%.

17 The historian Dr R. Wagenfuhr claimed that this was characteristic of the 'peace time' style of economy operated until 1942.

18 In 1939 the number of women in employment was 14.6 million, a figure which actually declined to 14.2 million in 1941 and peaked at 14.9 million in 1944.

19 The translation of this being 'children, kitchen and Church'.

20 This figure applies to native born Germans. By the middle of the war there were large numbers of foreign nationals working the land.

21 This figure also ignores the 1.7 million losses up to this point which had also been taken out of the labour market.

22 In the Nazi racial hierarchy, the Slavs came just above the Jews and were considered to be *untermenschen* or subhumans.

23 Polish workers suffered numerous restrictions from 1940 including the forced wearing a yellow badge marked with a P and not being able to use public transport.

[24] The horror of this project, code named 'Dora', was detailed by Speer in his book Inside the Third Reich.

[25] An example being the BMW engine for planes - the production of which increased by 200% between 1941-'43 with an increase of only 12% in the workforce.

[26] The changes associated with rationalisation contributed to the German economic miracle in the 1950's.

[27] The profits of IG Farben had more than doubled from 1936 to a figure of 300 million RM by 1940.

[28] After the *Anschluss* with Austria and the take over of Czechoslovakia in 1938, *Reichswerke* took over large sections of the countries' enterprises under Göring's instructions. This included companies such as Skoda and Steyr-Daimler-Puch.

[29] Pohl was in charge of the development of the WVHA which was the economic administration section of the SS. By 1942, he had control of 20 concentration and 165 labour camps. Pohl envisaged a role for the camps akin to the *Gulag* in the Soviet Union.

[30] Throughout the war, Hitler repeatedly promised the 'extermination of the Jews' in Europe.

[31] Eichmann was head of the innocuously named Department IV B2 of the RSHA which was the chief administrative office of the SS. Department IV was the state police - the Gestapo - and the sub section IV B2 was devoted to Jewish affairs.

[32] *Weltanschauung* is roughly translated as 'world view' or 'outlook'.

ALBERT SPEER

CHAPTER 6

WHY DID THE SPANISH SECOND REPUBLIC FAIL, 1931-'39?

Introduction.

The Spanish Second Republic failed as it was torn apart by issues and ideology. In attempting to reform the main institutions of established Spain - Church, Army and land - the Republic provoked and polarised active opposition from those who were instinctively anti-Republican. A similar response was provoked by a degree of decentralisation[1]. However, in not reforming far enough, successive governments served to alienate those whose expectations had been raised by the creation of the Republic in 1931. Therefore the political process from 1931-'36, triggered a spiral of polarisation and opposition which was reflected in increasing political and social violence.

The Second Republic failed also because its ideological divisions during the Civil War contrasted with the unity of the opposing Nationalists[2]. It was crucially undermined by foreign intervention on behalf of the Nationalists, and the lack of it on its own side. This resulted in Republican military inferiority which was to prove decisive in the war. Both intervention and non-intervention were ideologically inspired - fascist Germany and Italy coming to the aid of the Nationalists, whilst Britain and France failed to support a democratic republic they perceived to be tainted with Communism. The irony of 'non intervention' was that it pushed the Republic to accept aid from the Soviet Union which caused further internal political conflicts. These were the factors which ultimately led to the failure of the Republic.

By the 19th century, Spain was no longer the world power it had been two hundred years previously. Throughout that period it suffered turmoil and upheaval, the causes of which were to persist into the following century. Most obvious were a series of civil wars called the Carlist Wars[3]. Although these wars were superficially concerned with who was to rule Spain, the root cause was the differing definitions of what Spain was. Although the liberal constitution of 1812 had been accepted by the Bourbon King Ferdinand VII in 1814, it was only sporadically adhered to. His daughter, Isabella II, similarly paid at least lip service to liberal ideas, granting greater powers for the *Cortes*[4] and some regional autonomy by the *Estatuto Real* of 1834. The Carlist wars continued sporadically, until 1876. These wars and the only nominal acceptance of liberal constitutional structures, point to Spain's failure to develop into a mature state in the 19th century. It is true that by the constitution of 1876, the politician Antonio Canovas created a two party political and parliamentary structure similar to that of Britain. In 1890, universal suffrage was introduced. Yet these changes to the political structure obscured the extent of economic underdevelopment and the power of *caciquismo*. The *caciques* were the groups of landowners of mainly Southern Spain. They controlled society throughout the 19th century, using mainly economic levers. However, this control also extended to the electoral system - a fact which significantly undermined the suffrage law of 1890. Therefore 19th century Spain was beset with contradictions: a modernised and liberal democratic institutions coexisting with a semi-modern social structure and economic underdevelopment. By the 1851 Concordat, the Catholic religion was recognised as the sole authorised faith in Spain. The Church was also given wide ranging control of education and censorship which also undermined the semblance of a liberal country.

The defeat at the hands of the United States in the Spanish-American War of 1898 was a significant humiliation. By the peace treaty signed in Paris in December 1898, Spain withdrew from Cuba and handed over the Philippines, Guam and Puerto Rico to the United States. The consequence was a further erosion of confidence in Parliamentary government. This manifested itself in the emergence of an authoritarian conservatism, the development of socialism and the spread of regional (especially Catalan) nationalism. Such tensions were highlighted by the events in Barcelona in 1909 which became known as *Semaña Trajica* (tragic week). In protest to what was seen as an unequal system of military service, a general strike was proclaimed in Barcelona. This rapidly transformed itself into an orgy of looting and attacks on the city's convents and monasteries. As monks and nuns were massacred, so the government's repression was fierce - the leader of the anti-clerical opposition, Snr Ferrer, being executed. Such an outburst and the response to it reflected deep divisions.

Primo de Rivera

Although Spain was not a direct participant in the Great War, the increased demand for industrial goods from Europe's military machines placed further stresses and strains on Spanish society. Of note was the growth of major cities such as Madrid and Barcelona - the 1920's alone saw a population rise in Spain of over 10%. The issue of Catalan separatism developed in tandem with industrialisation. Calls for Catalan home rule by a Catalonian Union in 1919 and a mutiny of the garrison at Barcelona in 1923, helped to provoke the coup d'état of General Primo de Rivera in September 1923. From then until 1925, martial law came into force, the *Cortes* was dissolved, censorship introduced and the liberal constitution suspended. Although the dictatorship was formally ended in 1925, de Rivera remained as Prime Minister with a military cabinet until 1930. It is important to note that despite the repressive nature of the regime in the 1920's, this was also the period of greatest industrialisation and urbanisation in Spain - a factor with important consequences for the 1930's.

Creation of the Second Republic 1931

The resignation of de Rivera in 1930 plunged Spain into turmoil. Political leaders such as Alcala Zamora[5] and Marcellino Domingo called for the abdication of the monarch Alphonso XIII. The calls for a Republic were also supported by the middle classes who saw democracy as a potentially effective bulwark against communism as well as the means by which they could exercise greater political power. In Catalonia, many members of the middle class *Lliga Regionalista* viewed republicanism as the means of finding a solution to the issue of separatism without upheaval. Yet republicanism had a far wider base of support, appealing to artisans, industrial workers and peasants alike. There were limits to this support, however, and that was reflected in the results of the municipal elections of April 1931. The previously authoritarian monarchy had restored the constitution[6] in February 1931 and allowed these elections to take place. It was therefore judged by the outcome. Despite the fact that 45 out of 52 provincial capitals voted for Republican candidates, in rural areas there was a 75% vote for monarchist candidates. However, this was not enough to prevent the abdication of a monarchy which had lost even the confidence of the army. On April 14th, Alphonso XIII abdicated his throne and parliamentary elections in June resulted in a victory for the Republican-Socialist coalition[7] led by Manuel Azaña. In December, a new constitution was adopted by the *Cortes*. By it, there was to be a single-chamber *Cortes* which was to be elected every four years by universal suffrage. A certain degree of autonomy was granted to Catalonia with the creation of the *Generalitat*[8]. The attack on the church by the new Republic was swift in coming - Article 3 of the constitution proclaiming complete religious freedom and the separation of Church and state. Not only that, but Article 26 stipulated that education be completely secularised within two years. Such a reform was to prove antagonistic to those opposed to the anti-clericalism of the new Prime Minister Azaña and his supporters[9].

Yet the state went further - in January 1932 the Jesuit order was dissolved and its property confiscated.

Reforms 1931-32

Expectations of the new Republic, *la nina bonita*[10], were high. The reforms of the Army and of land in 1931-'2 were aimed at appeasing the supporters of radical change. In attempting to modernise the army, Azaña aimed to cut a huge officer corps by offering to many officers retirement on full pay[11]. The army lost its judicial rights and all those who intended to serve as an officer henceforth had to serve time in the ranks first. To ensure a more democratic army, 60% of places at the academy for officers were reserved for NCOs and the elite academy at Zaragoza was closed down. Such reforms provoked resentment amongst army circles as they were perceived as an attack on the army's role within Spain[12]. The issue of land reform was equally pressing and controversial and provided much of the tension which surrounded reform. In the South of the country, land holding came in the form of the *latifundios* - the large estates controlled by their landlords the *latifundistas*. Those who wished for redistribution of land put their faith initially in the reformist PSOE[13]. For those who wished for more radical change, the South also had a strong anarchist tradition centred in the CNT[14]. Others who pressed for land reform included the socialists' union, the UGT[15] which called for collectivisation on a model not too far distant from that being implemented in the Soviet Union. Such a prospect swelled the ranks of CEDA[16] which was formed to represent those who rejected the idea of agrarian reform. It appealed not only to the *latifundistas* but also the smallholding farmers of the more fertile north who feared collective ownership of the land. The whole issue of the land was intensified by the drought which hit Spain in late 1931. This caused a failure in the olive harvest in areas such as Seville with heightened unrest. As Minister of Labour, Largo Caballero attempted to improve the plight of the landless labourer with a series of decrees. In April 1931, a decree forbade the hiring of labour from outside the municipal boundary, thereby preventing landlords bringing in cheaper labour from outside. This was followed in May by legislation which created arbitration councils in rural areas to settle wage and other such disputes. In July, agricultural labourers were given certain rights by law including an eight hour day. Such reform infuriated the landowning classes who used their political influence to undermine further suggested change. In 1932 the Agrarian Reform Bill - which aimed to effect a transfer of land from *latifundista* to labourer, was effectively wrecked in the *Cortes* - the version passed in September 1932 being a mere shadow of the original. Such an action caused bitter resentment and radicalised many who had placed their trust in reform. This was more the case as the reforms which had been introduced were effectively blocked at local level.

Opposition and unrest 1932-33

The extent of opposition to the Republic was apparent in August 1932 with the revolt of General Sanjurjo in Seville. It was immediately crushed and

that opened the way for a spate of further reform including the Catalan Charter of Autonomy which was passed by the *Cortes* in September 1932. This created a Catalan President, Parliament and government. However, there were strict limitations to their scope of action. Despite having sole jurisdiction over agriculture, public health, poverty and local government - the *Generalitat* received only a third of the taxation raised in Catalonia and had to cede overall control in all other affairs to Madrid. Disillusionment with this settlement, added to the growing influence of the CNT, led to an attempted insurrection in January 1933. This sparked off unrest across Spain with incidents including that at Casas Viejas[17] in which twenty four workers died. Despite such tension, the government continued to suggest reforms. In May 1933, an Associations Law was passed which abolished all church schools and banned the involvement of religious orders in secular education. By the same legislation, all church property was seized by the state and all religious orders were banned from engaging in commercial activity. The reaction from the church was swift - the papacy condemning the Law in the encyclical *Delectissimi Nobis*. However, such reform did not tackle the fundamental social and economic issues in Spain. From 1933 onwards there was a perceivable decline in working class support for the 'bourgeois Republic' and increased militancy of the UGT and CNT. This was matched by growing conspiracy on the right, e.g. with the foundation of the *Union Militar Española* which was a group of lower and middle ranking officers committed to the destruction of the Republic. In the autumn of 1933, the withdrawal of the PSOE from the governing coalition with the Republicans sparked a series of strikes in Madrid. Such protest was to become the norm in the following years. In November 1933, the elections saw a collapse in the socialist vote, the parties of the right gaining 44% of the vote. The largest party in the *Cortes* was CEDA with 114 seats, yet the party's anti-Republican stance prevented it from forming a government. Instead the new Prime Minister was Alejandro Lerroux who was the leader of the Radical party[18].

Instability and Polarisation 1933-36

The new cabinet led by Lerroux included members of CEDA, a fact which caused a fierce counter reaction in Catalonia. In December 1933, a public transport workers' strike spread into a general strike, partly inspired by the fear of the loss of autonomy at the hand of the new Madrid government. It took four days for the police to suppress the unrest. In January 1934, Catalan elections resulted in a swing to the left and the new President, Luis Companys, attempted to persuade Madrid to agree to a shift in resources to the *Generalitat*. Such a plea fell on deaf ears, the Lerroux government being unsympathetic to the regionalist cause. The focus of tension between Madrid and the *Generalitat* was the Cultivation Contracts Law. The new (and temporary) central government led by Semper vetoed the Catalan legislation which would have given tenant farmers the right to buy the land they had been cultivating for at least eighteen years. Attempts to compromise on the part of Semper led to the collapse of his

government in October 1934. It was brought down by CEDA, which made it clear that it would not countenance any government which did not support the position of the landlords. The new government was again led by Lerroux but included three CEDA ministers. Such was the state of tension that the inclusion of these ministers precipitated the declaration of Catalonian independence on 6th October, 1934. The rebellion was immediately crushed and brought the suspension of Catalonian autonomy[19]. Yet this was not the only violence in the regions. The negativism of the Lerroux and Semper governments, their unwillingness to enforce the reforms of the previous years[20], the suppression of union activity and the use of police to end strikes[21] further alienated and radicalised the labour movement. In October 1934, a socialist inspired uprising took place in the mining area of the Asturias. Centred around Oviedo, the insurrection failed and was brutally suppressed. By the end of the year, Spain was bitterly and irreconcilably divided.

Throughout 1935, Spain suffered political instability. In September, the Lerroux cabinet fell to be succeeded by a series of weak right wing governments. Despite their obvious differences, the parties of the socialist and republican left came together to form a Popular Front for electoral purposes. The aims of this coalition were to return to the reformism of 1931-'33 and reverse the work of governments since. In December 1935, a governmental crisis had given Gil Robles and CEDA the opportunity to form a government but such an opportunity was blocked by President Zamora who called a general election instead. The result of this election in February 1936 was a close victory for the Popular Front which formed a government led by Azaña. However, there were serious weaknesses in the alliance. Although the government was supported by the socialists in Parliament, the PSOE was crucially divided. Not only did its leaders refuse to take governmental responsibilities, but the revolutionary stance of Largo Caballero seemingly confirmed the worst fears of the right that the Front was revolutionary at heart. Throughout the spring of 1936, industrial militancy led by the UGT and CNT (who also fought between each other) and land occupation in the south, gave further credence to the view that Spain was on the verge of social collapse. In April, the socialists in the *Cortes* engineered the dismissal of President Zamora and Azaña was elevated to the Presidency[22]. By now a military conspiracy, co-ordinated by General Mola, and supported by a cross section of the right, was being prepared. The trigger for uprising was the assassination of the monarchist leader Calvo Sotelo in July 1936. On July 18th the rebellion began.

Spanish Civil War 1936-39

The Spanish civil war was brutal from the outset. Across Spain, those supporting the rebellion attempted a military take-over. In Spanish Morocco, the towns of Melilla and Tetuan fell to the core of the Nationalist army, the *Africanistas*[23]. After seizing major towns such as Cadiz, Seville and Corunna, the Nationalists created a Junta of National Defence on July 30th with the purpose of co-ordinating the military effort. This coincided with the first instalment of German military aid - a score of Junkers to be used to ferry the *Africanistas* to the mainland. On October 1st, General Francisco Franco was declared Head of State by the insurgents. The following month, the siege of Madrid began but the strength of the Republican defence resulted in stalemate. From the start of the war, political and military divisions had emerged on the Republican side. In September, a Popular Front government was formed in an attempt to bring together all the political forces sympathetic to the Republican cause and end fears of revolution. Led by Caballero, the government even contained representatives of the Catalan and Basque nationalists. In November, its membership was widened further to include four anarchist ministers. The new government was committed to maintaining the parliamentary democracy as stated in the constitution of 1931. However, its efforts were undermined by the stance of non-intervention adopted by the leading democracies Britain and France, in late 1936[24]. This contrasts with the recognition given to Franco's government by Germany and Italy in November of that year.

In February 1937, Nationalist forces captured Malaga which was a crushing defeat for the Republic. Franco's forces then moved north to attack the Basque province. As part of the military campaign, the town of Guernica was bombed to destruction by the German Condor Legion. Meanwhile, the Republic was wracked with ideological division. The government of Caballero had attempted to end the expressions of revolutionary ardour which had been forthcoming across Spain since July 1936. Collective farms were closed down and the influence of central government reasserted. In doing so his administration was supported by the PCE[25] which gained influence as the government was forced to look to the Soviet Union for aid. The tensions which this caused were directly responsible for the infighting of the Barcelona May Days[26] of 1937. Such division and the ascendancy of pro-Stalinist communists was the root cause for the resignation of Caballero and his replacement by Juan Negrin in May 1937. This contrasted with the unification of the disparate forces of the right by the Decree of Unification in April 1937[27]. In 1st July of the same year, the church's establishment issued an episcopal letter in which it justified the uprising as a crusade against godless Communism. On the other side, the new government of Negrin reversed fragmentation of authority within republican ranks. This was done in a variety of ways including the creation of SIM[28] which was used to clamp down on those considered to be political enemies. By increasingly identifying with the Communists, however, Negrin's government undermined the Republic by altering its identity.

In June 1937, Bilbao fell to the Nationalists, the rebels then pushing on to Santander which they took in August. Bitter fighting took place in Aragon and a major counter offensive launched by the Republic to capture Teruel in late 1937. Although the newly formed Popular Army was initially successful in both campaigns, Tereul was recaptured by Franco's forces in February 1938. In April, the Nationalists took Vinaroz on the Mediterranean coast, thereby dividing Republican forces. A counter offensive at the River Ebro pushed Franco's forces back but in time they regained lost territory. The initiative was now with Franco and in December, the Nationalists began their offensive in Catalonia. With Italian help Barcelona was taken by Franco in January 1939. The following month Britain and France attempted to mediate an end to the war but in vain. On 28th February, Azaña fled to France to be followed by Negrin's government in March. A Republican military junta led by General Miaja attempted to negotiate peace terms with Franco but to little avail. On March 28th Madrid and Valencia surrendered unconditionally. The Republic had been defeated.

ANALYSIS

Introduction

The Republic failed as it was torn apart by issues and ideologies, the process of which polarised Spain. In attempting to reform, the left provoked a backlash which eventually undermined and divided Spanish society and politics. This contrasts with other seemingly weak regimes such as the French Third Republic which survived because of the inherent conservatism of successive governments. It should be argued that this division of issue and ideology goes a long way to explaining why the Nationalists won the Civil War.

Section A. 1931-'33. The Army

It is wrong to assert that the army was automatically antagonistic to the Republic. This is not the case as without a degree of acceptance from the army, the smooth transition from monarchy to democracy in 1931 would not have been possible. That is not to suggest that the army hierarchy was welcoming of the new regime - more that it was willing to adopt a neutral stance. Such an 'understanding' was undermined by two important factors: the issue of army reform and that of regionalism. There is little doubt that for all its moderation, the army reforms of 1931 antagonised significant groups within the military who perceived such reform as a direct assault on the army's position within Spain. The culling of senior posts within the army blocked the promotion prospects of many middle and lower ranking officers

who were to form the basis of *Union Militar Espaniola* and the uprising in 1933. Since the defeat of 1898, the army perceived itself to be the defender of Spain. However the Spain which it saw itself defending was narrowly defined - unified, Catholic, hierarchical and socially controlled. The granting of regional autonomy, the attack on the Church, the growth of worker militancy all acted to confirm perceptions in army circles that the Spain described above was in grave peril. Hence the attempted coup of General Sanjurjo in 1932 and the plotting which resulted in the uprising of 1936. In attempting to alter Spain, the Republic alienated significant elements within the army.

The Church

As the Concordat of 1851 recognised the Catholic Church as the state religion, it inextricably linked it to the social and economic interests of the governing classes. Yet economic change and the decline in attendance at Mass challenged the Church's dominance. Population mobility and the decline of the power of the *caciques* meant that in some working class districts of Madrid in the 1930's, church attendance had fallen as low as 7% of the population. The Church's implicit anti-republicanism developed from an increasing insecurity about its position within a changing Spain. The threat of religious liberty in 1923 and the reforms proposed in 1931 were part of a trend which divorced church from the central definition of Spain. Therefore, one should see the threat to the church as being long term. In 1937, the bishops declared their support for the uprising, ostensibly in reaction to horrific massacres at the start of the war[29]. Yet this declaration was not the consequence of such actions alone. Essentially the Church was interested in its own survival, and this was only guaranteed by the Nationalists - the constituent groups of which shared the same interests. Therefore the reforms of 1931 simply acted to accentuate the Church's hostility to the Republic. Their main significance is that they acted as an impetus for the Church to set up links with anti-republican movements such as *Accion Popular* and CEDA. The formulation of the Church's policy of accidentalism i.e. simply accepting the Republic's existence but nothing more, sums up its tacit anti-democratic line. A final point should be made. The Church and its role within society was a central pillar of the Nationalist cause. Of major importance to its credibility and ultimately its legitimacy, was its ability to present the uprising as a crusade to protect the Church and Christianity against the forces of 'godless Bolshevism'. The Concordat of 1953 which heralded an era of 'National Catholicism' and the full blessing of the Church for the regime in return for full control over Spain's intellectual life should be seen as important. It proves that the identity of Spain as defined by Franco and the Church was similar. Hence the Second Republic, by proposing reform automatically alienated the Church.

The question of land

An important area of reform in terms of confrontation and impact was that of land. Indeed one should point to the whole issue of agrarian reform as being central to the argument that the Republic foundered on issues which, once brought out into the open, simply encouraged further political and social polarisation. The two largest political parties each found large groups of support amongst the peasantry - the PSOE amongst the landless of the south, CEDA with the smallholding farmers of the north. It was the prospective reforms of the Republican-Socialist government which prompted the formation of *Accion Popular* and then CEDA in 1933. Much of the land in the south of the country was dominated by the *latifundistas*. The entire system relied on the existence of a large reserve of landless labourers to keep wages low. Therefore, any threat to improve the conditions of the labourer was a threat to the whole system. This was particularly keenly felt as a threat in the early years of the 1930's which were ones of world economic depression.

The series of reforms introduced by Largo Caballero between 1931-'2 had important repercussions for the future of the Republic. The series of decrees such as that limiting the employment of labour to that within the municipal boundaries were aimed at limiting the power of the landowning class. The intention was revolutionary in that the state was interfering to redress the balance of power in the countryside. In reality the effect was very different, the reforms were blocked at all levels - including by central government from 1933. A clear example is the 1932 Agrarian Reform Act which attempted to effect a redistribution of land, only 7,000 families ultimately benefiting. The most important aspect of these reforms is that they stimulated the opposition and organisation of landowners. This in turn led to action which antagonised and frustrated the rural peasantry. The rural socialist trade union, the FNTT, and the anarchist CNT were pushed into accepting more radical measures of protest by the frustration of their members. The most extreme example was the call to strike in 1933 which resulted in the massacre at Casas Viejas. Again one can argue that the proof of such polarisation can be seen in the ideology and structure of the regime post 1939. It maintained the *latifundos* to such a degree that one might argue that the war was fought to maintain that interest. The issue of agrarian reform divided Spanish society. The reforms proposed, alienated the landowning classes, the lack of real reform frustrated the landless. This was reflected on a national scale with the policies of successive governments from 1933-'36 aimed at minimising the impact of and preventing any further reform.

Regionalism

A sense of regional identity and separatism in certain parts of Spain were heightened by the advent of economic change. By the end of the 19th century, there was a 'dual economy' in Spain, the industrialised Catalonia and Basque country having little in common with the agrarian South of Andalusia for example. The only shared trait was an adherence of some to anarchism. In the south it was inspired by the Russian Bakunin and revolved around the idea of land redistribution. In the north it developed into anarcho-syndicalism based in the CNT union. Whatever the differences between the regions of Spain, the move towards autonomy such as that in Catalonia in 1933 alienated those which held *La Patria* to be sacred. However, the restrictive nature of the autonomy which was granted, e.g. the limited powers of the *Generalitat* - was to be a source of tension within and alienation from the Republic. The clearest example of this was the suppression of the *Generalitat* in 1933 in response to the declaration of independence in October of that year. It was this event more than any other which hardened the resolve of the army to destroy the Republic. Therefore, in attempting to deal with the issue of regionalism, the Republic set in train events which were to crucially weaken it.

Industrialisation

One should see the development of the Republic and the process of polarisation in the 1930's in the light of the rapid changes in Spain in the early part of the 20th century. In particular, industrialisation, urbanisation and the changing economic structure had important repercussions for the social structure, values and society's concerns in the 1930's. Rapid change created a society in which large sections were disempowered, e.g. the industrial working classes. The Second Republic, therefore, was burdened with the expectations of these groups post 1931. Its problems were in part due to the fact that it failed to meet these expectations. Yet in trying to do so it provoked reaction from groups which found the new democratic system threatening. That they were so threatened is due to the insecurity which was a product of economic modernisation. In the 1920's there was a 4.6% increase in the proportion of the workforce involved in industry. The same decade saw towns with a population of over 10,000 increase their collective size by 2 million. From 1911-'31, those involved in agriculture fell by 20.5%. The drift of population from the countryside was feared by those, including de Rivera, who were concerned about the declining influence of Church and *caciquismo* as agents of social control[30]. Events such as the strike at Oviedo in 1934 seemed to back up this fear.

It is important to note, however, that the Republic gained much support from those involved in the economic and social changes of the 1920's. Those who disliked the changes or felt threatened by them, such as large sections of the Church, shunned the Republic as the manifestation of those changes. A further example were the bulk of middle and small landowners who joined anti-republican groups such as the CNCA[31]. To them, the Republic was no better than a class dictatorship. The rapid changes of the 1920's had helped to create a new class structure yet it was imposed on an immature state. This made much easier the subsequent rejection and challenging of the new Republic.

Although it was not a class dictatorship, the new Republic initially raised the hopes of many on the left of a new Spain. The vision had its roots in the work of writers such as Ortega y Gasset who rejected the concept of Spain as one dominated by the *caciques*, Church and Castille. The new Republic appealed to the regionalists such as those in the Catalan separatist party *Estat Català*. It promised much to the landless labourers of the *latifundos* and the urban working classes which hoped for economic and social reform. Many members of the professional middle classes believed that with the Republic might be the chance to break the power of the Church and political patronage. To many on the left such as the PSOE, the Republic was the opportunity to implement real, even revolutionary, reform. The problem for the Republic was to meet all these expectations whilst allaying the fears of its enemies. In practical terms it couldn't and there lay the crucial weakness of the Republic. An example was the Agrarian Reform Act of 1932 which failed to tackle the problems of land redistribution but antagonised those who feared its potential consequences. The result, however, was that the Republic soon lost the confidence of many of the groups which initially supported it. The political left fragmented and the labour movement embarked on a series of strikes which further highlighted social divisions. The inability of the Republic to meaningfully reform also split the PSOE. This was important in that the flirtation of the left with extra-parliamentary action, as proposed by Caballero, alienated sections of the middle classes from the Republic.

Section B. 1936-9

Foreign intervention

The Nationalist victory in the civil war was underpinned by foreign aid. This was ideologically inspired as was the refusal of Britain and France to support the Republic. Without doubt, this was more important than any other factor in determining the result of the war and the fate of the Republic. French foreign policy was guided by the appeasement of the British Prime Minister Baldwin and the fear of the British Foreign Office of the threat (real or not) of communism. This explains the non-intervention agreement of September 1936 which had the ironic effect of forcing the Republic to buy arms off the Soviet Union - thereby accepting an element of interference which further divided, weakened and discredited the Republican cause. This also was a crucial factor in defeat. Stalin's interest was mainly concerned with preventing the spread of fascism. It led to the contradictory situation whereby those who favoured social revolution such as POUM were persecuted by Soviet backed agents. Furthermore, the use of political commissars and SIM weakened morale in the Republican army. It was Largo Caballero's refusal to tow Moscow's line and outlaw POUM in 1937 which led to his dismissal. The policy of Negrin of accepting greater communist influence as the price for continued Soviet support, had the effect of confirming for British and French Foreign Offices what they had always believed to be the case, i.e. that the Republic was tainted with Bolshevism. Perhaps the most important consequence for the Republic of accepting Soviet support was that it became financially reliant on it. This situation was exacerbated by the British and French freezing of Republican assets. Therefore, Negrin as Finance Minister was forced to transfer the national gold reserves (worth some $518 million) to Moscow as credit for arms purchases. This exacerbated the Republic's financial problems and made the chances of defeating the Nationalists more remote.

The intervention of the fascist powers of Germany and Italy was to crucial in the Nationalist victory. Credit facilities were offered to Franco's forces to the extent of $700 million. Money was raised for the Nationalists through donations and foreign businesses such as the Texas Oil Company which extended credits to them. The fascist countries also provided substantial military aid which made up for initial deficiencies. Both Germany and Italy provided air power, most notorious being the Condor Legion. Italy provided around 70,000 troops which took part in some of the most important campaigns of the war such as that in Catalonia in 1937-'8. The aid provided for that campaign, when Franco's stocks and reserves were perilously low, was of real importance in determining the outcome. This is not to suggest that the Republic was without support from Western Europe. The volunteers of the International Brigade numbered some 35,000 strong and stiffened the resolve of an army short on manpower. They fought in major campaigns such as at Tereil or the Ebro. Yet they were no substitute for official support from their countries of origin.

Nationalist unity

The Nationalists won the civil war through a mixture of foreign support, military effectiveness and terror. They also were far more cohesive both ideologically and strategically. This cohesion was a product of the common desire to defeat the Republic, a desire which was increasingly stronger than that of the government to defend it. A key point of the war was in mid 1937 when the contrast between the two sides is revealing - the Nationalists issuing the Decree of Unification whilst the Republicans were embroiled in the May Days and the circumstances of Caballero's resignation as Prime Minister. The Decree of Unification in 1937 curtailed the divisions in Nationalist ranks between Carlists and Falangists. The *Falange* was the movement created by Jose Antonio in 1933. It was both anti-liberal and socially radical. Its membership increased after 1936 as many of its ideas appealed to the working class in nationalist held areas. By the Decree of 1937, radicalism was buried although Franco allowed token gestures to the movement's origins such as the Labour Charter of 1938. This promised the right to work and holidays for workers. The *Falange* idea of creating national syndicates was incorporated into the principles of 'Unity, Totality and Hierarchy'. Just as the radical element of Nazism was removed from prominence with the purge of the SA in 1934, so the influence of the *Falange* was removed in 1937. The Nationalist movement was controlled by the class which believed itself to have been politically disinherited by the Second Republic i.e. the *caciques*, the old aristocracy, the Church and *latifundistas*. Through the Decree of Unification, their movement was formally defined. What is more, religion was used to justify the rebellion and propose the reconstitution of a hierarchical and unjust society. This degree of unity was vital for success. It helped to engender military efficiency and a consistency of purpose which was often lacking on the Republican side. The organisation of the Nationalist army was far superior to that of the localist militias of the Republic. While Franco's forces were able to conscript 600,000 soldiers into one fighting body, the government's cause was crucially weakened by poor communication between different militias. In the early days of the war, many militias were politically orientated and were constituted with the explicit aim of social revolution. When Negrin imposed greater discipline over the army after the May Days of 1937, the undermining of revolutionary fervour also lessened morale and the fighting spirit of many units.

Conclusion

The Republic ultimately failed as it lost the Civil War. The primary reason for this was that it suffered from problems created by its perceived ideology. This resulted in a lack of support from democracies and the backing of its opponents by the fascist states. Similarly, ideological divisions exacerbated during the lifetime of the Republic weakened the efficiency of its army. Conversely, ideological uniformity which was born out of a sense of adversity, strengthened the Nationalist cause.

From the beginning, the Second Republic bore the burden of Spain's ideological, regional, economic and social tensions. The causes of the failure of democracy in Spain in the 1930's are many. The immature and divided state of the 19th century was compounded in its division by the economic and social changes of the 20th century. The emergence of issues and the development of conflicting ideologies during the Republic, resulted in political and social polarisation which manifested itself in civil war. It was these factors which were the underlying reasons for the failure of the Republic in the 1930's.

1   Spain was dominated by Castille, the capital of which being Madrid. Other areas of the country - in particular Catalonia and the Basque country pressed their claims for a level of autonomy from Madrid.

2   'Nationalists' is the term used to collectively describe the forces of rebellion, 1936-'9.

3   In 1833, the dying King Ferdinand VII changed the succession to the throne to install his infant daughter Isabella and deprive his brother Don Carlos. In claiming the throne in 1834, Don Carlos gained support in those northern regions which desired autonomy and from conservative elements who disliked the liberal constitution.

4   The *Cortes* is the Spanish Parliament.

5   Zamora was a conservative yet believed that a Republic would act as a vehicle for stability as it had in France.

6   The monarchy had supported the dictatorship of Primo de Rivera and was seen as increasingly out of touch with a Spain in transition.

7   In the election, the left Republican - Socialist alliance won 200 out of the 473 seats. This was a considerable amount of seats in a *Cortes* which contained numerous regional and other parties.

8   *Generalitat* was the title of the medieval Catalan government which was independent from Castille and even asserted autonomy in the 17th century.

9   Opposition came not only from within the Church hierarchy, but even prompted the resignation of President Alcala Zamora in October 1931. He was re-elected President in December.

10   Translated as 'the beautiful girl'.

11   Around 8000 officers accepted this offer out of a total corps of 21,000.

12   Ever since 1898, the army saw itself as the guardian of a conservative, centralist Spain. Such a view was obviously undermined by the Republic's reforms.

13   The *Partido Socialista Obrero Espanol* (PSOE) was the main socialist party.

14   The *Confederation National de Trabajo* (CNT) was strongly committed to dividing the land and transferring ownership to individual peasants.

15   The *Union General de Trabajadores* was the trade union organisation of the socialist movement.

16   The *Confederation Espanola de Derechas Autonomas* (CEDA) developed out of other right wing organisations as *Accion Popular*. Closely allied to the Church, CEDA was hostile to democracy and the Republic. Its leader was Gil Robles.

17   Situated in Cadiz in the South, Casas Viejas was typical of a village dominated by the landowners. In 1932 it was estimated that over 80% of the labourers were unemployed.

18   The Radicals had gained 104 seats in the Cortes.

19   Immediately, Catalan language newspapers were closed and the Parliament suspended.

20   Not only did the Radical governments refuse to enforce the reforms, some were reversed. The official anti-clericalism came to an end and the Church was allowed to be involved in education.

[21] In 1934, the police were increasingly used to crush strikes. In Sama in September, six people were killed at a Socialist meeting.

[22] Azaña's replacement as Prime Minister, Casares Quiroga was notoriously indecisive - a fact which was to become significant in July when the rebellion began.

[23] The *Africanistas* were the core of the Spanish Army. An elite fighting force, they were stationed in Spanish North Africa.

[24] Britain and France's main concern was that victory for the Republic would hasten the onset of Communism. Included in non-intervention, therefore, was a ban on selling arms to the Republic.

[25] The *Partido Comunista de Espana* was the main pro Stalinist party. Its support for Caballero's government was inspired by the desire to see the curtailment in the influence of non - Stalinist Communist parties.

[26] The May Days was a brief period of ideological struggle. On the one side were allied the PCE/UGT - ranged against them the Trotskyite POUM and their allies the anarchist CNT. The fighting was short in length but ferocious.

[27] By this decree, Franco was declared *Jefe d' Estado* - state leader. All ideological considerations e.g. that of the Carlists or Falangists were to be secondary to the aims of the movement to build a Spain in their collective interest.

[28] The *Sevicio de Investigacion Militar* (SIM) was based on, and in part trained by the Soviet NKVD.

[29] Thirteen bishops alone were killed in the opening weeks of the war.

[30] One must avoid exaggerating the demise of social control in the countryside. The results of the 1936 election revealed the widespread control of votes.

[31] The *Confederacion Nacional Católico-Agraria* (CNCA) was the organisation of Catholic smallholders. Its membership was large and they played an influential role at a local level in CEDA.

FRANCO

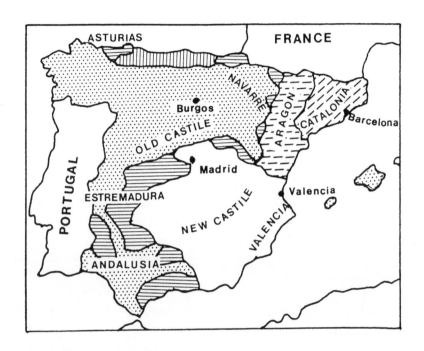

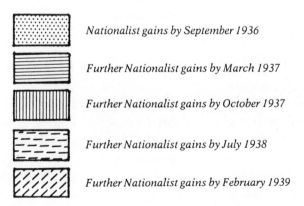

Nationalist gains by September 1936

Further Nationalist gains by March 1937

Further Nationalist gains by October 1937

Further Nationalist gains by July 1938

Further Nationalist gains by February 1939

SPAIN - CIVIL WAR 1936-9

WHY DID FRANCOISM COLLAPSE AND WHY WAS DEMOCRACY RESTORED IN SPAIN?

Introduction

The answer to this question lies in the nature of Francoism. As an ideology it represented the aims of the victors[1] of the Spanish civil war. The primary aim of the state post 1939 was to rule in the interests of these victors to the preclusion of others. To maintain that rule and control society, repression was used on a wide scale. Francoism did not survive its founder's death, however, as it had become increasingly anachronistic. The economic modernisation of the 1960's and the pace of economic and social change it provoked, rendered the regime obsolete as one whose ideology and methods of rule were grounded in the victory of 1939. The collapse of Francoism in the 1970s should be seen as a consequence of this factor and the perceived and real inability of the regime to deal with the political and social issues facing Spain.

Aftermath of War

April 1939 saw the end of the Spanish civil war and victory for the Nationalist[2] forces. The most important consequence for Spain was the division of society into two camps; the victors (*vencedores*) and the vanquished (*vencidos*). The vanquished, those who had sided with the Second Republic, were to be subjected to a vicious persecution. In the 1940's, 440,000 Spaniards went into exile and another 400,000 were to spend time in concentration camps, prison or working as forced labour.

During the years of the Second World War , Spain was isolated politically and economically. Although too weak to join the war formally, Spain supported the Axis powers wherever possible, sending troops to support the invasion of the USSR (the blue division) and supplying Germany with essential raw materials such as wolfram. Economically, the regime embarked on a policy of *autarky*[3] (self sufficiency) - partly out of necessity but also due to an ideological belief in its necessity for the consolidation of power. The policy was implemented through a series of protectionist measures and interventionist schemes such as the Industrial Law of 1939 or the Institute of Industry (INI) set up to direct investment programmes. By 1951 the national income had reached parity with pre civil war levels but, overall, the policy was an economic disaster with inflation, widespread poverty, shortages and corruption predominating.

The Structure of the Francoist Regime

The Francoist regime was created as an authoritarian one. Power came from above and emanated from Franco. He balanced his ministers who tended to represent the so called political 'families'[4]. The structure of the regime was flexible, however, and managed to allow for the articulation of the different interests which had supported the Nationalist cause. The Catholic Church had come out in favour of the rebellion in 1937 - a factor which allowed Franco to portray the war effort and subsequent regime as some kind of 'National Crusade'. The Church's reward was the Concordat[5] of 1953 which ushered in an era of 'National Catholicism'. The Church was given control over the intellectual and moral life of Spain. As an established religion, its bishops could sit in the *Cortes*[6] from its opening in March 1943. Most importantly, the Catholic lay movement gave the regime its bureaucracy and, to an extent, its dynamic element. This was centred in two movements, the ACNP and *Opus Dei*[7] - the latter being the driving force for modernisation in the 1960s.

The government of the state revolved around Franco as *Generalisimo* and '*Jefe del Movimiento*'[8]. It did not so completely rely on the party apparatus as in Nazi Germany or fascist Italy. The originally national socialist Falange party was effectively neutered by the 'Decree of Unification'[9] of 1937 whereby it was placed under the control of the *Jefe* and coopted into the *Movemiento*. This process was made complete by 1941 and was in response to the fact that the conservative groups that controlled the Movemiento - the army, Church, monarchists and landowners had no desire to see the primacy of a radical party. There was an acceptance of syndicalism[10] but precious little else. The new state was to be a monarchy as dictated by the Succession Law of 1947 - yet a monarchy without a king until Franco's death. Despite the fact that when he was declared heir to the throne in 1969, Juan CarlosII swore an oath to the principles of Francoism and the *Movemiento*, the concept of the monarchy was opposed by most Falangists.[12] The army was given its due in the regime as ultimate guarantor of its stability. The services were permanently represented in the Cabinet and the army was given jurisdiction over political offences. It was given police functions and could uphold the traditional view of what it perceived as Spain. This view was reflected in the Fundamental Laws, the Law of the Principles of the Movement (1958), and the important Organic Law of 1967. None of these elements of the 'constitution' challenged the 'unity of power' as exercised by Franco. So called 'Organic Democracy'[13] restricted basic rights and relied on a certain repressed non-participation on the part of the majority of groups within society.

From isolation to liberalisation

The regime was isolated politically and militarily after the end of the Second World War. In 1946 the UN recommended a diplomatic boycott of Spain and the regime was excluded from the Marshall Plan which helped in the regeneration of other parts of Europe in the late 1940s. Due to the outbreak of the Cold War, however, the regime's inherent anti communism won it American loans of $62.5 million in 1950 and outright US recognition and military alliance in 1953. In 1955, Spain was admitted to the United Nations. This recognition legitimised the regime and the $625 million of United States aid between 1951-57 propped up a system of autarky which failed to significantly raise living standards. With the tailing off of loans but the increasing dialogue with the western world, the regime moved towards a market driven economy as advocated by the new breed of

Opus Dei technocrats[14] led by Alberto Ullastres. The years 1958 /9 saw Spain join a variety of European and world economic organisations including the World Bank, International Monetary Fund (IMF) and the Organisation for European Economic Co-operation (OEEC). What should be seen as a turning point for the regime was the Stabilisation and Liberalisation Plan of 1959 which is discussed in detail below. This economic policy evolved into a market economy by plan as was represented by the three development plans of 1964-75. How responsible these plans were for the industrial boom of the period is debatable. What is without doubt is that the liberalisation of Spain's economy was at variance with what had been attempted previously. That Spain saw economic growth after 1959 was due to foreign investment, receipts from emigrant workers and tourism (in 1973 worth $3,091 million) and integration into the capitalist order which the regime had denounced for twenty years. Such growth, however, unleashed social and ultimately political tensions which were to highlight the regime's limitations and to discredit Francoism as an ideology.

Labour militancy

The relationship between worker and employer was governed, at least in theory, by national syndicalism. The Labour Law of 1944 gave large groups of the workforce job security. There was strict control of the unions, however, and the 1950s saw few open labour conflicts. The situation from 1962 onwards saw widespread union militancy - between 1964 -74 there

were nearly 5,000 strikes. The main cause of this was the introduction of collective bargaining. Large scale strikes such as that which led to riots in El Ferrol in 1972, discredited syndicalism as defined in the Syndical Law of 1971 and thereby the regime. The emergence of the 'independent' Catholic unions such as the CC OO[15] reiterated this point - hence its banning in 1968 in response to the demonstration of 100,000 workers in Madrid in October 1967 against the high cost of living. Student unrest after 1962 was frequent and similarly damaging - the response of the government in 1969 in declaring a state of siege again highlights the point. The demands of the students centred around political reform and explicitly political protest and in that were irreconcilably hostile to Francoism. By 1970 the student movement was large scale and a permanent reminder of the contradictions of Francoist rule - the unrest at Madrid university in 1972 being a case in point.

Regionalist Opposition

Although for the nationalists the civil war had in part been a war against separatism[16], in particular in Catalonia, developments from the mid 1950s showed the reality of Francoist rule to be divorced from its rhetoric. In particular, the violence spawned by the Basque terrorist movement ETA was a direct challenge to the effectiveness of the authoritarian regime. Numerous terrorist outrages which culminated in the assassination of Franco's closest political ally, Prime Minister Carrero Blanco[17], in June 1973 or the Madrid outrage in September 1974 which killed twelve, highlight the fact that the issue of separatism had not been resolved. The repressive response such as the Burgos trial of 1970 which sentenced nine ETA terrorists to death (their sentences were later commuted to life imprisonment) simply provoked violence and antipathy. The sixties had also seen a strong revival of Catalan nationalism.

Decline of 'National Catholicism'

The liberalisation of the economy was matched by a decline in the support of the Church for the regime. This was a consequence of new clergy, many of whom shared in the more liberal tendencies of the Roman Catholic Church world wide which were the consequence of the work of Pope John XXIII and the Second Vatican Council[18]. In encyclicals such as 'Mater et Magistra' (1961) and 'Pacem in Terris' (1963) the papacy supported the ideas of ideological pluralism, free speech and human rights. As time passed a younger clergy often was critical of the regime - in 1969 five Basque priests were imprisoned, between 1972 and 1975 priests were fined 11 million pesetas. In February 1974 the Bishop of Bilbao was placed under house arrest for openly criticising the regime. Although the sixties and early seventies did see some liberalisation e.g. the 1966 Press Law[19] which gave some freedoms to editors, the regime continued to repress - an example being the execution of the communist Grimau in 1962. Despite some Francoist politicians such as Manuel Fraga moving towards some forms of Christian Democracy they had real opposition from the old guard - the *Immobilists* led by Carrero Blanco. It was their rule

in the early seventies with the Burgos trial (1970), general strikes in Vigo and other provincial towns, closing of liberal papers such as '*Madrid*' in 1971 and continuing terrorism which finally dispelled any idea of ' national unity' or the 'peace of Franco'. In a sense these years paved the way for the restoration of democracy more than any other, 1974/5 seeing the execution of Puig Antich (a Catalan communist) and a state of emergency in the Basque country.

End of Francoism

On November 20th 1975, Franco died. All the main instruments of state, the monarchy, the council of the movement, the Council of the Realm were controlled by Francoists to ensure continuity. The first government under the Francoist, Arias faced economic unrest, particularly in the first three months of 1976. In March of that year five workers were killed in clashes with the police in Vitoria. The year also saw tension with continued ETA attacks and the refusal of the Francoist right to accept any reform of the Francoist constitution. This led to anomalies such as the Law of Political Association being passed in June 1976 which legalised political parties yet at the same time the *Cortes* refused to alter the Penal Code which made belonging to a political party illegal! The new government under Adolfo Suárez (minister for the Movement and a member of the ACNP[20]) which was appointed in July 1976 began to rectify the anomalies and thereby dismantle Francoism. In September 1976 Suárez met with army leaders who gave him the go ahead on the principle of political reform and in November, the Law of Political Reform created a legislature based on universal suffrage. Various steps were taken to recognise Catalan and Basque regionalism e.g. in January 1977 the Basque flag was legalised. Another important step in tackling the issue was in May 1977 when the main leaders of ETA[21] were released from prison and exiled. After the first democratic elections in June 1977, the Catalan *Generalitat* was re-established in September 1977 As part of the democratising of the political system, the Communist party (PCE) was legalised in April 1977, the same month the Movement was dismantled.

The new constitution on 1978 was introduced in the spirit of consensus as shown by the Pact of Moncloa of the previous year which set out an agreed strategy to tackle the country's economic problems. Although the constitution was introduced against a background of ETA violence, it defined Spain as a 'social and democratic state'. Three years after Franco's death, Francoism had been dismantled.

ANALYSIS

Introduction

In studying Francoism and its ultimate demise, one is presented with a series of issues. Primary amongst these is how Francoism was defined by its adherents. It is important to understand this, because it was this ideology which was undermined by the modernisation process. Equally important is to grasp that the central tenets of this mentality/ideology dictated government policy until 1976. By this date Francoism had become anachronistic. The manifestation of this anachronism was the social and, to an extent, the political turbulence and unrest of the 1960s and 70s which threatened the stability of the state. There is no doubt that democracy was introduced because the ideology of Francoism had become a discredited one by the mid 1970s. To the conservative classes whose interest Francoism protected, democracy now provided a better chance for the protection of their interests. This was particularly the case since their interests had altered from the 1930s. The failure Francoism as an ideology was that it did not evolve sufficiently to represent those interests.

The ideology of Francoism

Francoism was constructed as the antithesis of the Second Republic. It was developed as the collective ideology of those groups e.g. the Church, large landowners, who were threatened by the intended reformism of the Republic. What these groups feared was what became known as 'inorganic democracy' i.e. universal suffrage and political parties. The

Organic Law of 1967 summarised the belief in corporate suffrage i.e. representation of different groups as being truly reflective of the wishes of the Spanish people. The representative groups in whose interests the civil war was fought, were formed into the Movement with its National Council which was the ideological watchdog of the state. Therefore all institutions of power were controlled by individuals or groups whose shared principles were a critique of the Second Republic and an adherence to the ideals which defeated that republic.

It is the fact that Francoism was rooted in the thirties and the propaganda of that time which made it so inflexible. Any alteration of the script was simply a variation on the same theme, none more so than the role and cult of Franco. As the saviour of Spain, the defender of the principles of July 18th (the date of the outbreak of rebellion in 1936), deliverer from communism, Franco won some public support. It was Franco who decided his role to be that of 'constituent dictator' by two decrees of January 1938 and August 1939. Although this developed into the 'dictatorship of development' of the 1960's, the key element was still that of dictator. This dictatorship was deemed necessary in Franco's eyes because the government of the Republic had failed the nation. It was endorsed by referenda in 1947 and 1966, just as it was endorsed by the approbation of the large crowds organised for that purpose on certain occasions. To Franco, all unrest in the later years was still related to the civil war e.g. foreign hostility such as the ostracism of the United Nations in 1946 was put down to the hostility of communist states and

corrupt democratic powers. Yet despite his hold on power and absolutist control, Franco's dictatorship was not universally supported since it was not intended to be for the benefit of Spain as a whole but for Franco's sectarian and partisan view of Spain. This is contrasted to Don Juan's Lausanne Manifesto of 1945 which attacked Franco and expressed his own desire to be King of all Spaniards. As the supposed 'benevolent dictator' who brought material benefits to the Spanish people - nothing could be further from the truth. The economic reforms of the 1950s and 60s were introduced despite his only tacit acceptance as the policy of autarky had brought Spain to its knees. One needs to look no further than the apparatus of terror and repression to quash any concept of universal benevolence.

Just as the Civil War had been a crusade against the ungodly, so the rest of his regime was considered a continuing crusade to save Spain. The regime frequently boasted of 'the years of peace' and occasions such as the silver jubilee of Franco's rule in 1964 were entitled as 'twenty five years of peace'. Nothing could have been further from the truth as the regime's take over of power in 1939 did not initiate peace but ushered in a period of institutionalised revenge. The periodic executions such as that of Julian Grimau (garrotted in April 1963) or Puig Antich (a Catalan anarchist executed in 1974) took place against the background of widespread international opposition. Yet to Francoists they were part of the continuing crusade - even two months before Franco's death five members of FRAPP[22] and ETA were executed. The myth of

Francoism as represented by national holidays: April 1st the Day of Victory, October 1st the Day of the Caudillo[23] or at the huge monument to the Nationalist fallen at the Vaille de los Caidos was that the civil war was over and had been won. The reality in terms of policy and official attitude was very different. As time passed, however, to succeeding generations the spirit of revenge and the importance of the Victory became increasingly irrelevant.

Ideology triumphant and sustained 1939 -57

It could be argued that it was in these years that Francoism enjoyed its 'Golden Years'. It is true that Spain suffered economically yet this was blamed on numerous external factors by the regime. Most importantly, it was in this period that the regime experienced few open incidents of opposition. Brutal repression at home and isolation abroad fostered a form of political autarky which won sympathy or at least a certain apathy from many sections of society. It was also in this period that the image and policies of Francoism most closely coincided with the aspirations of many Spaniards. As a regime so closely linked to the civil war, it is not surprising that its greatest period of stability and legitimacy was just after that war. To many Spaniards, Franco's victory in the war was a deliverance from communism[24] and the forces of 'barbarianism'. The establishment had been rescued from democracy and flourished in the protection of autarky - of the thirty eight wealthiest figures in the banking world in 1944, sixteen had titles and another six were connected to the aristocracy. Central to the acceptance of Francoism

was the image of it as a deliverer against the godless both at home and abroad. The values and morals of Catholicism became all pervasive, the *curas* - the priest - took centre stage in society and an era of unquestioning 'National Catholicism' was ushered in. This was sealed by the concordat of 1953. Catholicism became the cultural driving force of Francoism and a Catholicism of the seventeenth century to boot! Catholics controlled the universities and the Council of Scientific Investigations founded in 1939, imposed an unquestioningly traditional Catholic view on Spanish intellectual life. Periodicals such as *Escorial* and *Arbor* rewrote history to match the Francoist/Catholic view e.g. the nineteenth century was godless, un - Spanish and therefore to be ignored. It was in this period that the views and values of the Church and regime were so closely intertwined to the extent that the Catholic Church played a leading role in the definition of the Francoist myth. To the Catholic lay groups of *Opus Dei* and the ACNP were given the spoils of victory, the running of a bureaucracy unhindered by democratic government.

Other groups whose cause the Nationalists had fought for, flourished post 1939. In agriculture there was hunger and falling yields but this was explained away by the regime as being the fault of the Reds or foreign powers refusing to sell fertilisers or tractors. The regime regulated agriculture by a series of decrees (such as that limiting the planting of orange trees in 1942) and by controlling prices and output. The farmers who benefited from this system were the larger farmers who were left to trade extensively in the black-market - the *estraperlo*. The *latifundios*, the absentee landlord of the South were encouraged to improve their land by Cavestany - agriculture minister in the 1950s - but there was no threatened land redistribution and labour was not only cheap but compliant. The civil war had been fought to protect the interests of large landowners and until the mid fifties their interest was well served.

To the conservative classes, the threat of organised labour was diminished. The creation of syndicates to replace unions was a token gesture to the *Falange* which had lost all real influence by the 1937 Decree of Unification. For the different components of the Nationalist side in the Civil War - the 'negatives ' against which they fought, e.g. democracy, reform, liberalism had been defeated. The 1946 Banking Act protected the banking status quo to the extent that profits increased for the five large banks so as their combined reserves grew from next to nothing in 1940 to 7,472 million pesetas in 1960. In the 1950s these large institutions gained a near monopoly over the financing of private industry. Again, it is easy to see how the civil war was central to the maintenance of power of the established elites. Until 1966, pre-publication censorship made possible the creation of a new hegemony - a fact made easier by international isolation until the mid 1950s. The monarchists were reassured by the Succession Law of 1947 and preferred the interlude of the dictatorship to republicanism. It was possible for all these groups to ignore the failings of autarky in its attempts to succeed in import substitution at the cost of shortage and rationing. The new regime had embarked on the process of restructuring Spanish life to ensure that their interests were protected.

Ideology confronted, 1957 -75

The cause of the disintegration of the Francoist myth was the economic modernisation which was undertaken to preserve it. That process produced political apathy through consumerism that enabled the regime to survive to 1975. It also produced social tensions and conflict which typify advanced or developing consumer societies. These tensions manifested resulted in change - in values, beliefs, behaviour and attitudes. The main tenets of Francoism were rooted in the past and therefore incapable of substantial or corresponding change. This period therefore saw the further development of a chasm between how the Francoist regime perceived Spain and the reality.

Modernisation

By 1956, Spain faced bankruptcy, its gold reserves had fallen to $40 million, autarky was discredited as austerity measures were introduced to combat spiralling inflation. The policy of protectionism and state intervention as represented by the INI had failed to bring about industrialisation. The series of reforms which were undertaken by the *Opus Dei* technocrats led by Alberto Ullastres, Mariano Rubio and Laureano Rodo is significant in that they represented official admission that autarky had failed. So central was autarky to the chauvinist critique of the world presented by Franco, that its abandonment highlights how divorced Francoism was becoming from reality. Franco only grudgingly accepted the changes as a means of maintaining a hold on power. Such policies as joining the IMF and the World Bank in 1958 fully contradicted twenty years of speeches criticising the decadent capitalist world!

The aim of the Stabilisation Plan of 1959 was to restore financial stability by restricting inflation. It also planned to liberalise foreign trade and promote foreign investment. In fulfilling this public spending was cut and protection was reduced and imports encouraged. The danger of this for the regime is all too obvious - opening Spain up to market forces - integrating her into an international system - contradicted the mentality of the closed Spain of Franco. Rapid industrialisation also reduced the effectiveness of the mechanisms of social control such as the Church. The rate of growth was rapid, Gross Domestic Product (GDP) grew by 7.2% p.a. between 1960 -73, industrial production by 10.2% p.a. The regime even tried to take credit for what was termed the 'economic miracle'[25]. In reality it was overtaken by the pace of social and economic change. Increasingly, the justification for Francoism became increasingly anachronistic in a modernising country. The ideology began to disintegrate.

Consequences of modernisation

The introduction of a market driven economy with all its consequences is central to understanding the evolution of many groups from passive acceptance to rejection of Francoism. An excellent example is that of the working classes. National Syndicalism was institutionalised through the introduction of the Syndical Organisation (OS) between 1938-40. Its aim was to create an alternative to capitalism and Marxism, to maintain social order and through the organisation, the syndicates were to provide the working classes with representation in the *Cortes*. As in Mussolini's Italy, however, the reality of their operation differed greatly from the rhetoric of intention. It is true that there was little labour conflict in the 1950s and large scale unrest such as the Asturian miners' strike of 1958 was rare. This was due to a stagnant economy and repression, however. The introduction of market forces contradicted the existence of syndicates as a critique of capitalism, it also necessitated free collective bargaining as an essential prerequisite of a capitalist economy. This made syndicates anachronistic despite attempts under José Solis Ruiz (Minister for the Movement from 1957) to reform them. The Organic Law (1967) and the Syndical Law (1971) are both examples of how reform could only ever be limited without fully compromising the ideals of Francoism. Therefore democracy in the unions was denied, both laws were restrictive and denied the idea of independent unions. The consequence was a contradiction; the working class were to be organised on the principles of Falangism which was a critique of the capitalist market economy being introduced. The development of the independent Catholic workers' councils - the CC OO undermined the syndicates although they cleverly worked with the structures of the OS. In 1962 they successfully won improvements in pay for miners in the Asturias, the demonstrations for better conditions they organised in Madrid in 1967 contradicted the official view of improving living standards. The CC OO was infiltrated and run by communists and dominated the labour movement to the extent that it was made illegal in 1968. It continued in operate in a semi legal fashion until 1975 although in 1973 nine of its leaders were imprisoned. The irony of the situation is clear - not only had the Francoist model failed - but the legacy of that failure was that the largest union in the workers' movement was dominated by communists such as Marcelino Camacho. The main reason for this was the introduction of free collective bargaining with its related consequence of rising material expectations. That these could not be delivered by the official syndicates was clear.

The consumerist values which were part of the modernisation of Spain were at odds with the principles, values and institutions of the Francoist ideology. Most striking was the rejection by the youth of the sixties of the previous generation's acceptance of an authoritarian political system. That many exhibited political apathy appears to be the norm and to an extent the aims of the *Opus Dei* technocrats were achieved - to create a stable, acquiescent society through consumerism, where it failed was in achieving social cohesion. However, that process, with its links to Western democracies and ever growing contact with the West, produced behaviour which was incompatible with and challenged Francoism. The student movement most of all showed up the shortcomings of the regime, the fallacy of its boasting to have brought social 'peace' and

ultimately it challenged the regime's legitimacy. Agitation began in 1956 but mushroomed in the sixties led by independent students' unions ranging from the communists to the Christian Democrat (UED). The importance of the strife was that it highlighted the regime's inability to reform meaningfully e.g. attempts to create a state controlled students' union in 1965 failed dismally. It also highlighted that repression was only a partially successful means of control; although the universities were often closed, such as Madrid University in 1968, it did not prevent near permanent student unrest such as the widespread strikes in 1973. Without the ability to prevent such behaviour, the regime's frailties were exposed.

The modernisation process created a crisis of identity in Francoism itself. The ascendancy of *Opus Dei* produced tensions within the Movement, in particular because of the marginalisation of the *Falange* by the 1958 Law of Fundamental Principles of the National Movement. The limits to political change can be seen in 'political development' the attempt to give the regime credibility at home and with the international community. The aim of 'political development' was to modernise the regime in line with the economy but all attempts foundered on the same point - that to enact real modernisation would undermine the regime. Therefore it simply ended up as a revamping of the Movement. Whilst Franco talked in 1962 of Spain being ' an example of democracy' a more realistic picture of the nature of the regime should be seen in the execution of Grimau a year later or the creation of a special court

- the TOP - in the same year to deal with public order crimes. The desire for greater liberalisation within the regime and a new law of association was led by Falangists, many of whom had no experience of the civil war. Led by politicians such as Solis and Fraga they highlighted the dilemma of Francoism without being able to enact real change. Control of government, first by Carrero Blanco from 1969-73 and then Arias Navarro 1974-5 brought repressive government without reform. In many senses these governments characterise the weakness of Francoism more than any other. Strikes were banned yet the general strikes at Vigo and Pamplona were a reality. Spain was in theory a Catholic country but the regime was at loggerheads with the Church.

 The liberalisation of the Catholic Church was due less to the consequences of economic modernisation and more the result of a significant shift in the philosophy of the church. The effect on Spain and the regime was of enormous importance. National Catholicism was all pervasive in the 1940s and 50s, it was the intellectual and moral basis of the regime as shown in the works of such authors as Raphael Calvo Serer. The rejection of National Catholicism by the Vatican through *Mater et Magistra* (1961), *Pacem in Terris*(1963) and the Second Vatican Council was a devastating blow. Neither Pope John XXIII or his successor Paul VI accepted National Catholicism and both ensured that new appointments made in the Church's hierarchy would assert the liberal view - most importantly the appointment of Enrique y Tarancon as Primate of all Spain in 1969. Added to this was the development of a younger more radical clergy which rejected the concept of the crusade and spoke out in favour of social justice, autonomy and democracy. By 1971 not only had the Bishop of Bilbao been placed under house arrest but the Assembly of Bishops and priests sought forgiveness for the church's partisan role in the civil war. The ideology was based on a protection of traditional Catholic values and institutions against the godless of the West and East. This view was completely undermined by the slow rejection of those values, in particular the attempted emulation of the West, and the liberalisation of the church.

The concept of Spain - 'One, great and unified' - was another mainstay of the nationalist uprising and of the principle of 'July 18th'. Despite cultural repression in regions such as Catalonia - the continued expressions of regional identity remained an example being the meeting of a Catalan Assembly in 1971. The terrorism of ETA proved that the repression of Francoism was no permanent answer to the problem of regionalism. The Basque region was industrialised heavily in the 1960s. This was not the main cause of the development of ETA but the regime's inability to deal with it in any other way but by using heavy handed tactics such as the state of emergency declared in 1968, led to a ground swell in sympathy for regional autonomy. The regime, as exemplified by the attitude of Carrero Blanco would and could not offer any form of autonomy. The consequence was a near permanent state of crisis as exemplified by Carrero's assassination in 1973.

The ideology dismantled 1975 -78

The transition to democracy and the rejection of Francoism was a product of the modernisation process which had undermined the legitimacy of the old regime. That it lasted to 1975 pays testimony to the remarkable achievement of Franco in staying in power until his death. How far the ideology had become anachronistic is highlighted in the level for support for change and the extent to which the new, democratic Spain rejected the values and institutions of Francoism. Whilst the issues which Spain faced were in some senses similar to the 1930s, e.g. regionalism or democracy, many issues were new. Therefore the ideology of the 1930s was inappropriate to deal with those issues.

The transition 1975 -'8

The transition to democracy was made possible because by the 1970s, the conservative elites in whose interests Francoism had been forged recognised that Francoism was a spent force. The contradictions and failures of the few months of the Arias administration in 1975/6 proves the point with the escalation of ETA violence, the stalling of reform such the refusal in June 1976 of the *Cortes* to repeal the Penal Code despite the new law of Political Associations and the massive strikes of January - February 1976.

The role of the monarchy was essential in dismantling the Francoist system and, even more important, bestowing a legality to the new democracy. Franco had installed Juan Carlos in 1969 as his successor to perpetuate the institutions of Francoism. From his succession and in particular from mid -1976, Juan Carlos played an important role in promoting those, such as Adolfo Suárez, who were prepared to introduce democracy. A constitutional monarchy was the best option available for the long term survival of the institution. From the point of view of placating the army, the monarchy was essential. As head of the army, the monarch's views had great influence in preventing the military from outwardly opposing the process of democracy. The legalisation of the Communist party by Suarez in April 1977, the opposition of the army and the diplomacy of the monarchy in assuaging their fears is a case in point. Yet even the army had changed, there were influential officers such as General Mellado who was appointed to the government and those who Suarez met in September 1976, who supported reform.

The period of transition was fraught with tension but lacked the polarisation of the thirties. The ministry of Suárez was particularly adept at creating compromise and trust. A consensus had emerged at the basis of which was a rejection of the Francoist system. Yet this consensus was also used to tackle the issues of government - in particular the economic ones. the Moncloa Pacts are an excellent example. These agreements signed in October 1977 brought together the industrial and business fraternities with the unions with the aim of bringing down the inflation rate (26% in 1977). The legalisation of the Basque flag and the amnesty granted in 1977 diffused an explosive situation, as did the re-establishment of the *Generalitat*[26] in September of that year. Yet all sides compromised to achieve a peaceful transition to democracy, the PCE, for example, accepted the monarchy and the process of negotiation as the means of change.

Conclusion

It is indeed remarkable how rapidly the Francoist structure collapsed after his death and how, for the most part, the change was peaceful. The extent to which Francoism had become an anachronism can be seen in the changes which took place. Central to the ideology of Francoism was the defeat of communism and the labour movement. The role of the CC OO has already been discussed but the real irony was that after legalisation in 1977, the PCE[27] became far stronger than in the 1930s gaining 10% of the vote in the 1977 election. Indeed after democracy was re-established in 1977, the explicitly Francoist parties gained only two percent of the vote. The legacy of Francoism was not a centralist Spain but one in which regions such as Catalonia pressed for autonomy. The rigid application of the centralist ideology left the new democracy the legacy of ETA. The so called 'pillars' of the regime crumbled; the Movement was dismantled by Suárez in April 1977, the army neutralised by the monarchy and the church actively supportive of political pluralism (it refused to back any party in the 1977 election). It should be remembered that Suárez and many in his government were members of the ACNP yet they managed to create a democratic consensus to the extent that Carillo, the leader of the PCE was prepared to call

the Church 'a factor for progress'. The liberal constitution of 1978 represented the formal end of Francoism.

[1] The victors being the Church, army, conservative elite, monarchists, falange, landowners and business. The first two in particular, became known as the 'pillars' of Francoism.

[2] The Nationalists were those who rebelled against the Republic in July 1936.

[3] The economic policy of autarky was also a feature of German and Italian fascism.

[4] The 'families' were the different interest groups already outlined above in footnote 1.

[5] A Concordat is an agreement between the papacy and another government. In this case it gave formal recognition and legitimacy to Franco's regime.

[6] The Cortes, the Spanish Parliament was a mere rubber stamp for the period in question.

[7] Both organisations were dedicated to influencing political and intellectual life.

[8] *Jefe* literally means boss. The *Movemiento* was the amalgamation of the different groups which supported Franco, and played the role of the single party in the state until 1975.

[9] The Decree of Unification was the means by which Franco pulled together the anti - republican forces in 1937. This was an important factor in the civil war victory.

[10] Syndicalism was seen as an alternative to trade unionism and socialism in the organisation of the working class. Within

syndicates, workers and employers were to collaborate for the national good. The syndicates were to be instruments of social control yet also the channel through which workers could be represented. In Spain, as in fascist Italy, they were as much propaganda as substance.

[11] Juan Carlos was the son of the heir to the throne, Don Juan, who remained in exile rather than sanction Franco's regime.

[12] The *Falange* were the Spanish equivalent of a fascist party. They were effectively sidelined by the Decree of Unification in 1937.

[13] 'Organic democracy rejected universal suffrage and a party system. Instead it promoted representation through bodies such as the syndicates, Church or army.

[14] A technocrat is an economic or technical expert who controls or influences government.

[15] The *Comisiones Obreras* - CC OO were independent trades unions formed in the late 1950's by Catholics and Communists. They became extremely influential.

[16] Separatism was a historic issue which was the result of the dominance of the province of Castille. From the late 19th century, the developing economy of Barcelona and the resurgence of nationalism led for the call for regional autonomy and independence. In 1933 the *Generalitat*, a semi autonomous Catalan state, was created by the Second Republic.

[17] Carrero Blanco was an unreconstructed Francoist and was seen as Franco's most likely successor.

[18] The Second Vatican Council reformed the Catholic mass and introduced innovations such as services being conducted in languages other than Latin.

[19] Before 1966 censorship was rigid in Francoist Spain. The new law did not permit press freedom, however. Editors could still be punished for attacking the regime.

[20] The *Asóciacion Católica Nacional de Propagandistas* (ACNP) were a leading Catholic lay movement.

[21] ETA were the military wing of the Basque separatist movement which undertook terrorist activity.

[22] FRAPP was a revolutionary terrorist organisation.

[23] This term was used respectfully to describe the 'leader'.

[24] This highlights the ideological nature of the civil war. Although the republican forces were not communist, there was increased communist influence as a consequence of Soviet support. This simply reinforced the misrepresentation of the Republic as extending communist influence.

[25] The 'economic miracle' of sustained growth was a result of a booming tourist industry, foreign investment and restrictive labour laws.

[26] The Generalitat was led by Josep Tarradellas who had been the Catalan president in 1936.

[27] *Partido Communista de España* - the Spanish communist party.

FRANCO

Chapter 8

WHAT WAS THE IMPACT OF INDUSTRIALISATION ON THE RUSSIAN EMPIRE 1890-1914?

Introduction.

Industrialisation in Russia from the 1890's was characterised by state intervention to hasten the process of industrial development. There had been emerging industry the Empire from the 18th century[1], but it was only with governmental intervention that there was significant growth[2]. It is important to point out, however, that industrialisation was encouraged by the autocracy[3] for political purposes, most importantly for its own preservation.[4] Of equal importance was the maintenance of Russia's status as a world power in the light of the industrial and technological advances of her Western competitors[5]. In judging the impact of change one should first measure against these intentions. There is no doubt that the industrialisation undertaken produced significant economic growth although this growth failed to match that of other leading industrial nations. Whilst attempting to create a role as an independent world power, the process of industrialisation created an over reliance on foreign capital and alliances. In undertaking such a process, the state created economic and social tensions which not only failed to bolster the autocracy but periodically threatened to undermine it. One should argue that the impact of industrialisation on the Russian Empire was great but that the impact was not that intended by the state when it undertook to direct the process from the 1890's onwards. Intended to solve the problems of Russia's backwardness, it created new and potentially far more damaging ones for the autocracy.

The Foundations of Industrial Growth, 1861-90

The Crimean War of 1854 -'6 highlighted the Russian Empire's technological backwardness in comparison to the industrial powers of Britain and France[6]. The consequence was not government acceptance of the need to industrialise for there was significant opposition within the autocracy to such a change. However, the war had shown the need to construct railways for military purposes, if no other. From 1861 -'90 the government created the financial conditions to attract foreign and other investors into building railways, The result was that by 1890 nearly 30,000 km of track had been laid and important lines constructed including Moscow to Kursk and the Ekaterine railway (1885) which linked the coal of the Donets Basin to the iron of the Krivoy Rog region of the Ukraine. The impetus this gave to other industry was considerable. In the coal and iron industries growth was impressive, output in the former rising from 18.3 million poods[7] in 1860 to 367.2 million poods in 1890. Foreign expertise was used to develop production in the iron industry. In 1869, the Welsh industrialist John Hughes was contracted to build an iron works at Lugansk which subsequently flourished with state help[8]. The railways were particularly important in overcoming the greatest obstacles to economic modernisation, that of the Empire's size and the difficulty of communication. Apart from railway building, encouragement by the state for industry was slow in coming. The Emancipation of the serfs in 1861 had removed an obstacle to economic growth but was not a direct stimulus to industrial growth[9]. In fact, in the short term, those industries (e.g. sugar production) which had relied on serf labour suffered a period of readjustment[10]. There were still restrictions on the mobility of labour, e.g. internal passports, which were potential restrictions to growth. Successive Finance Ministers in the 1880's, Bunge (1881-'6) and Vyshnegradskii (1887-'92), acted to stimulate industrial growth by using a series of fiscal measures. Until 1877, tariffs[11] on imported goods were low which stimulated light industries and those which relied on cheap imported raw materials such as the cotton industry. Major tariff reform in 1877, '81 and '82 helped to protect heavy industry form foreign competition, thereby acting as an impetus for growth[12]. The policies of Vyshnegradskii in particular, acted to generate investment for industry by raising domestic taxes and creating the conditions which would attract foreign capital. This policy worked to an extent as could be seen in the growth of the oil industry in the Baku region of the Caucasus.

The Influence of Witte 1892-1903

The most important decade for Russian industrial expansion is associated with the policies of Sergei Witte who was Minister of Finance from 1892 - 1903. To maintain Russia as an independent world power, Witte embarked on a deliberate programme of rapid industrial expansion. He built on the progress made in the 1880's and rejected the anti - Western view that there was an alternative to industrialisation for Russia. At the basis of Witte's reforms was state intervention to develop the railways and heavy industry. To this end, Witte followed a fiscal policy based on financial reform[13], protection through high tariffs, foreign investment and heavy domestic taxation. This policy was not new, what Witte brought was vigour and an increased role for the state. In the 1890's this policy seemed to work. The railways flourished with the state not only encouraging investment but undertaking actual construction. The linchpin of Witte's industrial strategy was the building of the Trans-Siberian railway linking Moscow to the Pacific Ocean at Vladivostok and completed in 1904. This construction acted as a huge demand on domestic heavy industry, and by that the state was compensating for the lack of domestic demand. This increase was particularly felt in the Ukrainian iron industry, railway demand accounting for one third of pig iron production in the 1890's. Overall, railway growth was spectacular, expanding from 30,595km in 1890 to 53,234km in 1900. The state invested considerably in such an expansion, by 1900 the national debt of 3.5 million rouble was the highest in the world. Yet Witte's policy was based on attracting foreign investment to mitigate the lack of domestic capital. By stabilising the rouble and, in 1897, by placing it on the gold standard (i.e. fully convertible into gold), Witte managed to attract significant investment from abroad. This was because with the rouble's value fixed against gold, investors could be sure of the returns in interest they would receive from their investments. From 1893-'99, foreigners invested 595.6 million roubles as opposed to domestic investment of only 215.5 million. By the turn of the century, there were some 270 foreign companies operating in the Russian Empire. Apart from sound financial policy, investors from abroad were attracted by the potentially high rates of return on Russian capital, in particular as interest rates were low world-wide throughout the 1890's. By 1906, 27.5% of all French capital investment overseas was in Russia.

Much of the foreign investment in the 1890's was in heavy industry which flourished accordingly. Partly as a consequence of a late start (which meant that all the new technologies available could be used), and also because of the new communications afforded by the railways, heavy industry grew dramatically. Between 1890 -'99 the average annual rate of growth of industrial production was 8.03%. Similarly the metallurgical industry was worth around 14 million roubles in 1890, heavy investment had increased its value to around 144 million roubles by 1900. Such developments were accompanied by a shift to large scale production units, by 1900, 10% of firms in the oil industry accounted for over 70% of production. Witte was a great believer in the theories of the German economist Friedrich List who had argued that high tariffs could enhance economic development. Therefore he modified and strengthened Vyshnegradskii's 1891 tariff which meant that throughout the 1890's, on average 33% of the value of imported goods consisted of tariffs. For certain industries the tariff was sufficient protection for growth to occur and there is no doubt that the taxes on imported goods were prohibitively high, e.g. on iron ore in 1891 it was 10.5 gold kopeks

per pood as opposed to nothing in 1861.

Lack of agricultural reform

Industrialisation was undertaken in the 1890's without compatible agricultural reform[14]. This was of particular significance as the Russian Empire was still largely rurally based. The need of the autocracy to maintain social stability meant that economically restrictive measures were still being introduced in the countryside at the same time as industrial growth was being pursued, e.g. in 1893 a law was passed preventing peasants withdrawing from the *mir*[15] on completion of the payment of redemption dues without a two thirds majority of the village community agreeing. The agricultural sector was squeezed in the 1890's by the increase in taxation to pay for industrial development. Between 1893 - 1912, anything between 20-30% of Russia's grain was exported and the indirect taxation burden grew by 450% between 1860 -1900. The countryside was still not immune to famine as the tragedy of the famine in the Volga region in 1898-'9 showed[16]. Between 1897-1901 a series of poor harvests across the Empire compounded the harsh conditions the peasantry faced. Perhaps most serious was the rapidly growing population which placed a huge strain on agricultural resources. The 3.55 times increase between 1811-1913 was mainly rural as only 13.7% of the populace lived in towns, even in 1897.

Slump 1900-1903

The industrial boom of the 1890's was followed by a sharp slump from 1900-'03. The reasons for this included the agricultural crisis mentioned above, and a decline in the construction of the railways. The Trans-Siberian was nearing completion: 1900 saw a fall of 10% in orders. Industrialisation was still reliant on state or foreign investment, the domestic demand remaining extremely weak. From 1899 there was an international downturn in the trade cycle which was exacerbated by the uncertainty caused by the Boer War which broke out in October of that year[17]. The Russian Empire was particularly severely hit, bankruptcies were widespread - in 1902 alone 2,400 interests closed. As a whole, overproduction led to a slowdown in rates of growth, from 1900-'06 the rate of growth of industrial production had slowed to only 1.43% p.a.. Emergence from depression in 1903-'4 was further slowed by the negative effects of the Russo-Japanese war to be followed by the 1905 Revolution and its aftermath, both were factors in reducing business and foreign confidence. This was particularly the case with the dismissal of Witte in 1903, blamed for the economic downturn. Because of the fragility of demand and the weakness of competitive capitalism, post 1900 saw the development of monopolistic organisations concerned with marketing. Known as syndicates, they were set up throughout the heavy industry sector and they wielded considerable influence. There were over 150 created by 1914 including *Prodamet* (1902) which controlled virtually all of the Ukraine's meat industry and *Med* (1907) which did the same for the nation's copper.

Economic upturn 1907-14

Despite years of depression in the early years of the century, the industrial economy boomed again in the years running up to the First World War. The main features of the boom years between 1907-'14 were similar to that of the 1890's. There was spectacular industrial growth, at an average of 6.25% p.a. in these years and the basis of that growth was foreign capital which financed government investment and foreign expertise and capital in specific industries. The process of concentration of industry in large enterprises continued apace, by 1914 over 40% of the industrial workforce worked in the 344 plants with over 1,000 workers. The state still was a major source of investment through the railways although the levels of investment were nothing in comparison to the 1890's e.g. between 1907 -'13 around only 1,000 km of track was laid a year. On top of this was the demand created by new contracts to supply the navy with new warships. Improved prices for agricultural produce after 1906 helped to create some domestic demand for consumer goods and domestic investment overall in this period outstripped that from abroad, 913 million roubles as opposed to 284 million between 1909-'11.

Social consequences of industrial change

From 1890-1914 the Russian Empire saw considerable economic change but this brought with it social tension, unrest and demands for political reform. The industrial workforce was not a large proportion of the Russian population, numbering only 1.7 million (1.28%) in 1900 and still only 2.3 million (1.4%) in 1913. However, their concentration made them a potential threat to social stability. This was compounded by poor working conditions and pay. In 1885 in the Morozov textile plant in Orekhove-Zuevo, over 6,000 workers walked out in an illegal dispute over conditions. This strike was symptomatic of unrest in other industrial centres such as Moscow where workers were the victims of blatant abuses such as the use of the truck system[18] and excessive fines. The government's response in 1886 was twofold. Primarily, it used repression to end the strike, deporting 600 strikers back to their home villages. Secondarily, in every sense, the state passed ineffectual laws concerning the creation of factory boards to oversee disputes and the outlawing of payment in kind (paying workers with goods or tokens rather than with cash) and other such measures. Overall, these laws tended to favour management rather than rectify the grievances of the workforce and the continued banning of unions reinforces this point. Despite this, the urban proletariat set up its own strike committees, in 1889 a Central Workers' Committee was created in St Petersburg to be followed in 1895 by the Union for the Struggle for the Liberation of the Working Class. Both organisations were central in supporting the strikes of 30,000 St Petersburg cotton spinners in 1896-'7. These strikes were countered by further repressive measures including the creation of a factory police force in 1899. The previous year had seen the creation of the Russian Social Democratic Workers' Party which was a milestone in the development of the Russian labour movement. The new century saw an ever increasing number of demonstrations, in particular those held on May Day. The economic downturn saw a proliferation of strikes throughout the country including that at Rostov in 1902. Despite the attempts between 1901-5 of various supporters of the autocracy e.g. Sergei Zubatov or Father Gapon to set up unions or workers societies not influenced by socialism, the attitude of the state to the proletariat continued to be one of hostility. The burden of exploitation fell equally on the peasantry and 1902 saw insurrections in the Ukrainian districts of Poltava and Kharkov. Such unrest was not inspired by Marxist thought but it spurred the development of a political movement based on such ideology. In 1902 Lenin published *What is to be Done* which formed the basis of revolutionary Leninism. The following year The Russian Social Democratic Workers' Party divided into two factions - the Bolsheviks led by Lenin and the Mensheviks led by Martov. Pressure for democratic reform was centred around the Union of Liberation created in 1904 by Milyukov and Struve and more radical in its demands for social justice than the more classical liberalism of the *zemstva*[19].

1905 Revolution and its aftermath

The Russo-Japanese War proved to be the catalyst for revolution in 1905. Russian expansionism in the Far East resulted in conflict with Japan and humiliating defeat at Port Arthur in December 1904. At sea, the Russian fleet was destroyed at the battle of the Tsushima Straits in May 1905[20]. Each defeat provoked demonstrations which were also partly fuelled by continuing industrial unrest. In January 1905 there was a walk out at the Putilov metal works in St Petersburg. On 9th January, a march of the strikers to the Winter Palace with the intention of petitioning the Tsar was led by Father Gapon organiser of a government sponsored union, the Assembly of Factory Workers. The crowd was attacked by police and Cossacks with many casualties on what was to become known as 'Bloody Sunday'. Order was temporarily restored to St Petersburg but industrial unrest spread, to be organised by newly formed soviets[21], the first appearing in the Urals in April. By far the most important soviet in St Petersburg, was founded in October 1905 and became the focal point for the general strike of that month. Started by the Union of Railway Workers on 7th October with demands for political concessions and improved working conditions, the strike spread across the Empire. The autocracy's response, as prompted by Witte, was to issue the 'October Manifesto'[22] which promised limited democracy and civil liberties. There was sporadic continued defiance from the strikers, in December in Moscow there was a brief uprising which was suppressed by the army. On 3rd December the St Petersburg soviet was closed down by the authorities.

The government moved to suppress further unrest, having split the revolution's supporters with the 'October Manifesto'. A loan from France of 2,250 million francs secured the autocracy's financial position and the return of the army from Manchuria made possible the widespread clamp down on revolutionaries, 2930 being executed between 1905-'9. The Fundamental Laws issued in April 1906 revealed that the autocracy was willing to accept only limited political reform. Included in its proposals was a limited and imbalanced suffrage, the possibility of government by decree and no ministerial responsibility. The weakness of the Duma was highlighted by the premature dissolution of both its first and second meetings and the passing of a new electoral law in June 1907 which altered the suffrage further in favour of groups loyal to the autocracy.[23]. Although the third and fourth Dumas were more conciliatory towards the state, by 1911 the alliance between the autocracy and its supporters in the Octobrist party had broken down.

Stolypin and Limited Reform

Unrest was not limited to the towns in 1905. In January and February, uprisings took place in Kursk and the Volga regions. From October 1905 to August 1906, there was sporadic revolt in areas as diverse as the Baltic provinces to the Caucuses. The autocracy's response was the repression mentioned above, with limited reform. Although land redistribution was not entertained, redemption payments were abolished from 1st November 1907 and the concept of a property owning peasantry was turned into reality by Stolypin's agrarian reforms introduced in November 1906. This was done by permitting peasants to own land independent of the commune, by making possible the consolidation of strips into fields and instructing ownership of land to be in the name of the head of the house alone. The effects of the reforms were not consistent across the Empire. In the south and west of the Empire, there was more of a move out of the *mir*, but in other areas change was slow. By 1915 only 22% of peasant households had individual land ownership. Further reform in 1910 which attempted to strengthen capitalism in the countryside by making individual land ownership compulsory in some cases, came to little. Not only was there attempted reform on the issue of land holding, the legal status of the peasantry was raised in October 1906 and educational facilities were made more widely available in 1908. The assassination of Stolypin in 1911 ended the limited reformism of the autocracy. In some sense this was the response to a perceived strengthening of the ruling classes due to the lack of discontent amongst the proletariat from 1907-'11. Social reform had given them the right to form unions in 1906 and insurance against accident in 1912. However, the shooting of 200 strikers at the Lena gold fields in 1912 signalled a further outbreak of unrest. In 1914 strikes swept across the Empire from the oil wells of Baku to the Putilov factory in St Petersburg. Many of the protests were aimed at the horrendous living and working conditions. Such was the boom in industrial production in the years running up to the war that St Petersburg alone saw a growth in the numbers of industrial workers from 150,000 in 1908 to around 210,000 in 1914. This was not matched by improvements in the conditions of the working classes which led to unrest.

ANALYSIS

Introduction

More than ever previously, by the end of the 19th century there was an acceptance amongst sections of the ruling class that reform was necessary to maintain the power of the autocracy. Yet there was one fundamental contradiction, to undertake reform risked undermining the social structure and stability on which the continued power of the autocracy relied. This factor more than any other, served to shape the nature of reform, in the case of industrialisation it coming 'from above'[24]. It also constrained the extent to which reform could take place i.e. that the promotion of heavy industry was not undertaken alongside compatible political and agricultural reform.

The impact of industrialisation on the economy was great yet it failed to match the growing productivity of the main Western economies. Perhaps the most important by-product was that industrialisation unleashed social and economic tensions which threatened to erode the basis of autocratic rule, that of hierarchy, order and stability. One should then argue that in an important sense the impact of industrialisation was the opposite of what was intended.

An economic 'Great Power'?

There is no doubt that the industrialisation programme of the 1890's and after provided the

Russian Empire with a significant industrial base.[25] The impact of the state's intervention and, particularly the railway building programme were keenly felt in numerous industries. Coal production grew from 367 million poods in 1890 to 995.2 million poods in 1900. The rate of growth of the iron industry was similarly great, output of ore rising from 106.3 million poods to 367.2 million poods within the same period. What this points to is an extremely high rate of growth, the figure of around 8% p.a. throughout the 1890's being virtually unparalleled in the history of industrial development. Even after 1906, when the rate of growth drops to around 6% p.a., this is still a considerable achievement especially when the fall in direct state subsidy is taken into account.

The impact of the railways

Although the Empire still lagged behind the rest of the world in terms of railway density (by 1913 it was 1km of track as opposed to Germany's 12km for every 100 square km), this picture distorts the real achievements of the railway building programme. The Trans-Siberian railway swallowed 250 million roubles of investment but the engineering feat of laying 6,400 km of track was as impressive as its economic potential was considerable. By 1913 the Empire had some 70,000 km of track which served as the arteries for economic communication. One should not overemphasise the impact of the railways, however. The military priorities of the regime as argued by many close to the Tsar e.g. General Kuropatkin led to the building of some lines

for which economic considerations were secondary, e.g. that between Orenburg and Tashkent. In fact much of the railway network was uneconomic and one of its most important consequences was that to further expand and meet running costs, the state fell in to deeper debt. By 1914, the national debt had risen to 8.8 billion roubles and foreign shares of this debt rose from 30% in 1895 to 48% in 1914. There is no doubt that the construction of the railways had a significant impact on industry, indeed it became the largest industry in itself with nearly half a million employees by the turn of the century. In judging the impact of the railways, however, one should recognise that a factor of equal importance was that the state had to finance a debt which could only be serviced by a continued squeeze of other sectors of the economy - namely agriculture. This meant that the industrialisation process undertaken left the Russian Empire with an imbalance between agricultural and industrial sectors. This had important social implications as is explained below.

Uneven growth

Another main feature of the economic 'landscape' was that the massive investment only had an effect on certain sectors of industry. The large businesses such as the Putilov metalworks in St Petersburg were an indication of the poor productivity of labour and the need to employ large numbers to reached required levels of production. Side by side with these new heavy industrial enterprises remained traditional artisan and craft production which still employed two thirds of the non-agricultural workforce. Most of these workers were employed in crafts related to the production of consumer goods. Industrialisation and the policies of Witte had little effect on production methods in these industries. The ratio between the value of output of light and heavy industries was 70 : 30 in 1887 but by 1900 that figure had been transformed to 53.5 : 46.5. By 1900, the Russian economy was one of contrasts and uneven development. Alongside the fact that vast swathes of industry continued to use outdated methods and were hampered by low productivity there were beacons of modernisation. By 1900, foreign investment had made the oil industry based in the Caucasus the most modern in the world (mainly due to British capital) producing some 701 million poods in 1901. Whilst some areas of the country such as the northern regions were relatively untouched by industrialisation others grew rapidly. The population of the town of Baku, which was at the centre of the oil industry, grew from around 14,000 in 1863 to just over 232,000 in 1914.

The impact on agriculture and living standards.

The impact of industrialisation has to be put into the context of the Russian economy as a whole. To finance the process, indirect taxation was raised on goods commonly used by the peasantry. Around 85% of revenue came from taxes on matches, sugar, kerosene, tea and vodka. On top of this increased burden of taxation was the continual repayments of redemption dues, by 1903 redemption arrears averaged 138%. In 1892, arrears on taxes owed for that year alone stood at 72%. Similarly, innovation

was hampered by increased tariffs on imported agricultural machinery, the 1891 tariff increasing the burden to anything up to 140 gold kopeks/pood. Consumption was also very much hit by the policy of high tariffs. The main point is that the government was prepared to depress living standards in the countryside to pay for industrial growth. Witte recognised as much in his famous memorandum of 1889 in which he stated that not only did Russians pay more as a consequence of the tariffs but that this formed a 'heavy burden' on the already impoverished. One consequence was a shift in the patterns of income which contradicted the desire of the autocracy to maintain the commune as the basic form of social control. As the financial demands increased on the peasantry, so many resorted to wage labour as a means to supplement their income. Including all types of wage earners, i.e. industrial, agricultural and other such as domestic service, the numbers of wage earners grew from around four million in 1860 to 17.5 million in 1913. Pressure for this change also came from the steep population increase in the 19th century (from 74 million in 1860 to 170 in 1913). Whatever the reasons, it altered the pattern of peasant life - in 1900 only 48% of wage earners lived with their families. This was particularly unwelcome to the autocracy in a period when agrarian policy was aimed at maintaining the status quo and stability in the countryside e.g. the use of Land Captains from 1882. As industrialisation helped depressed the agricultural sector, so it impoverished the most important sector of the economy. This in turn meant that the industrial sector was over reliant on state investment. The depression from 1900-'3 is a case in point when the poor harvests and weakness of the agrarian sector resulted in very weak demand helping to deepen the depression considerably.

For the Russian Empire to develop a robust and diverse industrial economy, fundamental reform of the agricultural system was necessary. Yet this fundamental reform was not possible because of the interests bound up in maintaining important elements of the old system. This was another factor which helped to limit the impact of industrialisation. Despite the levels of investment, industry still played a supporting role in the economic structure, agriculture contributing around 70% of GNP both in 1900 and 1914. Yet the impact of industry would always be limited without modernisation in agriculture. The reforms undertaken by Stolypin to reduce dependence on the *mir* and encourage peasant innovation and capitalism had only a limited effect by 1914. Such was the conservatism of the peasantry that only around 2.5 million households had been separated from the mir by 1915 and by the outbreak of war still 80% of peasant land was held in strips and not in consolidated fields which could be innovated upon. Another problem was that the population continued to grow at an alarming pace, up to 25 million births being recorded between 1905-'14. This placed a further strain on resources despite innovations such as the Peasant Land Bank created in 1883 to help peasants purchase land. Industrialisation and economic policy deflected from the fundamental problem, that of the need for agricultural reform. The policies of Witte deepened the crisis as reflected in the continuation of famine

on a large scale and the intensity of peasant unrest in 1905-'6.

The creation of a working class

Perhaps the most significant impact of industrial growth was the creation of an urban working class. In addition the autocracy was faced with the political demands to rectify the injustices suffered as a consequence of the introduction of capitalism. Yet there was the contradiction - an autocracy by its nature is undermined by dissent, opposition or pluralism - all of which can be seen as a consequence of industrialisation. The industrial economy the state encouraged from the 1880's produced tensions which could only be alleviated by economic and political reform, but that was not possible without undermining the autocracy. Therefore, the government acted throughout the period with the twin tools of repression and very limited reform. Such a policy failed to solve the root problems of dissent i.e. poor pay and working conditions and helped widen the base of dissent into demands for political reform. There are numerous examples of this. The ferocity with which the 1897 cotton workers strike and the 1905 demonstrations in St Petersburg were met helped to fuel support for the soviet and the demands in October 1905 for political liberty and social justice. Although the state allowed unions to be formed in 1906 it so severely limited their means of protest - no combination with other unions, political manifestos, police harassment and so on - that their effectiveness was limited. The violence of the strikes in St Petersburg in 1914 reflect the lack of social control the autocracy had in the cities. The extent to which the military was used from 1890-1914 reflects the insecurity of the regime. In 1893 troops were used 19 times in industrial disputes, by 1902 that number had risen to 522 times. However, in shooting at miners in the 1912 Lena gold fields' strike the military helped to provoke further unrest across the country. The courts used after the 1905 Revolution were brutally efficient in suppressing any further unrest, some 2,000 being executed between 1905-'08. The limitations of the Fundamental Laws, what Trotsky called 'the police whip wrapped in the parchment of the constitution' were followed by the 1907 electoral law which reduced the opposition in the third Duma to 19 Social Democrats and 54 Kadets. Meanwhile the government supporting Octobrists gained 154 seats and their allies on the right another 97 seats. Industrialisation had helped to create tensions which could only be resolved through reform, yet even the non reactionary Stolypin was unable to compromise as a minister of the Tsar. The revolution of 1905 polarised the political classes which feared the radicalism of the revolutionaries and many were supportive of Stolypin's conservatism in 1907. Yet growing urban unrest from 1912 frightened even the government's supporters amongst the Octobrists and forced a breach between them and the government over the need for political reform. It was the persistent underlying state of agitation in the cities as a result of the nature of unrestricted industrial development between 1890-1914 which helped to create a sense of crisis in the regime.

Urban growth and exploitation

The impact of industrial growth on the cities was great. There was persistent unrest in these cities and towns due to the continued poor conditions of the proletariat. Overcrowding in the major cities was endemic, St Petersburg's population alone growing from 1.3 million in 1897 to 2.1 million in 1914. Most of these workers were migrants from the countryside and many of them unskilled and illiterate. Not surprisingly, housing was extremely poor, in St Petersburg in 1904, with over half the working class families each sharing a single room. Exploitation was commonplace, the 1886 legislation providing no protection to workers. This was in the main due to the lack of factory inspectors. The loyalty of those inspectors which did exist was very much to the factory owners and the bureaucracy of which they were a part. In the cotton strikes of 1897, inspectors adopted a strong anti striker stance touring factories and warning potential strikers of the grave consequences of withdrawing their labour. Many of the new industrial workers were women, in St Petersburg the figure was as high as 60% due to the existence of a large textile industry. Overall, the numbers of women employed in St Petersburg' industries was around 25%. Yet the predominance of women simply accentuated the exploitation, in the metalwork industry in 1914, women were paid only 44.1% of a man's wage. Even skilled male workers were underpaid, the wage for a machinist in the metal industry being 500 roubles a year when the amount needed to afford a basic living for a family was above 600 roubles. Those who worked in the textile industry could expect only around 200 roubles a year. Working conditions in the factories were extremely poor and were not improved because of the state's hostility to intervention on behalf of the exploited, e.g. in 1893 the Council of State rejected a measure to compensate those injured in factory accidents as socialist. In 1913 over 14,300 accidents were reported in St Petersburg alone. For women, childbirth was a hazard, most women being expected to work until labour began and return immediately after the birth, in 1912 nearly 95% of women gave birth without medical assistance.

The government's legislation after 1906, e.g. accident insurance from 1912 did little to alleviate such hardship. Industrialisation created an explosive situation which was made even greater by the concentration of such large numbers of workers in each factory. The Putilov engineering works with its 40,000 employees was the largest in the world. The impact of the urban working classes was far greater than its size as a proportion of the population would suggest (only 1.4% in 1913). To overcome the injustices of their working lives they demanded reform but to the autocracy these demands were treated as subversion rather than as legitimate demands for improvement. This highlights very clearly the tension created by the incompatibility of autocracy and the effects of the industrial growth it promoted. The growing working classes were a major threat to economic and political stability.

There is little doubt that the effects of industrialisation provided a stimulus to the radicalisation of Russian politics and the creation of political parties which fundamentally opposed the autocracy such as the Russian Social Democratic Workers Party founded in 1898. Although their impact was limited before 1914, their influence grew and this created significant tensions.

The impact of foreign capital

The reliance on foreign capital as one of the main sources of investment capital had an important effect on Russian diplomacy and relations with the rest of Europe. It is wrong to assume that foreign investment led to foreign interference in domestic affairs as was feared by contemporary conservative and populist groups in Russia. The process of industrialisation and its attraction of huge amounts of investment, in particular from France was interrelated with political developments. By 1917 the French had invested around 740 million roubles in Russian industry, for the most part in mining and metal industries. The 1894 alliance with France was a by product of this growing mutual dependence but also stimulated further investment. The same can be said of the 1907 entente with Britain which also had significant investments in oil and cotton in particular. Foreign investors were attracted to Russian industry by the prospects of good profits and a stable and convertible currency. There is no doubt that it was in the interests of these investing nations that Russia was stable. The French loan to the Tsar in 1905 being a case in point. To go further and to state that reliance on foreign capital and especially French capital was the cause of Russia's entry into the First World War on the French side is harder to prove.

Catching up with the West?

It is indeed questionable that industrialisation from 1890-1914 achieved its aim of catching up with the more advanced economies of the West. Although productivity increased, the Russian Empire slipped from ninth to tenth behind Italy in the international rankings of industrial output between 1860-1910. The reality was that although Russian industry was developing, so was that of her competitors. Despite the use of new technology, productivity still lagged because there were many factors which held back industrial progress. Therefore, by the turn of the century, the output of a Ukrainian miner was still only half or even a third of his fellow miners in the west. Communication was still poor between regions and the social structure and governmental policy still acted as brake on economic growth e.g. the persistent state-supported anti-Semitism. There were groups within the bureaucracy which opposed industrialisation and their views were of a greater significance than the emerging industrial middle classes. Even the emergence of groups such as the Council of Representatives of Industry and Trade in 1906 could not prevent other factors such as internal security, taking precedence over industrial concerns in the formulation of government policy. In real terms, Russia also lagged behind her competitors, the 36 million tons of coal produced in 1914 comparing poorly with the U.K.'s 292 million tons or Germany's 190 million tons. Income per head was still low at around £10 ahead in 1913 as opposed to £30 in Germany or £68 in the US. The conclusion to be drawn from these figures is clear, the impact of industrialisation was great but not enough to narrow the gap with the west. The policy of Witte had made inroads but the Russian Empire had still predominantly rural economy in 1914. Perhaps the greatest test of this was war. Although Russian industry showed itself capable enough of meeting the needs of the military during the First World War, the poor transport system hampered delivery of goods and production began to fall from 1916 onwards in key industries such as iron and coal.

Conclusion

The economic impact of industrialisation from 1890-1914 was that it created for Russia a large industrial base comprising mainly of heavy industry. The aim of 'catching up' with the West was not reached although it was achieved in certain individual industries. Russian industrialisation was hampered by the structure and lack of reform in the agricultural sector which limited its impact. The substitution of foreign capital for home demand, however, had its own consequences on diplomacy and foreign affairs. Most important was the impact industrialisation had in creating economic, social and ultimately, political tensions which threatened to undermine the autocracy and in some senses was already doing so. Yet in this lay the contradiction, to maintain the autocracy, bureaucracy, ruling class and the social system on which relied, modernisation to a degree was necessary. Without it, the whole structure was in danger of being undermined by low productivity, poor communications and population growth. In modernising, however, the autocracy simply highlighted the fact that an autocracy and the systems on which it depends were incompatible with the forces unleashed by industrial capitalism.

[1] There was significant industrial development during the reign of Peter the Great from 1682 -1725. As the Empire's economy was very much based on serfdom, industry was imposed 'from above' with the state taking a leading role in promoting development. This was to be repeated in the 1890's.

[2] The first half of the nineteenth century saw only slow growth in Russian industry. There was development in consumer industries which was the consequence of a mixture of factors including protection, a growing population, new techniques of production from the west and a cheap serf labour force. Most importantly, the state did not intervene - conservative officials such as Count Kankrin (Minister of Finance from the mid 1820's to the mid '40's) believing that large scale industrialisation would result in social instability. This view was held by many bureaucrats even in the 1890's and Witte came up against considerable opposition to his plans.

[3] An autocracy is a system of government when there are no limits on the power of the monarch/head of state.

[4] The policy of economic change was supported by two conservative Tsars, Alexander III (1881-'94) and Nicholas II (1894-1917). Whilst rejecting the limited social and political reform of Alexander II (1855-'81), they both accepted that without industrial growth, the Russian Empire would fall further behind the West.

[5] This became particularly apparent during the Crimean War of 1854-'56.

[6] The Crimean War was essentially a dispute between Russia and France over Russia's claims to be the protector of Christians in the Ottoman Empire and custody of the holy places in Palestine. Military defeat in Russia at the hands of Anglo-French forces led to loss of land and neutralisation of the Black Sea at the Treaty of Paris in 1856.

[7] The pood is a Russian measurement of weight. One pood = 16.3 kg.

[8] The Hughes operation expanded to the extent that by the mid 1880's it was the largest producer of pig iron in the Empire. Such was Hughes influence that he had a town, Yuzhovska, named after him.

[9] The Emancipation Acts gave limited freedom to the serfs but not land. Each serf was to receive allotments of land but they were not given directly to the serf but to the village commune - the mir. The peasants were to refund the autocracy for the land via instalments (redemption payments) over a 49 year period. In that way the autocracy maintained the means of social control in the countryside.

[10] Some factories relied on serf labour. With emancipation that labour more often than not left and had to be replaced.

[11] A tariff is a tax on imports.

[12] Between the 1850's-70's tariffs on imported goods were low. This encouraged the growth of light industries but undermined heavy industries and those such as iron and steel which could not compete with cheap foreign imports.

[13] The most important financial reform was the placing of the rouble on the gold standard. This meant that the rouble could be freely converted into gold and was possible because Russia had built up sufficient gold reserves by having a favourable balance of trade since the 1880's. Such a measure increased the confidence of foreign investors.

[14] In many industrialising countries such as Britain, industrialisation was accompanied by innovation and change in agriculture. This resulted in a growth in production to meet the increased demand of an urban workforce for agricultural goods. In Britain, the agricultural sector became a source of investible capital and created significant demand for industrial products. This was not the case in the Russian Empire where innovation and capitalism in the agricultural sector was prevented by the land holding system and the mir.

[15] The mir was the village commune.

[16] The huge problems the bureaucracy had in dealing with the famines on 1891 and 1898 in particular, highlight the Empire's poor communications and administrative defects.

[17] The Boer War was a conflict between Britain and the Boers of South Africa. Although a colonial war, there were rumours from the start that there might be Franco-German-Russian

intervention on the side of the Boers. It seems that although the Russian foreign minister, Count Muraviev was keen, the other two nations showed little desire to intervene. These diplomatic manoeuvrings helped cause a down turn in the confidence of the international business community.

[18] The truck system was when an employer paid wages in tokens which then had to be used in the employer's shop - prices there being inflated and the quality of goods generally poor.

[19] The *Zemstva* were created in 1864 as local authorities. Their membership was made up of the rural gentry but almost immediately they became the focus for liberal opposition to the autocracy. As their already limited powers were reduced by Alexander III in 1890, they became increasingly vocal in their demands for further political representation i.e. national *Zemstvo* or *Duma*. This again highlighted the difficulties associated with the autocracy and reform.

[20] Under the command of Admiral Rodjestvensky, the only military success this Russian fleet had was against the British fishing fleet in October 1904. Whilst sailing through the North Sea on its way from the Baltic to the Far East, the Russian fleet fired on British trawlers mistaking them for Japanese destroyers. One trawler was sunk and what became known as the Dogger Bank incident strained relations between Britain and Russia.

[21] A soviet was an elected council of workers.

[22] The October Manifesto was issued to buy the autocracy time. It granted a constitution and a Duma with an extended franchise. It also promised to extend civil liberties. The result was to split the liberal opposition. Those within it who accepted the governments proposal's became known as Octobrists, those who wished for further reform such as a constituent assembly with far reaching powers on western lines became known as Kadets. In dividing the opposition and winning back the full support of the army, the autocracy achieved its aim and made restoration of order by force possible.

[23] The new law proposed that one deputy was worth the equivalent of each of the following groups' votes: 230 landowners, 1000 businessmen, 15,000 urban middle class people, 60,000 peasants or 125,000 urban working class. These figures alone give a clear indication of the mistrust felt by the autocracy towards the proletariat.

[24] 'From above' in this sense meaning that the main impetus for industrialisation came from the state.

[25] For further reading, the work of M.E. Falkus - *The Industrialisation of Russia 1700-1914* (Macmillan) is highly recommended for the clear overview it gives of Russia's industrial development.

SERGEY YULYEVICH WITTE

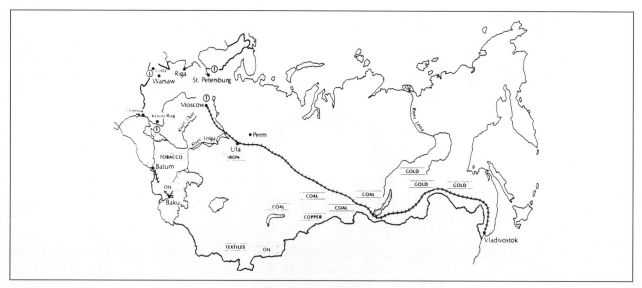

RUSSIAN RAILWAY

Chart on rate of growth

Index number of economic growth 1861- 1913

Year	Total ind A	Total agric B	Pop C	Urban pop D	Volume of grain exports E	Railways length F	Iron G	Govt revenue H
1861	1.00	1.00	1.00	1.00	1.00	1.00	1.00	1.00
1871	1.49	1.11	1.16	2.12	2.42	6.18	1.33	1.25
1881	2.52	1.12	1.36		3.59	10.50	1.67	1.60
1891	3.99	1.17	1.62		5.04	13.95	3.33	2.19
1896	5.33	1.96	1.70	4.25	6.47	17.95	5.33	3.36
1901	7.50	1.81	1.83		7.40	25.64	9.67	4.41
1906	8.10	1.89	1.99		7.25	28.91	9.00	5.57
1913	11.65	3.09	2.32	6.69	7.83	31.91	14.00	8.38

CHART OF ECONOMIC GROWTH

CHAPTER 10

HOW DID THE BOLSHEVIKS MANAGE TO GAIN AND CONSOLIDATE POWER 1917-'22?

Introduction

The Bolsheviks managed to gain power in October 1917 because they successfully distanced themselves from the policies of the Provisional Government of 1917 and, in particular, its continuation of the war. Through this, the Bolsheviks were able to win support amongst the strategically important soldiers and sailors stationed in the major Russian cities. As all other revolutionary parties[1] collaborated with the Provisional Government, the Bolsheviks' ability to reflect popular resentment in its policies won them significant support. As the power of the Provisional Government began to disintegrate from the summer of 1917, it was the Bolsheviks and Lenin in particular who had the opportunism to attempt to fill the power vacuum.

Attaining power was relatively straightforward, its consolidation far less so. The survival of the revolution was due to a variety of factors. In the short term, the Bolsheviks granted concessions to worker and peasant alike which won acceptance. Although ideologically motivated, the state was suitably pragmatic and ruthless when the situation demanded. A mixture of internal discipline and terror in dealing with her enemies led to victory in the civil war and the defeat of opposition within the broader revolutionary movement. Although Soviet rule was not assured by 1922, the state had gone a considerable way to ensuring that it would be very difficult to topple.

The First World War and the February Revolution.

On declaration of war in 1914, most opposition parties were prepared to put aside their domestic quarrels and to support the government. The defeat of Germany became the priority even for the revolutionary Plekhanov and many of the largest left wing movement, the Socialist Revolutionaries (the S.R.s). Widespread support for the autocracy ebbed away with the impact of growing economic hardship caused by inflation, prices rising four times over from 1914-'17. The consequence was that the rouble lost two thirds of its pre war value by 1917. Another destabilising factor was the failure of Russian arms. From the start of the war the Germans proved themselves to be better organised and equipped. The Russian army suffered a series of devastating defeats which began at Tannenberg in August 1914. In 1915, the Russian army retreated out of Poland at a cost of over a million men during the German offensive in Galicia. On September 5th, 1915, the Grand Duke Nicholas Nicolaievich was relieved of supreme command of the armed forces and his post taken by the Tsar. This had important consequences in that the Tsar's absence left the government at the mercy of the Empress Alexandra. Her German nationality and obvious hostility to the Duma, coupled with her fascination for the monk Gregory Rasputin[2], brought the government into considerable disrepute. This was compounded in 1916 by the appointment of the allegedly pro-German, Boris Sturmer as Chief of the Cabinet and further military defeat. In June 1916, the Brusilov Offensive was launched by the Russian army. Initially the Austrian army was pushed back along a 300 mile front but the arrival of German reinforcements signalled the end of any advance. The Russians failed to take their objectives of Kovel or Lemberg and the loss of over a million men led to discontent and demoralisation. Unrest on the home front was caused by growing food shortages and exasperation with the war. Opposition groups within the Duma pressed for reform and Rasputin was murdered in December 1916. On the January 9th 1917[3], 140,000 workers in Petrograd staged a strike in memory of Bloody Sunday which was followed by further sporadic action. On February 23rd another general strike took place. Two days later the Tsar ordered troops to take whatever action necessary to suppress such action. The response on the 27th was a general mutiny of the army in Petrograd. The same day the members of the cabinet resigned and the first meeting of the Petrograd Soviet took place. On March 2nd the Tsar abdicated in favour of his brother Michael who in turn abdicated in favour of the Provisional Government which was proclaimed the following day.

The Provisional Government

The first Prime Minister of the Provisional Government was Prince Lvov who ruled with the support of Liberals and Kadets. From February onwards, the government found itself sharing 'dual power' with the Petrograd Soviet which was dominated by S.R.s and Mensheviks. The latter gave conditional support to the former. The Soviet accepted the government's right to rule but only as long as it did not counteract the spirit of the revolution. Almost immediately, the government introduced a series of reforms including the right to strike, an amnesty for political prisoners and the abolition of capital punishment. However, on April 18th, the government pledged itself to the war against Germany via a note from the foreign minister Milyukov which promised to fight to a 'victorious end'. The Soviet on the other hand, had demanded a revision of war aims and the working towards a 'general democratic peace' without imperialist gains. In March, it had issued Order No.1 which removed authority from military officers and placed army administration in the hands of elected committees of soldiers. A counter order from the government was virtually ignored. This highlighted where real power lay, a fact which was underlined by the downfall of the Kadet-based government in early May and the creation of a coalition government which included two Mensheviks and the S.R. leaders V. Chernov and A. Kerensky. This new government continued with the war effort, Kerensky bringing new vigour to the post of Minister of War. The importance of this can not be underestimated as it meant that both socialist parties had become involved in the prolonging of the war. In June/July 1917, the Russians launched the ill fated Galician campaign. Despite initial gains, the Russian army was thrown back onto the defensive and routed in a series of battles which ended in August with the defeat of General Kornilov's forces at Riga.

Bolshevik opposition

Meanwhile, the Bolsheviks had begun to organise opposition to the Provisional government based on the message of unconditional opposition to the war. On April 3rd, Lenin arrived at the Finland Station, Petrograd after travelling across Germany in a sealed train[4]. Almost immediately he issued the *April Thesis* which placed considerable distance between the Bolsheviks and other parties of the left. In it the S.R.s and Mensheviks were attacked for their collaboration with the 'imperialist' government of Lvov. The 'thesis' promised an end to the war and no support for the Provisional Government. It went on to guarantee government by the Soviets, the immediate seizure of all land and the nationalisation of industry. The *April Thesis* was a comprehensive manifesto for change, promising also the abolition of army, bureaucracy and police and the end of Parliamentary government. It appealed to many of those who took part in demonstrations against the Galician campaign including the Kronstadt sailors who led the so called 'July Days' uprising. The response of the new coalition government led by Kerensky was to turn many against the Bolsheviks by accurately accusing them of accepting finance from Germany. Lenin was temporarily forced to flee to Finland but the Bolsheviks benefited soon after from the threat of a counter revolution led by General Kornilov. Acting with the support of many officers of the army, Kornilov indicated his intention to march on August 27th to march on Petrograd and restore 'order'. To defend the capital, Kerensky armed the Soviet and workers militia which included many Bolsheviks. Although the threat from Kornilov was removed by the railway workers, the incident served to further radicalise a working class ravaged by the effects of inflation. From January to October the real wage of the average worker had been reduced by 57%, in 1917 the rouble having only 10% of its value of 1914. Growing unemployment as a result of shortages in raw materials, coupled with increasing governmental intervention on the side of employers in disputes resulted in the election of a Bolshevik majority to the Petrograd Soviet on August 31st. Immediately it passed resolutions reflecting the demands of the *April Thesis*. Yet Bolshevik success was not limited to Petrograd, on September 5th they won a majority in the Moscow Soviet and later in the same month they won elections to the Duma in the same city. The response of the government on September 14th was to attempt to form some political consensus via the Democratic Convention (which was intended as a pre Parliament to pave the way for a democratically elected Constituent Assembly). However, such an exercise backfired with the Bolsheviks walking out and Kerensky forced to include Kadets in his cabinet who were perceived by many on the left as counter revolutionaries. All these events gave encouragement to Lenin who argued strongly that the European situation pointed to now being the time for revolution.

The October Revolution 1917

On October 10th, a meeting of the Bolshevik Central Committee in Petrograd decided on the course of armed uprising as proposed by the now present

Lenin. There were significant doubts, raised by Kamenev and Zinoviev in particular, of the consequences of failure of what was ideologically a premature revolution[5]. There were also worries expressed that the revolution would not be mirrored abroad and that it might not even find sympathy amongst a slogan weary Russian proletariat. The cause of armed insurgency was aided by the Petrograd Soviet's creation of the Military Revolutionary Committee on October 16th. Set up to co-ordinate the military defence of Petrograd in the case of a German attack, the effect was to provide the Bolsheviks with the means by which it could arm and organise the Red Guards. On October 23rd, Trotsky visited the strategically important St Peter and Paul fortress in Petrograd and won the support of the soldiers whose guns protected the Winter Palace. The same day Kerensky ordered that the Bolshevik press in Petrograd be seized and that the *Aurora* battleship stationed outside the Palace be put to sea. On the 24th and 25th the Red Guards countered these orders and seized strategically important points including the telegraph exchange and post offices. Kerensky fled Petrograd and the rest of his government was arrested after the Winter Palace had been taken on the night of the 25th/26th. Simultaneously the Second Congress of Soviets met with a majority of 300 Bolsheviks and 90 left SRs. As the Winter Palace was stormed, so the Mensheviks and Right SRs walked out of the Congress[6] leaving Kamenev to pronounce the success of the revolution in the name of the Soviets. Decrees were immediately passed on peace and land[7] and an interim government - the Bolshevik - only Council of People's Commissars set up.

Consolidation of Power, 1917-18

The new government had many enemies and immediately had to use force to counter the threat. Forces loyal to the Provisional Government under Krasnov were defeated in and around Petrograd from the 28th-30th October. Moscow was taken by the Bolsheviks after a fight on November 2nd. On the 27th October, the Bolsheviks began to close down the opposition press, a move hotly disputed at a meeting of the CC to ratify such a policy on November 4th[8]. The Bolsheviks were not in sufficiently strong a position to prevent the pre arranged elections to the Constituent Assembly on November 12th. Where the peasants' support lay was very clear, with the Right SR's receiving 17.1 million votes (41%) and 370 seats, the Bolsheviks gaining only 9.8 million votes (23.5%) and 168 seats. The Assembly first met on January 5th 1918 but was disbanded a day later on Lenin's orders. There was no time wasted in the introduction of decrees which destroyed the basis of the Tsarist social and economic structure. In November 1917 the legal system was abolished and on the 15th of that month workers were given control over the factories. Their obvious lack of experience and the potential consequences for the economy led to the creation of Vesenkha on December 5th to co-ordinate and impose state control. In mid December, the banks were nationalised by decree and on the January 28th 1918, the national debt was repudiated and all foreign loans cancelled. To protect itself and to counter opposition the government created the *Cheka* on December 7th. As it had promised, the new government immediately opened peace negotiations with Germany. Although Trotsky attempted a number of tactics to divert the Germans from insisting on their demands before peace could be signed, they were unyielding. With German troops advancing on Petrograd in February 1918 the Bolshevik government was forced to accept humiliating terms for peace which were signed at Brest Litovsk on March 3rd. The treaty was opposed by many within the Bolshevik leadership including Bukharin and Dzerzhinsky but Lenin and eventually Trotsky accepted peace at any cost. The Bolsheviks signed away Poland and the Baltic States to German control whilst accepting the independence of the Ukraine, Georgia and Finland. Such loss was too much for the left SRs who ended any remaining links they had with the Bolsheviks who now changed their name to the Communists. At the Vth Congress of Soviets[9] in July 1918, there was considerable tension between the Communists and left SRs who shouted Trotsky down and proceeded to assassinate the German ambassador in an attempt to provoke war. They capped this by arresting Dzerzhinsky on July 6th. The Bolshevik response was swift, the left SRs were removed wholesale from the Congress and a Right SR uprising in Yaroslav in late July was viciously repressed. This signalled the start of a Red Terror at the hands of the *Cheka*. In response to the assassination of the Petrograd *Cheka* chief Uritsky on August 30th[10], over 500 hostages were shot by Kronstadt sailors.

The Civil War 1918-'20.

The Bolshevik revolution faced considerable danger from a variety of forces. To counter the threat, the Red Army was created on February 23rd 1918 and organised into a highly effective military organisation[11]. The first threat to the Red army came in the east where a Czech army threatened in May 1918 by capturing Ekaterinburg[12] and Kazan in August. There was also considerable threat from Denikin's army in the South and the isolation of the Reds was shown by the creation of numerous governments including those set up in the summer by former allies (Chernov in the Volga region and Chaikovsky in Archangel). These governments were eventually subsumed under a more conservative government led by Admiral Kolchak who was pronounced Supreme Ruler of Russia in November 1918. To make matters worse there was foreign intervention, the British landing troops in Murmansk in March 1918 and a whole host of nationalities landing in the Far East throughout the rest of the year. Although their stated aim was to protect their interests and prevent weapons falling into German hands, there was considerable fighting between them and the Red Army in the spring of 1919. It was ended only with British and American withdrawal from Archangel in September and Murmansk in October 1919. In the Ukraine, the German army overran the country in March 1918. After the November armistice, the French occupied Odessa only to be expelled in April 1919.

The situation for the Communists seemed critical in 1919 with their army facing war on numerous fronts. In the East, Kolchak's armies had taken Perm and Ufa but this was the limit of their advance and by

November 1919, the Red Army had taken Omsk and forced the White Army to retreat to Irkutsk. Much prized for its oil, the region of Southern Russia was a target for the Red Army but their attempts to fill the vacuum left by the retreating German and Austrian armies were foiled by General Denikin in January 1919. The Whites then took to the offensive and had captured Kiev by September 1919, but they too were forced into retreat in December and in March 1920 Denikin turned his command over to General Wrangel. From April to October 1920 the Red Army was distracted by war with Poland which attempted to overrun the Ukraine. The war was ended by the preliminary Treaty of Riga of October 1920[13] which left the Ukraine to the Russian government. This left the Red Army free to pursue Wrangel's demoralised army which was finally evacuated from the Crimea in November 1920.

Economic problems and unrest 1918-21

The Civil War had caused severe economic problems which, with the ideological aspirations of the Bolsheviks, helped to shape the policy of War Communism. The loss of territory and the collapse of the currency dictated stringent measures. On February 19th 1918, all land was nationalised and a system of requisitioning the peasant surplus was introduced by the summer. Although a success in terms of the fact that the urban population was fed, requisitioning caused significant rural unrest. Meanwhile, in June 1918 all factories were nationalised, *Vesenkha* taking a leading role in organising industrial production. Industrial discipline

was tightened with strict penalties being introduced in May 1920 for absenteeism. The party too was reorganised, with ever increasing discipline replacing internal debate. At the VIIIth Party Congress in March 1919 the central decision making body, the *Politburo*, was formally recognised. However, greater centralisation of the decision making process was opposed by many within the party and dissent was rife[14]. The situation in the country was desperate as many peasants withheld grain and famine struck many areas. From February - March 1919, the sailors of Kronstadt Fortress in Petrograd (who had been in the vanguard of the revolution in 1917) revolted against the government and demanded the end to War Communism and free elections. The mutiny was crushed by the Red Army but forced the government into full retreat. At the Xth Party Congress in March 1921, the New Economic Policy was presented by Lenin and adopted by the delegates. It signalled the end of War Communism, requisitioning of grain and the introduction of a tax in kind on the peasantry. The commanding heights of the economy such as the banks and large scale industry were to remain in state hands but small scale business could operate again on the free market. It was a pragmatic step back from socialism but to force the NEP through Congress, dissent and debate within the party was abolished in March 1921.

The Nationalities issue

The nationalities issue was one which threatened the new Bolshevik state. Independent states were declared in the peripheral nations of the old Empire, in line with Lenin's Declaration of November 1917 that this was acceptable. Increasingly this became a threat to the government with states such as Georgia declaring her independence in mid 1918 and electing a Menshevik government. As it became apparent that the rest of Europe's proletariat were not going to rise up in support of the Russian revolution so policy changed. In 1921, Soviet governments were set up in Georgia and Armenia and in March 1922, these governments were combined with that of Azerbaijan to form the Transcaucasian Socialist Soviet Republic despite fierce opposition in Georgia. On 30th December 1922, the USSR was brought into being.

ANALYSIS

Introduction

The Bolsheviks gained power in October 1917 because of the distance they had placed between themselves and the Provisional Government. In particular, they won vital support by opposing an unpopular war with which all their rivals were associated through their dealings with the Kerensky government. Most importantly, power was gained and then consolidated by the Bolsheviks' flexibility in policy and their ideological pragmatism. This may seem a somewhat generous description of a government which introduced War Communism yet even this can be argued as a practical step to ensure victory in the civil war. From the *April Thesis* to the NEP, the Bolsheviks frequently followed policies which reflected populist aspirations and gave the regime a breathing space. In that they won significant support from strategically important groups including enough of the peasantry who had been given their own land. This factor must be placed in a context, however. Gaining and maintaining power had much to do with the organised use of violence and coercion. It was the ability of the Bolsheviks to militarily and politically outmanoeuvre a divided opposition which gave them a significant advantage until 1922.

The War

In continuing the war, the Provisional Government fatally misunderstood one of the main causes of the

February revolution - the war's unpopularity. This factor, more than any other sapped the government's legitimacy. A clear example was the Petrograd Soviet's 'Order No. 1' issued in March 1917 which gave the Soviet the semblance of governmental authority and revealed the government to be out of touch with the mass of the armed forces. Even more significant was the government's continuation of the military campaigns in search of a decisive victory. Although it superficially accepted the demands of the Soviet in March that the war was not one of conquest but 'revolutionary defencism', this was never clear. The involvement of socialists and Mensheviks in the government from May onwards tarred them with continuation of the war, whatever the aims. Indeed, Kerensky's desire to continue the war with the aim of revising the war's aims was naive. The Galician campaign, which was undertaken in June with this in mind was a military catastrophe, thereby further provoking social unrest and a breakdown in army discipline. Thousands of peasants deserted and returned home demanding land. The turmoil of the situation was not addressed by a government which failed to recognise the corrosive effects of the war. In the cities, rampant inflation radicalised the workers whilst in the country, expectations of land redistribution were not met by a government which found itself unable to enact radical legislation whilst the war continued[15].

This contrasts with the support the Bolsheviks gained from implacably opposing the war. The *April Thesis*, with its uncompromising stance on the issue, brought the party a tenfold increase in membership to around a quarter of a million members by October. It also ensured the support of many in the armed forces who wished to see an early end to the slaughter. This support became crucial in the Bolsheviks' seizure of power, the Petrograd garrison being unwilling to prevent the seizure of power in October. The sympathy amongst soldiers also ensured the victory against Krasnov's counter revolutionary forces immediately thereafter. There is no doubt that the slogans of 'Bread, Peace and Land' won huge support. These were the predominant slogans in the 'July Days' demonstrations which had initially been organised by the Congress of Soviets to rally support for the Galician offensive and Kerensky's government. The war also created the conditions in which the Bolshevik slogans found ready support from a population suffering the effects of a collapsing economy. Although the support was not a majority one, as shown by the elections to the Constituent Assembly in November 1917, it was a strategically important one. In Petrograd and the other major cities, the workers suffered increasing deprivation as the war progressed. As 1917 progressed, bread prices rose as the supply dried up, whilst inflation reduced the rouble to 10% of its 1914 value. Against this background of economic collapse, the employers used a policy of lockouts, partly due to raw material shortages, but also because it was an effective weapon to deal with labour unrest. The result was increasing unemployment, over 60,000 were sacked in Moscow from late July to September. It was from the discontented proletariat that the Bolsheviks recruited their core support, from the 10,000 strong Red Guard in Petrograd to those who elected a Bolshevik majority at the Second All Russian Congress of Soviets in October. The war politicised and radicalised large sections of the population. The Bolsheviks simply responded to and reflected their desires whereas the other parties of the left discredited themselves by involving themselves with a government which so obviously didn't. Despite the unpopularity of Brest-Litovsk, the Bolsheviks managed to withdraw from the war thereby ensuring that they did not fall into the same trap of the Provisional government of not fulfilling expectations.

Policy flexibility and ideological pragmatism.

As already shown above, the Bolsheviks responded to the demands of whole sections of the populace. This was often done counter to ideology but in the interests of ensuring the revolution's and hence Bolshevik survival. The policy adopted on land distribution and the peasantry in general highlights this point very clearly. In the *April Thesis*, Lenin promised the peasantry that all landed estates be confiscated and nationalised. It is true that this was confirmed by decree in February 1918 but the important legislation was the Land Decree passed on the evening of the 26th October 1917. By this, the peasantry were allocated family plots which very much countered collectivist Bolshevik ideology. Indeed, from 1917-'22 there was very little discussion on the collectivisation of land[16]. This is because Bolshevik influence was weak in the countryside and yet it was also politically wise to placate the peasantry. Such a policy was to serve the Bolsheviks in good stead during the civil war and

after. Although the seizure of grain alienated many within the peasantry - armed bands of peasants emerged such as that led by Nestor Makhno - such a procedure was often undertaken by the Whites in the areas they controlled as well. What the granting of land did was to ensure that the peasantry did not resist Bolshevik rule wholesale. Despite the excesses of War Communism, many peasants were still prepared to believe that they might hold on to the land under the Reds who were, therefore, preferable to the Whites. There were peasant uprisings such as in the Tambov region in early 1921, yet there was no general uprising despite the reduction of yields - in some areas such as the Ukraine by up to 80%. Lenin was determined to maintain the alliance of peasant and proletariat (the *smychka*) as the means by which the revolution could be consolidated. Therefore, even though some requisitioning was violent and random, from January 1919 a system of quotas was introduced by which only the surpluses were removed. The revolution survived because the peasantry was able to seize land as had been the general desire of 1917. Even with the advent of War Communism, there was no widespread revolt in the countryside in favour of the Whites who advocated the return of the gentry and the subsequent loss of the peasantry's recent gains.

The February Revolution had raised the expectations of many within society for change and social improvement. That these expectations were not met, resulted in an ebbing away of support and legitimacy from the government from an early stage. By promising to implement policy which had strong revolutionary appeal, the Bolsheviks managed to gain support in the Soviets in particular which was crucially important in the quest for power. After October 1917, the Bolsheviks managed to bolster their support and consolidate the regime by doing the complete opposite of the Provisional Government. From the early days, a great number of revolutionary decrees were passed on a variety of issues which met the aspirations of their supporters and gave the Bolsheviks a base of support which was to prove invaluable during the Civil War. The support of the proletariat was consolidated by the numerous decrees on factory control such as that of November 14th 1917 which handed over the factories to worker committees. The Bolsheviks immediately enacted legislation on women which delivered the long promised emancipation[17]. Up to the end of 1918, women won the right to vote, were given equal pay, given paid maternity leave and access to divorce amongst other rights. The most progressive legislation in the world towards women was crowned in 1920 with the right to free abortion. Women also benefited by the labour legislation which amongst other things banned night work for women. This and other decrees were brought together in the Labour Code of 1922 which had the aim of providing workers with rights in the workplace. The significance of this legislation is that it provided the Bolsheviks with concentrated support in the cities from the *April Thesis* when many of the promises were made through the revolution and beyond. That the Bolsheviks survived in power is because through their ideological commitment they built a committed following who were prepared to defend the revolution[18]. This following was transformed into a coherent and cohesive force through party and Red Army reforms. The strengthening of the party structures e.g. the creation in January 1919 of the Organisation Bureau (Orgburo) acted to channel the energy of the support the Bolsheviks had gained into the running of the state.

There are many other examples of the regime's ideological flexibility. Despite the promises of pre revolutionary speeches and works such as *State and Revolution*, the attempted transition to Communism was carried out not by some automatic transfer of power to the masses but by reasserting many of the features of the autocracy. This was because the near permanent state of crisis demanded action to prevent economic and social anarchy. A clear example is the case of worker ownership of factories. Despite being given immediate ownership of the means of production in November 1917, the most significant developments in this area were the creation of *Veshenka* the following month and the reduction of the power of labour in decision making introduced in April 1920. The arguments in the party over Trotsky's desire to the militarise and control labour which ended at the Xth Party Congress in March 1921 were an example of the tension caused by the divergence of action and ideology. Although the leadership's policies were challenged by groups such as Workers' Opposition[19] and the Democratic Centralists, the reality of maintaining power took precedence over ideological considerations, even the role of the proletariat. This is crucial in explaining how the Bolsheviks managed to maintain power.

The revolution was able to survive because of the ideological pragmatism of the leadership, its desire to place revolutionary survival above any other factor. In particular, the introduction of the NEP in 1921 should be seen as an example of the regime's commitment to the continuation of power. A return to small scale capitalism contradicted the legislation of the previous three years, e.g. the nationalisation of all enterprises (June 1918) and of land (December 1920). The ideological element had to be weighed against the scale of devastation caused by the years of war and revolution. By 1921, the economy was on the verge of collapse, industrial production overall being a fifth of what it had been in 1913. Just as the regime had managed to gain support by ideologically inspired measures, so it managed to keep hold of power by dropping the ideology when necessary. The uprisings in the Tambov region and the Kronstadt Fortress in 1921 highlighted the unpopularity of the regime. That the NEP was an unpopular innovation amongst party members is without doubt, but the banning of dissent imposed on the party at the Xth Party Congress ended any effective opposition to it. The NEP gave the regime breathing space as its reintroduction helped to stimulate the required economic growth and defused the simmering unrest in the countryside. Therefore it helped to play a significant role in the regime's survival. Without doubt, the NEP is the most obvious example of Lenin and the leadership's pragmatism and also the extent of the reintroduction of autocratic means of decision making.

The 'Nationalities question'

The Bolsheviks consolidated their power through centralisation of the party as mentioned above but also of the country. Despite Brest Litovsk, the area controlled by the new regime contained many different nationalities. The 'nationalities question' became an acute one with the recovery of land which had been lost in 1918. On gaining power in 1917, the new government saved little time in granting the nations of the old Empire self determination to chose whether they wanted to be a part of the new state.[20] The new state was to be a federal one, the RSFSR[21], yet these ideological decisions were to be overtaken by the practical considerations of the threat to the regime of the creation of independent states which formed on the borders of the old Empire[22]. The failure of the European proletariat to effect a revolution which would support that in Russia meant that security considerations became an overwhelming priority. Nationalities policy became heavily influenced by the decisions of Joseph Stalin, who, as Commissar for Nationalities was instrumental in creating the USSR in December 1922 as a means of curtailing the autonomy of those outlying republics. The resistance of the Communist Party of Georgia[23] to the move to assimilate their country into a new union and the dismissal of their complaints reflect the limitations of Lenin's nationalities policy and the extent to which policy did not reflect ideology, the new USSR imposed strict control from Moscow.

The Red Terror - violence and coercion.

The fundamental reason why the Bolsheviks came to power was that they were prepared to use violence to overthrow the government in October 1917. They also had the means and organisation to carry out their aims. Similarly, the consolidation of power was primarily a consequence of the regime's willingness to use unrestricted terror on its enemies and populace as a whole. This was coupled with the organisational efficiency of the machinery of terror, the Red Army and *Cheka*. Despite all the doubts raised, the Bolsheviks were best placed to carry out a revolution through their dominance of the Soviet and in particular the Petrograd Soviet military defence committee set up on October 9th. Through this body, the Red Guard were armed and organised[24]. Although it was not a particular threatening military force, the Red Guard had little opposition in October 1917, such was the state of disintegration of the government and regular army. The same can not be said for the opposition during the Civil War. Yet there were significant differences between the two sides which were prove crucial in the war's outcome. Most importantly, the Red Army was far better organised and more co-ordinated than its enemy. Even the appointment of Kolchak as central commander in November 1918 had little impact, the Whites failed to copy the single command structure created by Trotsky for the Red Army in 1918. The Whites were politically divided with groups as diverse as the reactionary elements led by Kolchak to the short lived socialist government at Ufa led by Chernov. This was a contrast to the ideologically motivated and policed Red Army. There were also geographical factors which helped the Reds to victory - they were in control of a centralised area - whilst their opponents were spread over a disparate area with poor communications.

Undoubtedly the foremost weapon the Bolsheviks used in crushing opposition was the secret police force created by *Sovnarkom* decree on December 7th, 1917 - *Cheka*. To counter opposition from sources as wide as royalists to disillusioned Soviets, *Cheka* was given virtually unlimited powers to act as it saw fit. The state formally sanctioned the use of terror through decrees, e.g. that passed on the September 4th 1918 which allowed for the taking of hostages and the decree of the following day which demanded an intensification of terror[25]. These decrees legally recognised what was already happening, e.g. in Petrograd on August 31st, Zinoviev ordered the execution of 512 hostages. Although there were attempts within the Bolshevik party to limit the excesses of *Cheka*, culminating in the agreement of the Central Executive Committee in February 1919 to end mass terror, these attempts were to have little practical effect. There were other methods used to suppress opposition apart from assassination and terror, forced labour camps being created in 1918 and two years later having a population of around 50,000. The victims of the terror came from all parties including the left SRs. How many people died is difficult to ascertain but has been calculated as high as 200,000[26]. The terror ran its full course unhindered by any legal system, the Tsarist structure being dismantled in November 1917 and any legislation passed pre 1917 discarded a year later. Instead 'justice' was delivered by Revolutionary Tribunals which were created with the sole purpose of maintaining Bolshevik rule. Yet many in opposition did not reach the tribunals, e.g. the Kadet leaders Shingarev and Koksokin who were murdered in late 1917. The significance of the Red Terror is that it cowed the population and removed effective internal opposition to Bolshevik rule. Execution was random and often arbitrary, the brutality across the country extreme. Lenin and the leadership of the party ordered and justified the levels of violence in terms of saving the revolution and in Felix Dzerzhinsky[27] found a reliable executioner.

Conclusion

The Bolshevik seizure of power was due to their ability to seize the opportunity to fill the vacuum caused by the disintegration of government. They gained significant support in strategically important groups such as the soldiers, sailors and proletariat by reflected populist discontent in their propaganda and by disassociating themselves from the government and war effort. In retaining and consolidating the power they had seized, the Bolsheviks relied heavily on the use of terror and violence. Just as their seizure of power had been reliant on their preparedness to use military means, so power was consolidated only with the creation of the ruthless Red Army. Added to that, the Bolsheviks displayed an ideological flexibility which met the expectations of their followers in the short term whilst buying the regime time. Such flexibility was made possible with the centralisation of decision making and the virtual restoration of autocracy. Underpinning this was the work of *Cheka*. It is ironic that the Bolsheviks consolidated power at the expense of those in whose name they seized it.

[1] Most important amongst these were the Socialist Revolutionaries, the SRs, and the Mensheviks.

[2] Rasputin's influence stemmed from his ability to reduce the bleeding of the Tsarevich Alexis who was a haemophiliac. It was also a consequence of sexual dealings at court which were legendary.

[3] The dates are of the old Russian calender which was, until Febrary 1918, thirteen days behind the Western calender.

[4] The German High Command calculated that by allowing Lenin to travel through Germany from Switzerland, the pro-Allied government would be suitable undermined. The Provisional Government, were able to use this to great effect against the Bolsheviks and Lenin in particular who was for ever being labelled a spy. During the July Days of 1917, the government was able to use such anti-Bolshevik propaganda to turn demonstrations against the Bolsheviks.

[5] In Marxist ideology, revolution occurred in mature, industrialised economies through the actions of a thoroughly exploited and politicised proletariat. That Russia was not yet a fully fledged industrial economy, therefore caused many on the left severe doubts about enacting revolution. It was Lenin who convinced the Bolsheviks that revolution was right within a European context. Uprisings abroad would bring socialist solidarity which would support the Bolsheviks through their problems whilst undertaking revolution in the name of the proltariat.

[6] As they left the hall they were taunted by Trotsky shouting his prophetic "Go where you belong: to the dustbin of history."

[7] The land decree ordered the immediate breaking up of large estates and distribution of that land to the peasants.

[8] Such were the continuing doubts of many in the Bolshevik leadership about their own ability to carry through the revolution without support of others on the left, that five members of the CC resigned over the muzzling of the press including Kamenev.

9 These events overshadowed the fact that at this Congress the new Soviet Constitution. By this, Soviet 'democracy' was established with delegates being elected from local Soviets to represent them at provincial Soviets and from there to the All Russian Congress. All elections would be held on occupational basis, thereby creating the 'dictatorship of the proletariat'.

10 The same day saw the attempted assassination of Lenin by Fanya Kaplan.

11 Trotsky insisted on conscripting 50,000 officers from the Tsarist army and organising troops along traditional command lines. By 1920, the army had only 5 million men whose resolve was stiffened by 180,000 political commissars whose task is was to ensure loyalty to the government.

12 Before the Communists withdrew from Ekaterinburg, they shot the Tsar and his family who had been held prisoner there.

13 The formal treaty was signed in March 1921.

14 An example of such dissent was Zinoviev's violent attack on Trotsky in 1919-'20 over the issue of whether labour should be treated in the same manner as the soldiers as part of the war effort.

15 Land redistribution had become the peasantry's main expectation in the aftermath of the February revolution. Throughout the early months of 1917, the goverment attempted to use force to stem the growing tide of land seizures. Unwilling to enact radical legislation concerning land redistribution in wartime, the Kerensky government laid itself open to charges of betrayal.

16 The policy of giving land to families was one which mirrored the manifesto of the SRs rather than the Bolsheviks.

17 Lenin had been a longstanding advocate of women's rights and was strongly supportive of the Women's Department set up under the supervision of feminist Alexandra Kollontai. The legislation of 1918-'20 reflected her radical agenda.

18 There were many in the party prepared to defend the revolution although purging of the party ranks and the civil war reduced figures to 150,000 by late 1919. By 1921, however, numbers had risen to around 732,000.

19 Worker's Opposition had strong support amongst party members discontented with the drift in policy. The leaders of the movement, Alexander Shliapnikov and Alexandra Kollontai demanded a return to union independence and proletarian influence in the work place. The organisation was banned at the Xth Party Congress.

20 This was done via the Declaration of the Rights of the Peoples of Russia in November 1917.

21 The RSFSR stood for the Russian Soviet Federal Socialist Republic.

22 Many regions took advantage of the new government's early idealism and declared independence, e.g Lithuania and Moldavia in late 1917, the Ukraine in early 1918.

23 Known as the Georgian Affair, it highlighted differences of opinion between Stalin and Lenin over the extent of autonomy for the nationalities.

24 The Red Guard had also been armed at the height of the Kornilov Crisis and had kept hold of the weaponry.

25 Hostage taking became a common place occurrence. The hostages were often high ranking officials of the Tsarist period who were shot if Soviet officials were attacked. The practice was intensified during the Civil War.

26 Any figure set is highly unreliable due to the turmoil of the time and the continuation of the Civil War.

27 Dzerzhinsky was the ruthless leader of *Cheka*.

Lenin

CHAPTER 10

TO WHAT EXTENT WERE THE PURGES AND LABOUR CAMPS THE CONSEQUENCE OF STALIN'S ECONOMIC AND POLITICAL PROGRAMME 1929-'53?

Introduction.

From 1929 -'53 the Soviet Union experienced upheaval which was unparalleled in history. In this period the country underwent a process of violent economic modernisation, at the basis of which was the forced collectivisation[1] of agriculture and rapid industrialisation on an unprecedented scale. The consequence was massive social turmoil which was compounded by war against Nazi Germany between 1941-'45. It was the pace, the tempo of this revolution which dictated the violence against Soviet citizens - which cost up to 20 million lives. To meet the unrealistic targets for industrial growth, the state enslaved millions of Soviet citizens in the labour camps of the Gulag[2]. In stamping out opposition to collectivisation it enslaved many millions more. The partial failure of such policies demanded scapegoats and these were to be found in the purging of party and economic institutions. The economic policies of Stalin and the corresponding social violence were inextricably linked.

The economic and social revolution of the late 1920's and early 30's had a political element which manifested itself from 1934 in a widespread purge of the Communist society and the social elite. Purging was the political response of Stalin and the bureaucracy to the economic and social chaos produced by the convulsions of 1929-'34. It was the means by which opposition was silenced and autocracy restored as well as being the tool with which

central control was reasserted and nationalism crushed. In this it destroyed the original Bolshevik party and any dissent or criticism of the policies embarked upon since 1929, thereby preserving and completing Stalin's revolution. Therefore, purging was as much the political programme itself as a consequence of it. Until Stalin's death in 1953, purging became the means by which he imposed his political will on the Soviet elite and nation as a whole.

It is important to note, however, that the purges gained a momentum of their own which shaped their development. It is argued that although the violence was linked with policies imposed from above, it was sustained by a radical populist base. This was shown in the widespread denunciations which led to the imprisonment of so many citizens.

The Debate

By 1927, the NEP[3] had fulfilled its primary aim in restoring the industry to the production levels of 1913 yet the Soviet economy lagged further behind those of the West. There were conflicting views within the Communist Party of how modernisation[4] of the economy could proceed in a manner that was compatible with the philosophy of revolutionary socialism. There was no dispute that the main source of capital was the countryside, yet differences of opinion surfaced about how a surplus in agricultural produce could be extracted from the peasantry. On the one hand was the policy of 'socialism in one country' associated with Nikolai Bukharin[5]. This proposed that the peasantry be allowed to prosper by using modern production methods. Through this excess grain would be produced which could be sold abroad which would provide the capital for investment in industry. Although these proposals would mean only the gradual introduction of a socialist state it had at its cornerstone the *smychka*[6] between peasant and proletariat as envisaged by Lenin in 1917. Against these proposals were the so called 'left opposition' led by Trotsky[7] and Preobrazhensky and their ideas of 'permanent revolution'. By this the peasantry would shoulder the burden of rapid industrialisation through taxation, procurements of grain and depressed living standards. The resources generated by collectivisation of farming should be redirected into heavy industry. Stalin allied himself for political reasons with Bukharin as Trotsky was his most obvious rival for the leadership of the party.

SECTION A-Agriculture

The move to requisitioning 1928-29

Once the left had been defeated in December 1927 and Trotsky and Zinoviev exiled by the XVth Party Congress, Stalin and his supporters began to assert an independent line from Bukharin which was more closely associated with the policies of the recently disgraced. Almost immediately, Stalin pressed the Central Committee to allow the requisitioning of

grain by force[8]. The reasons for this were partly ideological and partly a consequence of an impending crisis in agriculture. Like many other Bolsheviks, Stalin perceived the peasants as the enemies of the revolution, the forces of reaction and conservatism, the antithesis of modernisation and the epitome of nineteenth century Tsarist Russia. In particular, Stalin reserved his hatred for the wealthier peasant class - the *kulaks*[9]. Added to this was the so called 'scissors crisis' of late 1927. Rising prices in consumer goods due to scarcity led to peasants selling less grain as there was little use for cash, especially as grain prices were falling[10]. The government reduced the prices of consumer goods but grain prices fell by 20%, further reducing the incentive of the peasantry to produce. By December 1927 the state agencies which bought grain off the peasantry had only managed to buy 50% of the previous year's total. To most activists at the XVth Party Congress this was evidence of the deliberate hoarding of the *kulaks* and the best excuse possible to reassert Bolshevik control and destroy the *smychka*. In January 1928, Stalin and officials visited Siberia. They set about requisitioning grain by force and arresting dissenting peasants under Article 107 of the Criminal Code.[11] This was to become known as the 'Urals-Siberian method' and it destroyed any confidence the peasantry had in the state. It also opened up a rift between Stalin and Bukarin who opposed forced requisitioning of grain. Despite the demands of the July CC plenum to end the practice it continued apace into the spring of 1929. The right was increasingly discredited in party organisations and institutions. In December 1928, Bukharin was forced to resign as editor of *Pravda* following the publication in September of the article 'Notes of an economist' which implied criticism of Stalin and his methods. He was finally discredited in November 1929, by being expelled from the Central Committee[12]. Meanwhile, eager party officials had been 'encouraging' farmers into collective farms and setting grain quotas for their regions. The process of collectivisation was already underway and Stalin claimed in his article of November 7th 1929, 'Year of the Great Breakthrough' that the time was ripe for an all out offensive against rural capitalism. The following month was marked by celebrations of Stalin's fiftieth birthday[13] and a speech on December 27th in which he explicitly called for the liquidation of the kulaks.

Forced Collectivisation, 1930

On January 5th 1930, the CC announced the programme for the forced collectivisation of agriculture. By spring, some 30 million hectares were to have been collectivised, the process to be undertaken by 25,000 party activists who would be joined by around 125,000 workers and troops. In February 1930 a decree was passed which gave the go - ahead for the elimination of the *kulak* class[14]. By the beginning of March the countryside had been thrown into complete turmoil. In two months it was claimed over 10 million households had been forced into collectives. Churches were ransacked and by the end of the year up to 80% of the village churches in Russia had been pillaged. In many areas such as the Ukraine and the Caucasus there was widespread resistance and across the Soviet Union peasants

slaughtered their cattle rather than let it fall into the hands of the hated collectivisation brigades. Around a fifth of the country's cattle and a quarter of the country's livestock as a whole was slaughtered in the first two months of 1930 alone. Such was the opposition and turmoil, Stalin ordered a temporary respite in 'Dizzy with success' printed in March 1930. This article blamed the excesses of collectivisation on over zealous local officials. In addition it ordered the re-establishment of the principle that farmers could join the *kolkhozes*[15] voluntarily could leave if they so wished. The stampede out of the *kolkhozes* left a rump of only six million households collectivised in June as opposed to around fifteen million in March. The rationale behind this was to ensure the harvest was sown in the spring which it duly was. At the XVIth Party Congress in June 1930, Stalin again signalled that collectivisation was central to the process of building a socialist state in the Soviet Union. The consequence was that the forced process of collectivisation was restarted. From the summer of 1930 purges of the agricultural bureaucracy became commonplace. In September over a thousand party members including the former Minister of Food, N.A. Kondratiev[16] were arrested and accused of belonging to the anti - collectivisation (and completely fictitious) 'Toiling Peasant Party'.

Famine, 1931-34

Collectivisation was undertaken with little planning and kolkhozes were often run by members of collectivisation brigades with little or no experience of agricultural affairs. Although Machine Tractor

Stations (MTSs)[17] had been set up from 1929, the impact of mechanisation was limited. Because of fine weather, the harvest of 1930 was unexpectedly good, in all 77 million tons of grain was produced (out of which the state still only managed to take 22 million tons). This output was the exception to the rule, however, and was to provoke considerable problems later on when the state demanded quotas based on 1930 figures. Across the Soviet Union there was turmoil on an unprecedented scale. At a conservative estimate, over 2.5 million *kulaks* alone were exiled in 1930-1[18]. Collectivisation was implemented from the Ukraine to Siberia with harrowing consequences. After the initial wave of destruction came famine. From late 1931 to mid 1934 the state continued to demand high quotas of grain and other foodstuffs whilst hunger spread across the Soviet Union. Hardest hit was the Ukraine where the absurdly high quota of 7.7 million tons of grain (36% of the total harvest) to be handed over to the state was set in 1931. This figure was set at the 1930 level when the harvest had been over 5 million tons larger. Despite numerous protests from the Ukraine and other regions, at the XVIth Party Congress in January 1932 Stalin's ministers Kuibyshev and Molotov demanded no let up in the seizure of quotas and the elimination of the *Kulak* class. In 1932, the Ukraine was set a quota of 6.6 million tons yet only 4.7 million was collected. The consequence was a purge of the Ukrainian Communist party including the wholesale replacement of many of the party's district committees.

The peasantry was made subject to a series of harsh decrees which had the intention of controlling all aspects of rural life and closely resembled serfdom. In 1931, all peasants became liable for six days a year mending the roads. Such decrees passed in 1932 banned trade in the *kolkhozes* until quotas had been met, reintroduced internal passports and passed a sentence of execution for theft of *kolkhoz* property. With such a high proportion of grain seized by the state, complete administrative chaos and no incentive for the *kolkhoznik* to work, famine was inevitable. In the Ukraine, perhaps as many as between five million people died between 1931-'4. Such was the hunger that cannibalism was widely reported. Despite this, the state continued to export grain throughout the famine, in 1931 exports peaking at just over 5 million tons. In February 1933, the Politburo relented and seed was issued to the Ukraine. Three months later food was issued to the starving and a decree issued which ended the indiscriminate deportations of *kulaks* from across the Soviet Union. By the end of 1934, some 70% of households were collectivised, the figure rising to 90% by 1936 through the imposition of high taxes and quotas on those who remained outside the system.

The squeezing of the peasantry 1935-45

In 1935, a model statute to govern the workings of the *kolkhozes* was introduced. By this peasants were allowed small plots of land (no more than 0.5 hectare per family) and ownership of a cow, sow and four sheep. This limited private property was to become the major source of peasant income and payments to *kolkhozniks* was to depend on the number of labour days (*trudondny*) completed and how much produce was left after the state and the MTSs had taken their share. The *kolkhoz* was somewhat ironically defined as a voluntary co-operative yet tightly controlled by local party and government. Living standards continued to be depressed and procurement levels high throughout the 1930s. In 1939 these were increased further by demands for grain being made against the total area which could be cultivated rather than the actual sown area. The war placed further massive burdens on the countryside with industry and military operations taking precedence. Vast areas of the countryside were overrun and subjugated by the Nazis including the fertile lands of the Ukraine. There was vast depopulation, some 60% of the Soviet army being from the countryside and no agricultural occupation being treated as a 'reserved profession[19]'. In tandem with this fact was a de-mechanisation[20] which together resulted in a fall in production, in 1943 agricultural output being at only 38% of its 1940 level. This simply provoked the regime into squeezing the agricultural sector even more tightly with the help of political commissars sent in to run the *kolkhozes* in November 1941. The peasantry were forced to work harder by even more draconian regulations, in April 1942 the minimum work expected from each peasant was increased and failure to fulfil one's labour day quota rendered the individual liable to punishment. During wartime, the state requisitioned practically all produce from the countryside but it turned a blind eye to the black market.

Post War Continuity 1945-'53

Despite the huge sacrifices of the agricultural sector during the war in terms of a decline in living standards[21], increased labour and lives lost, the resumption of peace saw a return to the strict regulation by central authority of the pre war years. In September 1946 the state passed a decree demanding the return to the *kolkhoz* of all land the system had previously owned. The state continued to collectivise in its newly acquired territories, in 1947 the Baltic States saw the introduction of the *kolkhoz* with the inevitable deportations of those who opposed such a move. The burden of taxation was again placed on the *kolkhozes* and procurement levels of grain and livestock were increased by 50%. That the state maintained a strict control over agricultural affairs can be seen in Stalin's 'plan for the transformation of nature' introduced by decree in October 1948. Based on the ideas of the dubious character Trofim Lysenko, it resulted in the planting of 1.5 million hectares of trees by 1951.[22] In 1950, a drive to amalgamate smaller *kolkhozes* into larger ones was undertaken by Nikita Khrushchev and a proposal made to set up large agro-towns. The former proposals resulted in a decline in the number of *kolkhozes*, the latter came to nothing. In some ways this was a further attempt to reduce the dependence of the peasant on his/her private plot. Until the death of Stalin in 1953, there were no measures introduced which improved the life of the *kolkhoznik*. State prices paid for goods in 1952 were lower than in 1940 and greater taxes on the private plot led to a decline in output.

Analysis

Introduction

The collectivisation of agriculture was the linchpin of the modernisation process undertaken by Stalin from 1929. Most importantly, it was to ensure a grain supply to the towns at any cost and create a source of investment capital needed for rapid industrialisation. It also had its political dimension in that it was the means of asserting communist control over the countryside and crushing nationalist sentiment. The elimination of the *kulak* class and the recreation of what can only be described as neo-serfdom was central to these processes. One should go further and argue that the attack on the *kulaks* was not simply a consequence of economic or political policy but was a central part of those policies. The peasantry were perceived as anti Bolshevik and the epitome of the old order, the evidence plain to see in the period of the NEP and the periodic grain crises. Their elimination, the subjugation of the remaining peasants either on the land, as forced labour or as newly created proletarians served two key purposes. It won the state complete control of the countryside and formed the basis of an industrial economy.

The purge of the kulaks

In attacking the *kulaks* from 1928/9, Stalin and the party began their civil war to subjugate the peasantry. By their analysis the peasantry could be divided in to three classes, in descending order of wealth the *kulaks*, *bedniaki* and *serendniaki*. It should be recognised that this analysis was not simply that of Stalin but was shared by the majority of the party. The XVth Party Congress in 1927 strongly supported the concept of the rapid collectivisation of the agriculture and the elimination of the *kulak* class. Similarly, collectivisation itself was undertaken on a local basis, there were few directives from central government and much was decided by members of the 'collectivisation brigades' who roamed the countryside enforcing the newly defined ideology. Collectivisation actually took place at the hands of 25,000 party activists who were more than willing to implement what they saw as a renewal and a completion of the Revolution of 1917. This was heightened by the NEP and period of the mid 20's in which the step back into communism had provoked fierce debate within the party but also doubt about the future of the revolution. By eliminating the *kulaks* and forcing the peasantry to accept what they believed was modernisation, the party was ensuring the future of what was begun in 1917. To this end conflict was inevitable, yet opposition had to be crushed. Stalin evoked the revolutionary aspect of collectivisation when he talked at the XVIth Party Congress of his 'rural October'.

The 'scissors crisis' of 1928 gave Stalin the perfect excuse to revert to a policy of forced requisitioning of grain. There was an important political element to this, however, which shows how closely linked the process was to the rise of Stalin and his consolidation of power. After the discrediting of Trotsky in 1927, Stalin needed to distinguish himself from his only other clear rival, Bukharin. The means by which he did this was to adopt much of the policy of Trotsky whilst giving it a revolutionary and populist basis. Once achieved, Stalin could then dismiss all those who opposed such a policy as anti-revolution such as Bukharin in 1929 and his allies Rykov and Tomsky in 1930. Such a formula was also applied to the countryside whereby the term *kulak* was not only applied to all those who had land and were wealthy but those who opposed collectivisation. With the sanction of exile or execution behind it, such a formula was successful and became the norm through until 1953. In the initial stage, 'dekulakisation' came to mean the stripping of all assets of the wealthier peasantry and their transportation to Siberia. In total perhaps as many as 10 million peasants were moved off the land, a figure given by Stalin himself. Of that number perhaps two to three million lost their lives between 1929-'32 although a figure of as high as 6.7 million between 1930-'37 has been suggested.[23] The key point is that through 'dekulakisation', all opposition was crushed whatever the economic cost. It should be remembered that the *kulaks* were the most productive and experienced members of the agrarian classes. Yet this was not the issue, 'dekulakisation' was part of a cultural revolution, a transformation of Soviet social and economic norms. The new socio-economic system was based on a subjugated peasantry. When the process of collectivisation was undertaken in the Baltic States in 1947, those who opposed were denounced as *kulaks* and treated as in the early 1930's. Any peasant who flouted the draconian laws imposed from 1931 could be and was denounced as a *kulak* with the normal consequences. All of this allowed the state to manipulate agricultural production with impunity although the figures show that collectivisation did not increase production overall, in 1953 grain production was still less per capita than it had been in 1913. Yet this was not the point, what collectivisation did was to allow the state to take what it wished. The fruits of this policy continued during and after the war when the agricultural sector had huge demands placed upon it but without any opposition. The 1946 decree took back into *kolkhoz* ownership some 140,000 head of cattle and returned around 450,000 *kolkhoz* administrators back into productive work. Despite the fact that the private plots were the lifeline for the *kolkhoznik* (they also accounted for between 40-50% of all agricultural production in 1950), the state persisted in its attacks on private production.

Another aspect of the attack on the *kulak* class was that it created a pool of forced labour without which a policy of rapid industrialisation was impossible. Between 1930-1 around 380,000 *kulak* families were sent to the *Gulag* and a figure of perhaps as high as 4.3 million souls between 1929 -'38. Similarly it created an excess labour force which fled to the cities and worked in the new industries for little reward. When one defines 'forced labour', it should be remembered that the status of the *kolkhoznik*[24] was not much better than those in the *Gulag*. Deprived of any liberties and subsisting only through the private plot, the peasantry worked for little reward on the *kolkhoz*. It was only after procurements had been made and the MTS and other agencies paid that the *kolkhoznik* could claim their share. When the harvest was poor, as in 1946 when it was only 39 million tons, the *kolkhoznik* received practically nothing from the state.

The attack on the nationalities

Of importance to collectivisation was the attack on the peasantry in the Soviet Union's non-Russian regions. The nationalities were attacked and suppressed as a key part of Stalin's political programme - Russification and centralisation. As the vast majority of non-Russian citizens were peasants, it was via the creation of the *kolkhozes* that they were brought to accept Soviet rule. Therefore, the implementation of collectivisation was faster and more zealously implemented in those regions which were perceived to stand apart for Moscow's rule. By the middle of 1932, 70% of the Ukrainian peasantry had been forced into collectives as opposed to 59% across the Soviet Union. There is little doubt that the Soviet state used famine as a weapon of terror in the Ukraine but other areas as well. By setting absurdly high quotas for requisitioning and by limiting the supply of grain, the state crushed the ability of the peasantry to resist its will. By 1932 the Ukrainian agricultural system was capable of producing only 14.2 million tons of grain. The quota demanded by the state, however, was 7.7 million tons as it had been in 1930 when the harvest had nearly reached 30 million tons. Despite being reduced to 6.6 million tons the targets were impossible to reach and caused famine on a vast scale. The scapegoats for failure were the local party officials who were purged in huge numbers, yet the motives for such a purge were as much to do with stamping out any form of Ukrainian nationalism. In 1932 the secretary of the Central Committee, Postychev, was sent to the Ukraine with the task of purging the party hierarchy which he did ruthlessly. Thousands were purged: from Skrypnyk the Ukrainian Commissar of Education - to hundreds of local party secretaries. At the XVII Party Congress in 1934, Postychev claimed that nationalism had been destroyed. The tool used was collectivisation, the cost in terms of human life vast. In the Ukraine alone perhaps 5 million died as a consequence of famine and a further 1.5 million in Kazakhstan. Proof of the fact that famine was used to bring these areas under control was that there were other regions of the Soviet Union which suffered no famine whatsoever, in particular the grain growing areas of Central Russia. The purge of the Ukrainian and other non Russian peasantry was not simply a consequence of political or economic policy but was the policy in itself. This was to Stalin the solution to the age old Russian problem of how to control the different nationalities within her Empire. The bitterness it generated could be seen in the manner in which in 1941 the German army was considered to be a liberating one by many non Russian peasants. The response of Stalin was to deport whole nations he suspected of collusion to Siberia including the Crimean Tatars in June 1944.

Purging as a means of creating scapegoats for failure

The timing of agriculture related purges was closely

linked to the fortunes of the collectivisation programme and the need for scapegoats to explain inevitable failure. Whilst the peasantry were placed under a new form of serfdom, the party had to explain why the programme of modernisation had not delivered the much trumpeted improvements in productivity. Those who administered the changes became the scapegoats for its failure. In this sense the purges were the direct result of economic policy but one should be more specific. In this case as in others, purging was the consequence of the failure of that policy. In January 1933, the CC issued a decree which blamed wreckers and saboteurs for the problems in the countryside. Important experts were persistently denounced and arrested for their supposed role in the failure of the agricultural sector. The whole episode of the promotion of the ideas of Tromfin Lysenko is a case in point. Through the promotion of his ideas as 'Marxist', Lysenko was able to engineer the purging of 3000 biologists from the agricultural establishment between 1948-'51. Their 'crime' was to have dismissed as hogwash Lysenko's idea of planting three bands of trees, each 5000 km long, as a means of controlling temperature, their folly was to attack ideas from a man with Stalin's backing. Much of collectivisation was undertaken without any planning whatsoever, it wasn't until 1935 that *kolkhozes* had their role defined. In consequence there were numerous charges of 'wrecking' which affected thousands of officials and bureaucrats. A clear illustration was the fabrication of a supposed 'Toiling Peasant Party' which had the fictitious aim of undermining the whole collectivisation programme. In 1930 hundreds were arrested, including the former

Minister of Food, Kondratiev, and charged with membership. Even during the war it was assumed that poor economic performance could be improved with ideological stimulus. The introduction of *politotdely* (political commissars) in late 1941 was to prevent a further decline in productivity and implement state policy in the countryside. Implicit in their appointment was that the peasantry were in some senses wreckers in that they did not work as hard as they might. Despite all the purging of agricultural officials and administrators, the situation did not improve because the problems of agriculture lay not with the implementation of policies but the policies themselves.

Conclusion.

The purges and enslavement of millions in the agricultural sector between 1929-'53 was not only a consequence of Stalinist policy but a mainstay of that policy. In implementing forced collectivisation, the Communist party aimed to crush the economic and ideological independence of the peasantry once and for all. A secondary aim was to destroy nationalist sentiment and any form of opposition. Therefore, collectivisation was the means to the end of extending absolute Soviet control to the countryside and all nations of the Empire. It had its economic rationale in that by crushing any opposition through the creation of a *kulak* class, the state had complete control of the agricultural economy for the first time. All of this was done at a speed which resulted in the liquidation of all who stood in the way. In that the purges and forced labour was not just a by-product of the policy of collectivisation, it was the means by which the process was implemented and sustained.

SECTION B - Industry

Introduction

From 1928 the Soviet state embarked on a programme of rapid industrialisation the like of which had not been seen previously. All the nation's resources were used to build an economy with its foundations in heavy industry which would ensure the Soviet Union's status as a world power. Such was the scale of the task, the pace of change, the problems to be overcome that the whole programme teetered on the brink of failure. It was sustained by the huge sacrifices made by millions of Soviet citizens who were bolstered by the revolutionary spirit of the enterprise. Yet there were millions more who were forced into the Gulag and formed the basis of the workforce which slaved to achieve the targets set by the 'Plans'. In this sense, as with agriculture, forced labour was not a consequence of economic policy, it was an intrinsic part of it. In basic terms, the economic demands of the state were so vast they necessitated the enslavement of millions of its citizens.

As industrialisation was undertaken without relevant expertise and training so there were failures on a grand scale. In fact the whole process was chaotic and the scapegoats for this were to be those deemed as wreckers, often the most skilled engineers and managers who were sceptical of often fantastical targets. As the plan for economic reform was so vast, so the fulfilment of it became

all important. The revolutionary spirit was evoked but that in Soviet terms inevitably meant the creation of 'class enemies' to be persecuted and eliminated.

The pace of economic change and the process of industrialisation transformed the role of the state and its functions. Such a revolution had a political element which was based on the restoration of an autocratic system of power. The economic reform was mirrored in all walks of life. It was absolute in nature and therefore government was structured likewise. Therefore, the purging of the party, army and all the administrative and bureaucratic elite was not the consequence of any political policy - it was the policy. By that all opposition to the reforms was silenced for good. To an extent Stalin completed the revolution of 1917 and did so with considerable public support. It is wrong to assume that the purges were the product simply of a despotic government. At their base they had a radical populism which backs up the belief that they were recognised as the legitimate means of safeguarding the state's interest. In some perverse way the purges gave the Communist government a form of legitimacy it had previously lacked. One should therefore argue that the purges and forced labour were not so much the consequences of political and economic policy from 1929-'53 but the means by which they could be achieved.

The first *Piatiletka*

The history of state directed industrialisation in Russia goes back as far back as Peter the Great[25]. In 1927, however, the communists faced specific problems which narrowed their choices of how it was to be achieved. Although the NEP had resulted in the growth of industrial production back to the levels of 1913, it did not provide the long term answers to the problems of rapid industrialisation in a socialist society. In May 1927, Britain broke off diplomatic relations with the Soviet Union and poor relations with the outside world generally convinced most Communists that the threat of invasion was real. From late 1926 the state had been involved in heavy capital projects including the vast Volga-Don Canal and the Turksib railway line linking Siberia to Turkestan. At the XVth Party Congress in December 1927 and with the defeat of the Left behind him, Stalin proclaimed the virtues of such schemes and further industrialisation to stave off the impending invasions. When this scare had receded, another enemy was created, the mining engineers of the Shakhty region. In April 1928 a so called 'conspiracy' was 'uncovered' and fifty engineers were placed on trial charged with wrecking, i.e. trying to sabotage the industrialisation process. The pace of reform intensified with planning agencies vying with each other to produce fantastic plans for growth. In April 1929 a plan drawn up by the two foremost planning agencies, *Gosplan* and *Veshenka*, was adopted by the XVIth Party Congress. Setting quite fantastic targets, the *piatiletka* was backdated to October 1928 and set to run to mid 1933. By it, steel production was to rise from 4 million tons to 10.5 million tons between 1928-'33 (the actual figure reached was 6 million tons). To power the new industries, the target for electricity production was 22 million kilowatt hours in 1933 as opposed to 5 million in 1928 (in the end 13.4 million kilowatt hours were achieved). The rate of growth of investment was set at a very high level, peaking at 23.8% in 1932-'3.

The wreckers' trials

The drive to transform Soviet industry was accompanied by a revolution in education and the re-establishment of harsh social discipline. As part of the offensive to rapidly modernise, technical education was made widely available as the basis of a cultural revolution. In June 1929, all graduate training in technical related subjects was speeded up as part of the process of creating a new elite. At the beginning of 1930, Stalin launched the so called 'socialist offensive' to reach the *piatiletka's* targets. However the tempo of the undertaking of such an enterprise caused massive upheaval. In November-December 1930, a number of industrial experts led by Professor Ramzin were placed on trial for supposed wrecking. All defendants confessed their guilt to the infamous President of the Court, Vyshinsky, and five of the eight were condemned to death.[26] Simultaneously the system of the *Gulag* was being created to deliberately mobilise labour. In February 1931, Stalin made an unintentionally prophetic speech to Moscow workers in which he attempted to justify the tempo of change. It is important in highlighting the urgency with which industrialisation was undertaken; "We are fifty to a hundred years behind the advanced countries. We must make good this distance in ten years or they will crush us".[27] The following month those in positions of responsibility who had previously been Mensheviks were arrested and charged as conspirators in a plot to organise a foreign invasion of the Soviet Union. They were also charged with sabotage of the industrial process. Most of the so called saboteurs were not seen again. Their crime more often not had been to raise doubts about the realistic nature of the plans. The director of the Marx-Lenin Institute and the last outspoken independent intellectual, Ryazanov, was caught up in this purge and discredited. Simultaneously, work discipline was tightened with prison sentences for offences which broke labour discipline being introduced in January 1931. This was followed in February with the introduction of labour books for all factory workers. Not all the incentives to work hard were negative. In June 1931, Stalin reversed the official policy of sanctioning attacks on the 'bourgeois engineers', their technical skills were too important to industry. The same month he signalled the end of equal wages for all work and introduced differentials between skilled and unskilled labour. This process was part of an overall strategy of building a new elite based on technical education and loyalty to Stalin. By the start of 1932 the *politburo* was packed with Stalin supporters such as Ordzhonikidze and Kirov.

The years 1932-'3 were extremely hard years with a decline in living standards and a further reinforcement of discipline. Crisis gripped the economy with inflation rising sharply and famine in the country. As conditions worsened in the Soviet Union, so there were rumblings of discontent. In August 1932, M.N. Ryutin, who was an officer of the CC Secretariat and an influential communist, issued a damning critique of Stalinist policies. He was expelled from the party with his fellow conspirators but sentenced to only ten years imprisonment. This highlights the fact that Stalin's grip on power was no means absolute at this stage.[28] The worse the

economic and social conditions, the more frequent was the unmasking of conspiracies. Despite his volte face on the purging of engineers, in January 1933 workers from power stations (including six Britons) were charged with sabotage in what became known as the Metro-Vickers trial.[29] The same month, old Bolsheviks A.P Smirnov, Tolmachev and associates were expelled from the party and imprisoned for suggesting that Stalin should be removed form his post as General Secretary. So as to retain some control of the party, to embark on a new revolutionary course and to silence internal dissent, the party was purged of nearly 1 million members (nearly one third of the total membership) from the start of 1933 until 1935. The whole process of 'disciplining' the party was co-ordinated by Nikolai Yezhov head of the NKVD. The party was to be transformed in the same manner the economy had been. By December 1932 the first *piatiletka* was officially declared to have been completed and *Gosplan* laid the plans for the second piatiletka which was to run from 1933-'37. The targets were less ambitious than those of the first in the light of the poor economic performance in 1933, but followed the same lines i.e. mechanisation in agriculture, investment in heavy industry and the expansion of education. In fact the plan adopted by the XVIIth Party Congress in January 1934 was distinctly pragmatic. Stalin stressed the need for increased productivity, consolidation, better technical skills and respect for the previously hounded 'bourgeois specialists'.

The Great Purges

The Congress in 1934 had a far wider significance

than the adoption of the second *piatiletka*. Because of the significant hardship of the previous years there was some opposition to Stalin at this supposed 'Congress of Victors'. Behind the overwhelming praise of Stalin from figures including those previously associated with opposition such as Bukharin, Tomsky and Kamenev, was a move to replace him with Kirov as General-Secretary. In the secret ballot for the Central Committee, almost a quarter of the electorate (270 delegates) voted against Stalin. The dictator bided his time to revenge himself on the old Bolsheviks of the Congress. In July 1934 the whole apparatus of repression was reorganised, the NKVD swallowing up the OGPU and thereby gaining control of the *Gulag* empire and secret police. At its head was *Yagoda* with Yezhov taking the leading role in implementing Stalin's instructions[30]. The 'Great Purges' date from the 1st December 1934 when Kirov was shot dead in the Smolny Institute, Leningrad by a young communist named Leonid Nikolaev[31]. The following day the NKVD was given powers to arrest, try and execute suspects. Within weeks a 'Leningrad centre' (of opposition) had been identified and its supposed leaders shot. Thousands were arrested in the wake of the Kirov assassination including leading Bolsheviks, Kamenev and Zinoviev who were placed on trial in January 1935 as being responsible for Kirov's death. They were both imprisoned for five and ten years respectively. The purging continued apace as the machinery to do it developed. In April 1935 the death penalty was extended to be used on those as young as twelve when appropriate. Three months later a form of hostage system was introduced whereby all members of a family could

be punished if one of their members was deemed to be disloyal. Important communist institutions came under suspicion, *Komsomol* (the youth organisation) was purged and later in 1935, the Society of Old Bolsheviks was disbanded and its archives seized. This was particularly important as they contained information on all Bolshevik membership pre and post 1917.

All of this happened against an improving economic background. From 1934-'6 was known as 'three good years', there being significant growth in sectors such as the metal industry. Investments made from 1928 were now bearing fruit and the second *piatiletka* saw a flourishing of new enterprises, around 4,500 in all as opposed to 1,500 from 1928-'33. There was also a rise in labour productivity which was partly fuelled by the Stakhanovite movement[32]. Although the planned rise in investment in consumer goods industry did not materialise, this was mainly due to increase in defence spending - in 1933 it accounted for 3.4% of expenditure whereas in 1937 this had risen to 16.5%[33]. On the other hand, rationing was phased out in 1935 and money wages nearly doubled between 1933-'37 with real wages also rising. The drive to educate a new technical elite continued, there being in all 290,000 engineering graduates between 1928-'40. A new constitution was presented to the Soviet Union in June 1936 which promised numerous liberties including freedom of speech, religious belief and assembly, the right to work, equality between the sexes and universal suffrage. Although it even recognised the right of republics to withdraw from the Soviet Union, the constitution was as much a vehicle for institutionalising the role of the party.[34] Its introduction masked the preparations made for the campaign to denounce and eliminate all those considered to be 'enemies of the people' i.e. enemies of Stalin.

In July 1936 accusations were made against Kamenev, Zinoviev and Ivan Smirnov[35] that they and others had organised the attack on Kirov and that they were planning to assassinate the rest of the Soviet leadership. In the end, 'confessions' were wrung out of fourteen of the supposed 'Trotskyite-Zinovievite Centre' and all sixteen defendants at the first show trial were shot in August. This was an important turning point for from now on, all 'opposition' was to be treated without mercy. To prove the point, the following week, Stalin ordered the execution of around 5,000 supposed members of the 'opposition' who had been removed to the *Gulag*. The ever loyal Yezhov replaced Yagoda as NKVD chief in September 1936 and he enthusiastically prepared the ground and extracted the relevant confessions from the next group to suffer a show trial. The defendants included Radek and Piatakov. The former spent the trial repeating all that the NKVD told him to say, including the repeated and unprompted mentioning of Marshal Tukhachevsky who was overall commander of the Red Army. Despite the interventions of his boss, Ordzhonikidze who was Commissar of Heavy Industry[36], Piatakov was indicted on charges of sabotage and wrecking despite the fact the it was he more than any other who had planned the *piatiletka*. He was shot whereas Radek was only imprisoned.

The *Yezhovshchina*.

The period spanning the years 1936-'8 are known as the *Yezhovshchina* which literally means the 'years of Yezhov'. A whirlwind of denounciations, arrests and accusations swept the country completely destabilising all social institutions. The turning point was the February-March CC plenum of 1937. At this not only were Bukharin and Rykov denounced and arrested, but Stalin clearly hinted that the forthcoming purges would be extended to comprehensively cover the whole Soviet elite. In June 1937, Marshal Tukhachevsky and eight other leading members of the Red Army High Command were arrested. They were tried[37] and shot almost immediately and their families imprisoned or executed. Yet this was merely the tip of the iceberg. The military elite was arrested, summarily tried and imprisoned or shot without mercy. In all some 43,000 of the most experienced officers were purged including 3 out of 5 marshals, 50 out of 57 corps commanders, 154 out of the 186 divisional commanders and 221 out of 397 brigade commanders. The Old Bolsheviks were simultaneously purged. Of the 1,966 delegates to the XVIIth Party Congress, 1,108 were executed as were 98 of the 139 members of the CC they elected. In Leningrad, from May 1937 a vicious assault on the party hierarchy was unleashed by Zhdanov, partly because of the level of mistrust Stalin held for the city but also because all NKVD units were given their quotas to fulfil. The Ukrainian Communist Party was obliterated, e.g. only 3 out of 102 members of its CC surviving as were the ranks across the Soviet Union of those who had led the industrialisation process. By the end of 1937, the *Gulag* is estimated to have had over six million inmates, perhaps as many as 600,000 being former Party members. The *Yezhovshchina* developed a momentum of its own with denunciation common. Yet punishment for those denounced was quite often shooting on the spot. It is reckoned by Alexander Solzhenitsyn in *The Gulag Archipelago* that over 500,000 political prisoners were shot by Yezhov's men although the figure has been put as high as one million. Not all of these executions were demanded from the centre, many people became simply caught up in a tide which engulfed the whole of society.

The Great Purge Trial.

In January 1938, Yezhov was replaced by Beria, his task completed. The numbers purged began to drop and by 1939 some prisoners were actually released from the Gulag and rehabilitated.[38] This was overshadowed by the Great Purge Trial of Bukharin, Yagoda, Rykov and the last remaining Old Bolsheviks held in March 1938. The trial was of individuals from many parts of the Soviet establishment in the attempt to present all the different types of opposition from Rightists to Trotskyites as having some link. There were a variety of charges ranging from treason, the murder of the writer Maxim Gorky[39] and Bukharin was even charged with attempting to overthrow Lenin in 1918. Not all admitted their guilt and Bukharin infuriated the trial judge Vyshinsky by admitting overall guilt but denying all specific charges. All defendants were found guilty and all bar three shot almost immediately. Although wholesale purging was publicly deemed unsuitable at the XVIIIth Party Congress in March 1939, it was by no means over. Indeed, under the guidance of Beria, arbitrary arrest and deportation were to become no longer emergency measures but instruments of power. The XVIIIth Party Congress adopted the third *piatiletka* which was much in tune with the previous plans, i.e. giving precedence to heavy industry (around 5,400 new industrial projects being planned). This continuity was reinforced with further measures to tighten discipline. In 1940 a new labour law was introduced which extended the working day by an hour, made a criminal offence of absenteeism[40] and abolished the right of labour to switch jobs.

The Second World War.

The outbreak of the Second World War in 1939 saw the Soviet Union maintain her neutrality as a consequence of the Molotov-Rippentrop Pact[41] signed on August 23rd 1939. Almost immediately thereafter on September 28th, Germany and the Soviet Union agreed to partition Poland placing 13 million Poles under direct Stalinist rule. The Baltic States similarly fell into the new Soviet sphere of influence from late 1939. The consequence was the round up and deportation of millions to Siberia who were perceived as being 'enemies of socialism'. Nearly 700,000 Lithuanians were sent eastwards as were up to 1.25 million Poles in 1940 alone. On June 22nd 1941, the Nazis unleashed *Operation Barbarossa*, their military campaign to defeat the Soviet Union and destroy communism. The war which followed was a 'total war' in the truest sense of the phrase. Yet at the moment of invasion, the armed forces and state apparatus was taken completely by surprise, such was the consequence of the army purges of 1937-'8 and the misreading of the situation by Stalin. As the *Wehrmacht* made rapid progress, reaching the Crimea and the outskirts of Moscow by October, so Stalin made scapegoats of the military commanders whose forces had been overrun. So deep had the *Wehrmacht* penetrated by the end of 1941 that the civilian economy lay in tatters. To deny the invader any sustenance, Stalin ordered a 'scorched earth' policy - everything was to be destroyed. Important areas such as the coal and iron producing Donets region were lost to the Germans early on. In all some 45% of the Soviet Union's industrial capacity was lost to the invader. The nature of industrialisation in the 1930's - its totality, the speed at which it occurred, the imbalance between heavy and consumer industry was to be of importance in 1941-'2. As intended, the basis of a wartime economy had been laid in the 1930's. Despite the loss of industrial capacity as a result of the invasion, whole factories were dismantled and moved 1500 miles or so eastwards to the Urals, Central Asia and Siberia. There they were reconstructed and began to produce for the war effort. By the end of 1941, 1,523 factories had been reconstructed in the East.[42] Some factories such as the Kirov tank factory in Leningrad moved almost immediately in June 1941. Included in the enterprises moved were some very large concerns e.g. over 100 aircraft factories. By the turn of 1942/3 the Soviet Union was out-producing the German economy in terms of quantity and quality[43] of munitions. During the war the state invested vast sums in building 3,500 new factories, the main result being that by 1944, munitions production was over a third greater than in 1940. During the war, Soviet industry produced over 95,000 tanks and 108,000 planes. Such an effort was the cause of the eventual defeat of the Nazis. Having been turned at Stalingrad in the winter of 1943, the *Wehrmacht* was pushed ever further back. Soviet industrial superiority was underlined by the victory of its tanks at the monumental battle of Kursk in July 1943. From then onward followed what became known as Stalin's 'Ten great battles' which propelled the Red Army to the gates of Berlin and victory in May 1945.

The role of forced labour in the war was considerable. Because of the shortage of manpower available, forced labour was used widely in industry by the end of the war. In 1941, the population of the *Gulag* stood at around 1.9 million - this figure was high as it had been boosted by the new arrivals from the Baltic States. The figure was to fall to around 1.2 million by 1944 due to the appalling death rate in the camps, it is likely that 20% of the camp population died of disease and malnutrition between 1942-'3. Some camps were also over run by the Nazis and there are examples of mass executions of prisoners by the NKVD[44]. Whatever the human cost, the labourers were essential to the economy making up some 10% of the workforce. Over half a million prisoners were used in non-*Gulag* enterprises, many of them arrested under the catch-all Article 58 of the Criminal Code which punished all 'anti-Soviet' activities. As the Red Army re-conquered lost territory, so the *Gulag* population rose as those accused of collaboration with the Nazis were arrested[45]. The war had seen some loosening of state control, in 1942 the army had been given a degree of independence and political commissars abolished. It was not until the end of the war that the party reasserted a level of control, in 1946 the greatest of the Red Army generals, Zhukov, being downgraded from the CC and sent to be commander of the Odessa military district.

Stalinism triumphant, 1945-'53

The post war years saw a re-establishment of the repressive Stalinist regime and the planned economy.

There is no doubt as to the devastating effect of the war on industry as a whole, not least the loss of 20 million lives. By 1945, fifty one percent of workers in industry were women, nearly 4.8 million of them. Over 65,000 km of railway track had been destroyed during the war and some 3.5 million homes. The fourth *piatiletka* was introduced in 1945 with the aim of restoring heavy industry to its pre war levels and to an extent it achieved those aims, e.g. electricity output was higher in 1950 than ten years earlier. Although this re-industrialisation was not accompanied by the same level of political violence, purging was reintroduced as a means of centralisation and control. From 1946-48 was a period of so called 'party renewal' - the *Zhdanovshchina*[46]- which took the form of an attack on artistic and literary life as part of an attempt to restore the ideological supremacy of the Communist Party. During the war Zhdanov ran the Leningrad Defence Council and the first act of 'ideological regeneration' in August 1946 was an attack on two literary journals from that city, *Zvezda* and *Leningrad*. This was followed by the widespread denunciation and humiliation of those who had supposedly strayed from the conformity of 'socialist realism'[47]. Those who were expelled from Writers and Composers Unions included some of the great luminaries of the Soviet arts. In the summer of 1946, the writers Anna Akhamatova and Mikhael Zoshchenko[48] were denounced by Zhdanov but they were to be the first of many. The great film makers Eisenstein[49] and Pudovkin were ostracised and the composers Shostakovich and Prokofiev attacked in February 1948 for writing elitist and 'non Russian' music. The post war era was one of state sponsored xenophobia and Russian chauvinism, even after Zhdanov's death in 1948, all forms of art and culture considered to be anti-Russian were denounced.

Anti-Semitism, 1948-53

As the war was defined as 'the Great Patriotic War', so those nations within the Empire which were considered to be anti Russian were attacked. Ukrainian nationalism was suppressed and Soviet Jews came under attack, particularly after the declaration of an independent Israel in 1948. Such was the nature of the Stalinist state that any supposed 'dual allegiance' on behalf of Soviet citizens was completely unacceptable. A leading Jewish actor, Solomon Mikhoels died in suspicious circumstances in 1948 the same year that the Jewish Anti-Fascist Committee was closed down[50]. Although in 1934 the Jews had been designated a homeland in the far East - the Birobidzhan Autonomous Province, it was virtually uninhabitable. Yet in the last years of Stalin's life, the Jewish people suffered considerable persecution[51]. By 1952, there were quotas for Jews in most universities, Jewish schools had been shut and Jewish employment in state organisations was limited. This anti-Semitism peaked in August 1952 with the arrest and execution of Solomon Losovsky (who was an ex-deputy foreign minister) and twelve leading Jewish writers and scholars. In the bizarre 'Doctors Case' of 1952/3, nine doctors were named as having conspired to kill Stalin and having murdered Zhdanov. Their supposed motives were treachery, in that they were inspired by foreign powers, and that six of their number were Jews and therefore the 'enemy within'. Such accusations were not thrown solely at the nationalities and Jews of Soviet Russia. There was an annual purge of the party post war of some 100,000 members and all supposedly 'cosmopolitan' influences were attacked. In 1949, the Leningrad Communist Party was purged in what became known as the 'Leningrad Affair'[52]. Under the supervision of the chief of the security police, Abakumov, evidence was falsified against leading party and state officials including Politburo members Voznesensky and Kosygin (the former being eventually shot). As his health failed in early 1953, the rumours of further impending purges began to circulate. Such rumours were only to end with Stalin's death on March 5th 1953.

ANALYSIS

Introduction

The purges and forced labour were the tools with which rapid industrialisation was achieved. The *Gulag* provided the pool of labour necessary to undertake labour intensive projects at little expense. Although the purges damaged the process to the extent that it deprived industry of many skilled managers and engineers, they also served to eliminate all opposition to the pace of change and the emphasis of the whole industrialisation programme. They also served as the means by which autocratic rule was re-established in the Empire, any semblance of democratic debate or distinct identity crushed. In this sense, it should be argued that the purges were the means by which the Communist leadership established complete control over the Empire. This helps to explain why, although reduced, the process of purging continued after the war despite the victory which had been achieved in 1945. One should not see purging as a phenomenon which emanated solely from the centre. There is little doubt that there was widespread support for the elimination of enemies of the state, real or unreal. Therefore one can argue that the process acquired a dynamic of its own, sustained by state propaganda and public acquiescence. So neither the purges or forced labour were the product of policy, they were the tools by which policy was introduced and the means by which change was sustained.

The pace of change

The purges were very much linked with the pace of

industrial change and in that were an intrinsic part of that change. So great were the demands of the *piatiletka*, so vast was the undertaking that a change in social attitudes, a new hegemony[53] was sought. Yet this new hegemony could not be introduced over years, as was envisaged by Bukarin and, to an extent, Lenin. The 'cultural revolution' became central to the whole process of change. The early show trials from 1928-'32, e.g. the Shakty or 'Industrial Party' trials were essentially of the skilled e.g. engineers who were not communists. They signalled that the economic reforms introduced were of such importance that they demanded complete acceptance in society. All those who stood apart, i.e. those who had done well during the NEP or those who from experience questioned the nature of the changes, were targeted as popular enemies. As with collectivisation, any prospective success in industry relied on popular acceptance of the view that industrialisation was the means by which 'The Revolution' could finally be won. Such revolutionary ardour led in 1928 to the first *piatiletka* being woefully over optimistic. Yet industrial transformation was made synonymous with a revolutionary renewal. To question the *piatiletka* was therefore to question the Revolution itself. This was the justification for the means by which the *piatiletka* was introduced and the arrests of countless millions from 1928 onwards. In this way, the state introduced the means by which it could maintain complete control over the process yet deflect criticism for undeniable failure.

The creation of scapegoats for industrial failure

It is very clear that there were significant problems in introducing the first *piatiletka*. It is true that huge schemes were undertaken, e.g. the Magnitogorsk iron and steel complex or the Turksib railway lines, but these achievements hid the near total confusion and chaos. Many plants were not built as there were simply neither the means or the resources. The new workforce which flooded in to the cities between 1928-'32 was unskilled and uneducated. Although new resources were created, old ones were destroyed and the purging of the skilled as scapegoats for failure was in its turn a cause of further problems. From April 1929, Stalin warned of so called 'Shaktyites' in all industries and such was the fever whipped up against the 'bourgeois wreckers' that at the 'Industrial Party' trial some half a million workers trudged past the courthouse demanding the death penalty. Many of these were conscripted into demonstration, but there were many who help a grudge against those who had done well during the NEP and such purging of the technical elite was often popular on the shop floor. Yet the real problem of the *piatiletka* was not addressed, the shortage of skilled personnel. It was calculated that the plan required up to 450,000 technicians and engineers yet in 1928 only some 120,000 were available. The role of purging was not to make good that shortfall but to provide an excuse for its effects. It also provided the element of class struggle which gave the first *piatiletka* its revolutionary identity.

A new elite emerged from 1928 with a commitment to the modernisation process which was needed to sustain it in its progress. It was this elite and their aspirations which not only supported the purges but drove them on. The purging of specialists was a key part of a wider social revolution. Expert baiting became the norm and although Stalin specifically denounced the practice in June 1931, it still continued such as the Metro Vickers case in 1933 which coincided with the economic low point. What industrialisation did was to transform social status in the Soviet Union. From 1930-'33, over 600,000 workers became administrators and thereby part of the new elite. These were the loyalists to the new set of values, the new hegemony and they became the shock troops of its defence. If one studies the composition of Stalin's later *Politburos*, many of the elite took their first steps up the party ladder during this period of turmoil including Khrushchev and Kosygin. The pace of change engulfed society as well as the economy and in consequence there were inevitably, losers. It must be argued that this process took precedence even over industrial growth. The fact that the economy had practically collapsed by 1932 and that the purges of those 'responsible' continued, despite the harm it did to the economy, proves the primary importance of purging as the means of sustaining and justifying the policy.

Forced labour

The relationship between political autocracy, industrialisation and forced labour was a close one. To reassert autocratic control, the state introduced a reign of terror organised by OGPU. The *Gulag*, which was the system of labour camps to which all 'enemies of the revolution ' were sent, became an integral part of the industrialisation process. Such rapid growth demanded cheap and expendable labour and the *Gulag* was the means by which this labour was provided. Whilst there was a clear difference between the status of the *Gulag* inmate and the industrial worker, there was a level of discipline introduced into the life of the latter which became an integral part of industrialisation. By no stretch of the imagination was the use of forced labour economic, for the most part it was far too unproductive. The numbers involved, however, made it an important part of the Soviet economy. Figures vary to the numbers imprisoned in the *Gulag* at any one time but by 1939 there were up to three million forced labourers. If that is the case then they constituted up to 2% of the population as a whole. What this mass of labour did was to enable the planners to indulge their obsession with gigantic projects. These projects such as the White-Sea-Baltic or the Moscow-Volga Canals used up large pools of labour. Forced labour was particularly used to build up infrastructure and mine raw materials. Without the low labour costs that forced labour afforded, it is unimaginable how these essential components of the *piatiletkas* could have been developed. By 1938 the NKVD which controlled the *Gulag* was the largest construction agency in the Soviet Union. The work undertaken was often in inhospitable regions such as on the Kola Peninsular through which a railway was built from Murmansk to Kem. There are numerous other examples of other railways constructed by forced labour despite the elements - the Salelhard to Igarka or the Vim to Vorkuta being just two of many. Their value was in the transportation of the raw materials from the vast *Gulag* labour camps complexes. The largest were in the Far East and in the Komi Autonomus Republic to the North West of the Soviet Union. In both, the business of extracting coal, gold , uranium and other essential raw materials was undertaken without any concern for human welfare or life. It is likely that mortality in the camps was as high as 20% p.a. by 1938, yet that was of little importance since the flow of new inmates was never ending. In his important account of the system of forced labour, *The Gulag Archipelago*, Alexander Solzhenitsyn likens the constant topping up process of the *Gulag* to waves, each bringing in their new consignment. So as there were the engineers between 1928-'31, there was the party elite of 1936-'38. The *Gulag* was never short of new arrivals because once the system had been created and the economy relied on the forced labour element so it took on a dynamic of its own, in 1939-'40, Baltic nationalists, 1943-'44, Cossacks, Chechens, Tatars and so on.

The importance of the *Gulag* is underlined by the role it played in the war economy. Although the numbers in the *Gulag* dropped in wartime to perhaps around 1.2 million in 1944, this was because many inmates had been farmed out to industrial enterprises across the country, perhaps another quarter of a million prisoners. Because of the all embracing nature of Article 58[54] of the penal code, citizens could be sent to the *Gulag* for the most trivial offence. This served the system well for camp mortality rose further to 21% in 1942. By 1945, perhaps one tenth of all Soviet workers were forced labourers and yet this was still a woefully unproductive form of labour. What it was, however, was captive, controlled and expendable and in the short term that is what the

regime's policy demanded most. The rapid modernisation programme demanded complete acquiescence from the labour force as any form of questioning or doubt could signal disaster, such was the economy's permanent state of crisis. This helps to explain why forced labour was continued after 1945 when the regime seemed to have defeated its enemies. The devastation caused by the war and the onset of the Cold War, resulted in plans which aimed to restore the industrial base and build the technical and defence industries. As in the early 1930's, there was a foreign threat to counteract (that of the USA and her allies) and therefore a real urgency to build. In this atmosphere, human considerations continued to be ignored in contrast to the priorities of the plan.

Labour discipline

Forced labour should be viewed in a wider sense than simply the *Gulag*. The programme to turn the Soviet Union into a major industrial power demanded great sacrifices from its citizens, in particular the peasantry, as already has been discussed, but also from the urban working class. Living standards remained depressed until after the war when wages rose until in 1952 real wages stood on a par with 1928. The horrors of collectivisation produced a cheap workforce yet conditions and wages for this workforce were extremely poor, in 1935 only one in twenty working class families having more than one room to live in. Not only that, strict labour discipline was introduced thereby removing any rights from the labouring population. Workers lost the right to bargain collectively or to unionise. The system of work books (1931), harsh punishment for absenteeism/lateness (1932), internal passports (1932) and restricted mobility of labour (1940) coupled with the constant threat of the ubiquitous Article 58 can be explained by the need of the plans to exploit the workforce to the full. It is true that this was coupled with measures which were designed to encourage hard work. These included higher wages for skilled workers introduced in 1931 or propaganda based on the revolutionary spirit during the first *piatiletka* or the *Stakhanovite* movement during the second. Such a 'carrot and stick' approach did succeed in raising productivity but only to a point, output per hour in 1940 being only 115% of its 1928 figure. This helps to explain why the harsh 1940 Labour Law was introduced as labour productivity was beginning to stagnate. For most factory managers, the threat of purging for under achievement led them to try and have low production seem as the norm. The important point is that rapid industrialisation demanded productivity increases from the workforce. Trying to induce greater production through political propaganda i.e. *Stakhanovism*, often cause more problems than it solved, workers who did not qualify for 'overproduction bonuses' often producing less in consequence. During the war, new movements sprang up to emulate the overproduction of D. Bosyi and F. Bunkin. There is no doubt that the war did engender patriotic feelings which did help increase production.

Central planning and the pace of change gave the industrialisation process military characteristics.

Therefore, it is not surprising that the main tool the state used to achieve targets was discipline. As the process went into periodic crisis, so the discipline increased as it was too crude, too unsophisticated, too simplistic to respond any other way. A clear example of this response, and its limitations, was the policy during wartime. As the *Wehrmacht* swept across the Soviet Union, so stricter working conditions were imposed on labour. By the decree of 26th June 1942, public sector workers were expected to work 54 hour weeks and all workers could be ordered to do 3 hours overtime a night. For those in essential industries such as railway or munitions workers, the conditions were even harsher, both groups being 'conscripted' and therefore liable to military discipline for mistakes or failures. The figures for convictions under the discipline laws are quite astounding, one million a year being charged with absenteeism, over 200,000 of dereliction of duty[55] (which was defined as three or more cases of absenteeism/lateness). What these figures prove is that the state was prepared to subject the workforce to the harshest discipline and that this was its main form of control. The high number of prosecutions point to the extent to which the workforce was unwilling or unable to accept such levels of exploitation. The labour discipline imposed in this period was the main tool of coercing the workforce to carry out the orders of the bureaucracy. Therefore it was also not only a consequence of the policy but an integral part of it.

Purging as a traditional tool of control

The Stalinist political revolution very much reflected

the nature of the economic one and the two were very much interrelated. In this relationship, purging had a key role in establishing the centre's authority and ensuring hegemony of its ideas. Stalinism demanded the subordination of all interests to those of the central authority. Therefore purging became the means of re-establishing an autocracy and giving the regime a legitimacy it did not have up until the end of the NEP. It was the manner in which the revolution was imposed on the Soviet Union but in doing so it swept away the ideology and party of 1917. Yet purging was not simply the invention of Stalin. The Soviet and Tsarist political systems had no tradition of imposing their will through legalistic means and the rule of law which underpinned Western democracy simply did not exist. It is this fact that gives the purges their distinct character in that there were no defined limits to the brutality or the extent to which the purges took place. Purging had been commonplace in Bolshevik politics pre 1928. For example, in 1919 up to 15% of the party had been expelled. To ensure acceptance of the NEP amongst the party, despite its ideological flaws, Lenin embarked on a purge which saw the expulsion of 25% of the membership. Then as in the 1930's such expulsions were deemed necessary as the price paid to preserve the revolution. How the 1930's differed from the early '20s was in degree. Industrialisation led to the building up a state apparatus dedicated to coercion. That apparatus - the NKVD, the *Gulag* and so on - was created to ensure that the state's policy was implemented.

Purging as the tool of autocracy.

This helps to explain the *Yezhovshchina* of 1936-'38 which saw the purging of bureaucrats and the country's elite. The early 1930's had seen a dramatic growth in the size of the bureaucracy, many of them the new technical elite which had blossomed as a result of the opening up of education. It was to break the security of the provincial elite that the 1936-'8 purge was undertaken, for in an autocracy such independence was a contradiction. Stalin had been humiliated by the failure of Yagoda and the NKVD to deal effectively with the Ryutin conspiracy of 1932 and that helps to explain why Yagoda was one of the first to be arrested after the February-March plenum of 1937-which initiated the process in earnest. Figures fluctuate widely for the numbers arrested and killed during the Yezhov years; it has been suggested that up to 90% of the membership of the republic's CCs were arrested and in all up to seven million arrests[56]. What is for sure is that the purge succeeded in crushing provincial independence which Stalin so feared. This theme runs through the period and the treatment of the Leningrad Party is a very clear example. As a power base to rival that of Moscow, the Leningrad party was treated with suspicion by Stalin throughout his dictatorship. Not only was his closest rival Kirov shot in the Smolny Institute in 1934, but Leningrad was singled out for special treatment in 1937. The purger in this case was Zhdanov who filled the Party with his own men, e.g. Kuznetsov and Voznesensky. Yet these men in turn were purged during the Leningrad Affair of 1948. It is very clear, therefore, that in attempting to assert complete central control, the new autocracy used the tool of purging as a means of asserting its political will on the provinces.

Purging as a tool of 'Russification'

Yet one can extend this further, as purging was also used as the means by which the state reimposed the Tsarist ideal of 'Great Russia' upon the Empire. Rather than having to undergo Russification as they had pre 1917, those nationalities deemed disloyal to 'the Revolution were' purged wholesale. This was made possible by extension in the machinery of government. There are numerous, tragic examples of the wholesale suffering of nations which, in Stalin's view, stood apart from the new Russian hegemony. Industrialisation had set the pace in how the state implemented its policy. The removal of whole nations to the *Gulag* or death was rapid and efficient. Any nationalities new to the Empire were ruthlessly purged, in 1940 700,000 Lithuanians and 1.2 million Ukrainians being sent into exile. This process continued as the Red Army chased the *Wehrmacht* westwards, from 1943-'49 approximately 3.3 million members of non-Russian nationalities being deported. Whole nations were accused of collaboration such as the Chechens, Kalmyks or Cossacks. Their fate was removal form their homelands en masse. The definition of the war as a victory for 'Great Russia' helped to further institutionalise the chauvinism of the regime. Despite the suffering of the Jews during the war, their 'otherness' led them to being singled out and viciously persecuted post 1945. The Stalinist regime did not tolerate cultural pluralism and purging was a means by which it was prevented. From the arrest of Solomon Mikhoels in 1948 to the 'Doctors Plot' of 1952 the Jewish people were subjugated to systematic persecution. Yet they were not the only ones, the *Zhdanovschina* attempting to impose cultural uniformity on society as a whole. Those who were purged in this time - and there were many from the artistic world imprisoned - all were perceived as a threat to the cultural hegemony of the period.

The destruction of the 'Old Bolsheviks'

The most pressing question is why Stalin decreed the destruction of Lenin's party, since in preserving the Revolution, he destroyed the original revolutionaries. The answer is that the Revolution of the 1930's was a very different from that envisaged by the 'Old Bolsheviks'. There was considerable opposition within the Bolshevik Party to the scale and the tempo of industrialisation and this became acutely apparent in 1934 at the XVIIth Party Congress. In the vote for the CC almost one quarter of the party voted against Stalin. This was indicative of a party in which internal debate was seen as compatible with one party rule. Despite the fact that party dissent had been outlawed in 1921, Stalin still had to suffer the indignity of being outvoted in the *Politburo*, e.g. Ryutin's ten year imprisonment rather than the death penalty as demanded by Stalin in 1932. The party, its hierarchy, structures and leading members were all incompatible with the restoration of an autocracy which Stalin believed was essential for economic change. Terror was therefore unleashed to destroy the party and ensure the transition to one person rather than one party rule. One should not underestimate the extent of opposition to Stalin's methods amongst the party in the early 1930s. Of the 1,966 members of the XVIIth Party Congress, 1,108 were executed in the following years. These individuals were the core members of Lenin's party, just as were those executed after the great show trials. Yet this was the political aim, to destroy the party of Lenin and create a new elite which was compatible with the aims and methods of the 'second revolution'. Hence the death of Bukharin, Rykov, Kamenev and others who had been so close to Stalin. All those who could even theoretically pose a threat to this new elite were in their turn eliminated as part of the necessity of ensuring the desired outcome, the eventual victory of communism. This victory could only be achieved in Stalin's eyes by undertaking the policies he did, and in political terms that meant the ruthless elimination of all those capable of opposition. So purging became the political policy and there were no limits to its practice. The consequence was the destruction of those such as Marshal *Tugachevsky* in June 1937 and the wholesale slaughter of the armed forces command chain thereafter. Similarly, after the war, the demotion of Marshal Zhukov should be seen as part of the overall process of demoting any who might be perceived as of significance.

The radical populist base

As a central feature of the Stalinist state, purging did not simply emanate from the leadership but was sustained by a populist base. Although it was sanctioned by the leadership (there is clear evidence that Stalin and the *Politburo* signed many a death warrant) the *Yezhovshchina* developed a momentum of its own. By 1937 the NKVD had quotas of their own to fulfil which drove them to arrest and extort confessions almost randomly. There were large sections of the populace untouched by the purges and many unsympathetic to the elites who had now met their downfall. For those engineers who were arrested from 1928-'31 there were others ready to take their place and benefit accordingly. Similarly, the destruction of the upper echelons of the party from 1936-'8 was an opportunity for the next generation of communists whose only loyalty was to Stalin and who viewed Lenin's party with suspicion. There was a genuine and widespread belief that these people were in some sense 'enemies of the people' and that their fate was in some sense justified. At Piatakov's trial in 1937, a crowd of over 200,000 assembled to demand the death penalty this being a feature of many of the trials and reinforced by the 'confessions' of most accused. As a means of intimidating the population as a whole, purging also terrorised it into complying through denunciations. At the peak of the *Yezhovshchina*, thousands of citizens informed on their neighbours or fellow workers. This allowed personal scores to be settled but also allowed grievances to be aired, of which there were many. One must not also forget the popular enthusiasm during the first *piatiletka*, the revolutionary spirit which was engendered or the patriotism shown in abundance during the war. There is no doubt that the regime demanded sacrifices from the citizenry in terms of living standards. One should argue that it did enjoy a support and legitimacy as the provider of industrialisation and an improvement in the lot of those who were favoured.

Conclusion.

The purges and forced labour were a central element of economic and political policy from 1929-'53. Once set in place, they became the tools by which the state could dominate the economic sphere and create autocratic rule. That this was possible was due to the extension of the machinery of government as a result of the developing role of the state in the economy and the level of coercion necessary to implement reforms. Yet purging had a popular base; it also achieved a momentum of its own which, although it does not absolve Stalin and his henchmen form any of the guilt, helps to explain its extent. Millions were swept away in the cause of 'the Revolution' as the destabilisation of society became to be that revolution. Therefore, the purges and *Gulags* were the most important element of Stalinist policy.

[1] Collectivisation should be defined as the collective ownership of the land.

[2] The *Gulag* is the term used for the Soviet labour camp system. The letters are a form of anachronym for the Chief Administration for Corrective Labour Camps.

[3] The NEP was the New Economic Policy which was introduced by Lenin in 1921 to stimulate economic growth. As a pragmatic move it accepted some element of capitalism in agriculture, thereby encouraging the peasantry to increase production which it duly did.

[4] Modernisation should be defined as introducing modern means of production.

[5] A leading Bolshevik intellectual, in 1917 Bukharin was a leader of the party's left wing opposing Brest Litovsk. He became a convert to the NEP. Politically he was no match for some of his peers but intellectually he had few to match him. It was his grasp of theory, a skill which Stalin so patently lacked, which made him such a threat in the late 20's and early 30's.

[6] *Smychka* means alliance between the urban and rural.

[7] Creator of the Red Army and seemingly natural successor to Lenin, Trotsky was expelled from the party in November 1927 after a period of infighting. He was eventually murdered by Stalin's agents in Mexico in 1940.

[8] This tactic of taking grain by force had been used during the Civil War with disastarous consequences.

[9] *Kulak* is the term used for a rich peasant. They did not exist as a distinct class but *kulak* became a catch-all derogatory term for anyone who opposed collectivisation.

[10] This rise of the price of consumer goods and a relative fall in agricultural prices, led to a price 'scissors', hence the name given to the crisis. In 1923 when this previously happened, the state reversed price increases in consumer goods.

[11] This article had been passed in 1926 and made speculation a criminal offence.

[12] The Central Committee (CC) was the party's governing body although it came to be dominated by the smaller *Politburo*.

[13] From Stalin's birthday celebrations in December 1929 is dated the beginning of the cult of his personality.

[14] There was no economic definition of the *kulak*, it was an artificial class created to provide a scapegoat. Therefore throughout the collectivisation process, any opposition was labelled as kulak and punished accordingly. Similarly, those wealthier peasants or those which owned cattle under the NEP were labelled as kulak often out of sheer jealousy.

[15] *Kolkhoz* is the Russian for a collective farm.

[16] It was Kondratiev who proposed that trade cycles operate over

fifty year periods. He was, a leading and eminent economist.

17 Initially in the 1920's it was proposed that collectivisation would occur through the creation of MTSs which would be rural centres of mechanisation and work to encourage collective farming.

18 These figures are based on the calculations of the historian Roy Medvedev who used Soviet statistics as the basis for his analysis, hence the suspicion that they are conservative.

19 The agricultural workforce was reduced by anything up to 19 million people between 1941-'44.

20 The MTSs were starved of technicians and machines, all tractor factories temporarily producing tanks until 1944.

21 Procurement prices did not rise from 1940-'7 despite the fact that prices overall increased twenty times over in the same period.

22 Many of the trees died as they were planted in unsuitably dry areas. The planting of trees did not help to increase crop yields as intended, its main consequence was to divert scarce *kolkhoz* resources from where they were needed most.

23 The issue of the numbers killed by collectivisation is a contentious one. The higher figure of 6.7 million *kulaks* killed was proposed by Robin Conquest, the lower figure by Roy Medvedev.

24 *Kolkhoznik* was one who worked on a collective farm.

25 As Tsar of the Russian Empire from 1689-1725, Peter the Great was the first of many to attempt an industrialisation from above.

26 In fact none of the defendants were executed and Ramzin was later rehabilitated and even decorated.

27 In June 1941, *Operation Barbarossa* commenced, the German invasion of the Soviet Union. It was ten years and four months after Stalin's speech. Such was the progress in industrialisation and the total control of state over the industrial process that the Soviet Union was able to outproduce the economy of Germany by 1943.

28 The fact that a CC plenum sentenced Ryutin to only ten years angered Stalin considerably. In the subsequent purges, many leading Bolsheviks were forced to being part of the 'Ryutin Plot'. In 1937, Ryutin himself was shot after a trial lasting under an hour.

29 Although found guilty in April 1933, the Britons were allowed to leave the country soon after.

30 The NKVD became an elite organisation. Its security side GUGB was staffed by Old Bolsheviks who were well acquainted in methods of state security. As an elite, their turn to be purged was to come after they had completed Stalin's dirty work.

31 There is no doubt that Nikolaev was acting on Stalin's orders despite the outward show of grief Stalin showed at Kirov's funeral.

32 This was named after the Donbass miner Aleksei Stakhanov who was said to have overfulfilled his production quota by 1400%. Those who also overfulfilled their quotas were given special privileges as 'Stakhanov' workers.

33 Such spending was the response to Nazism's rise to power in Germany.

34 If ever there was need of an example to prove that a written constitution didn't automatically lead to the protection of citizen's rights, this is it.

35 Smirnov was an Old Bolshevik whose revolutionary credentials included the 1905 revolution, leading the Vth Army against Kolchak during the Civil War and being proposed as General Secretary before Stalin was chosen. The fact that he had been in prison in 1933, making conspiracy to assassinate the leadership somewhat difficult was dismissed at his trial as irrelevant!

36 Ordzhonikidze was one of the last independent voices in the Politburo and pleaded with Stalin to end the purges. In February 1937 he was found dead, supposedly having committed suicide.

37 Tukhachevsky was charged with 'crimes' ranging from treason to espionage. One of the more common charges against all those in the military was that they were agents of the German Army.

38 Solzhenitsyn puts this figure at only around 1-2% of the total Gulag population.

39 Gorky died poisoned in June 1936.

40 This was defined as being over twenty minutes late!

41 This was a non aggression pact signed between the Soviet Union and Nazi Germany. It also provided for the neutrality of each country if it was attacked by a third party.

42 This did not mean that these factories functioned automatically. Still by the end of 1942 some 50 factories were not in operation because of the lack of labour.

43 The Soviet army was equipped with vastly superior tanks, the T45 and Soviet KV. On top of this, aid from the US included 4,100 planes and over 138,000 motor vehicles giving the Soviets the advantage of the quarter ton jeep.

44 One of the most notorious examples was the massacre of 3,000 prisoners at Lvov prison in 1941.

45 At the end of the war, whole nations were incarcerated in the Gulag from the Chechens in February 1944 to the Balkars later that year. Those who collaborated with the Nazis and followed the renegade General Vlasov were sent to Siberia as were any surviving POWs. Most tragic were the cases of servicemen captured by the Germans who had to put up with inhuman conditions only to be reimprisoned on their repatriation by a government which accused them of treachery for 'allowing' themselves to be captured. The end of the war and the following period saw a stream of Ukrainian nationalists arrested and sent to do forced labour.

46 *Zhdanovshchina* literally means 'in the time of Zhdanov'.

47 Socialist realism was the cultural bedfellow of Stalinist ideology. Defined in the period 1932-'34 and reflected in the works of writers such as Michael Sholokhov, socialist realism rejected the abstract or romantic as 'bourgeois'. Instead it defined acceptable cultural expression as that which reflected the regimes' ideological message.

48 Zoshchenko's Adventures of a Monkey were deemed by Zhdanov to be particularly offensive. In the story a monkey escapes from his cage into Stalinist society. Such is his experiences, however, that he endeavours to return to the comparative freedom of his zoo cage.

49 Eisenstein was by far the most celebrated Soviet cinematographer, producing classic films including *Battleship Potemkin* and *October*.

50 This committee had been founded during the war to win support for the Soviet war effort, in particular in the United States.

51 This was despite the fact that Stalin's son Yakov and daughter Svetlana both married Jews.

52 Stalin had always been suspicious of Leningrad as a rival centre of power. Many of the most senior communists purged/eliminated had their power base in that city including Kirov.

53 Hegemony is the acceptance of received beliefs and values.

54 Passed as part of the Criminal Code of 1926, Article 58 was a catch-all section concerning anti-Soviet activity. This was widely interpreted as Solzenitsyn pointed out.

55 The penalty if found guilty, could be a lengthy prison sentence of at least five years forced labour.

56 Figures this high were claimed by historians such as R. Conquest and R. Medvedev. They have been revised downwards since the opening up of KGB archives. As yet there are no definitive figures as the data is insufficient.

STALIN

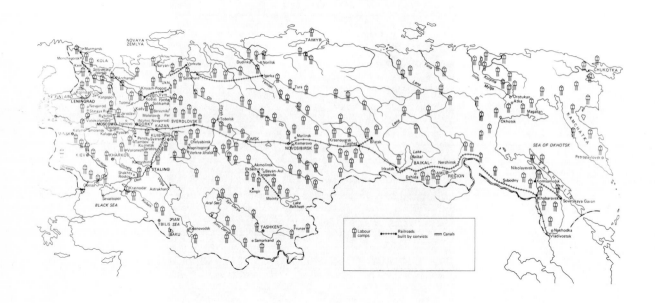

GULAGS

CHAPTER 12

ASSESS THE EXTENT OF DE - STALINISATION, 1956 -'64.

Introduction

From 1956- '64, the Soviet Union lived with the legacy of the all encompassing systems and structures created during Stalin's dictatorship, from the role of the Communist party to central planning[1]. The efforts to reform and change these systems and structures - to de-Stalinise - was limited by one fundamental factor, that it was impossible to reform the system without undermining it. The era of Stalinism had left the Communist Party and the bureaucracy with total power in Soviet life[2]. The attempts to reform these institutions were similarly limited by the condition that reform could only be undertaken if it did not alter the status quo. These points are the important context to the supposed de-Stalinisation within the era of Nikita Khrushchev. Whatever reforms were undertaken, were within and thereby limited by, the Stalinist system. Similarly, the reforms of the era 1956-'64 were only ever temporarily accepted by the party elites[3] for many of them threatened the institutional basis and security of their position. In some senses the term de-Stalinisation is perhaps inappropriate. There were not so much attacks on the fundamentals of the Stalinist system but more of an attempt to reform it into the mould of a new leader. This helps to explain the limited thawing of cultural attitudes under Khrushchev. That this attempt failed was because the effects of reform were seemingly threatening to those with vested interests in the continuation of the Stalinist structure.

The struggle for power, 1953-'56

On March 5th, 1953, Stalin died leaving a huge political vacuum to be filled. Immediately there was a thawing of the Stalinist system with the release of 1 million political prisoners and a reversal of the Russification[4] process which had been undertaken by Stalin. These actions were undertaken by Beria who was the head of the Ministry for Internal Affairs (MVD) i.e. the security forces. Such was the fear of the man, however, that at the first chance to discredit him, i.e. the East German unrest in June 1953[5], he was purged. It is probable that Beria was shot in June or December 1953. The political legacy he left was a programme of restricted de-Stalinisation within the system which was to be adopted by Khrushchev.

With the death of Stalin, the position as nominal head of government fell into the hands of Malenkov who became Prime Minister. The party was in the control of Nikita Khrushchev who became first secretary of the CC in September 1953. It was between these two that the battle was fought for leadership of the state, the battlefield was the economy. Malenkov proposed economic growth through an intensification of agriculture. This would entail improving the yield of existing land using better production techniques. This was countered by Khrushchev who, in February 1954, proposed an opening up of previously uncultivated land, the 'Virgin and Idle Land' Programme. This was to till the soils of the far flung Soviet Republics such as Kazakhstan and Siberia. Despite local opposition, in February 1954 a CC plenum agreed to the cultivation of 13 million acres of virgin land. This was extended in August 1954 by a government - party decree which extended the virgin soils programme to a target of 30 million new hectares under cultivation by 1956.

Khrushchev was able to use the CC plenum as the vehicle for the promotion of policy whilst increasing the relative importance of the party in relation to the government. This was at the root of the power struggle between him and Malenkov and was reflected in other policy areas. In 1955, as part of a decentralisation of economic planning, Khrushchev placed the running of certain businesses into the hands of the 15 Soviet republics. The party was near triumphant with the downfall of Malenkov in February 1955. Following an editorial by D.T. Shepilov in *Pravda* which attacked his industrial policy of concentrating on consumer goods he offered his resignation as Prime Minister and took over the enviable job of Minister in charge of Power Stations. This was followed in 1957 by the creation of over one hundred *sovnarkhozy*[6] which were economic planning councils dominated by the party. Their creation went hand in hand with the proposed dissolution of Moscow based industrial ministries. When those in the Presidium who bemoaned the loss of governmental economic influence objected, they were brushed aside as being anti the party. This brought the power struggle to a head and at a Presidium meeting in June 1957, Molotov, Malenkov and Kaganovich conspired to remove Khrushchev from

his position as First Secretary of the party. Although outnumbered, Khrushchev managed to hold out until a CC plenum met a week later which not only supported him resolutely but condemned the Anti-Party group. The Presidium was expanded to include new members such as Leonid Brezhnev and Andrei Gromyko who were loyal to Khrushchev. The shift to the party in terms of power was complete.

1956 and Cultural issues

At the XXth Party Congress in 1956, Khrushchev broke new ground in two ways. He introduced the concept of peaceful co-existence with the West. He also expressed the desire to trade and cooperate in technological matters. What stunned the Congress was his so called 'Secret Speech' given at the end of the Congress. In this speech Khrushchev catalogued the excess of Stalin's reign of terror post 1934. Although it did not bring into question the process of industrialisation and collectivisation, the speech criticised the military purges of 1937, the role of Stalin during the war (the real hero Zhukov[7] being given the credit he deserved) and the attack on Lenin's party. The speech matched the spirit of cultural liberation after the death of Stalin. In September 1954, Ilya Ehrenburg's seminal novel *The Thaw* was published which gave its name to the period. The rehabilitation of writers such as Dostoevsky was followed in 1956 by the publishing of two works which criticised the party and its past. In *Not by Bread Alone* by Vladimir Dudintsev, Stalin's role in creating an elite was vilified. Another important work to appear was *Dr Zhivago* by Boris Pasternak which was awarded the Nobel Prize for Literature in 1958. The tension between the conservative literary establishment as represented by Vsevolod Kochetov and the new intelligentsia constantly threatened to boil over into strict censorship. The sensation created by Alexander Solzhenitsyn's *A Day in the Life of Ivan Denisovich* (1962), which was an account of life in the *Gulags* (prison camps), resulted in the author writing little more until 1967. The same spirit of limited toleration was not extended to the Churches during the Khrushchev era. As the state embarked on a systematic programme of church closure and restriction on religious freedom, the number of churches open declined by two thirds between 1959 and 1962[8]. In 1961 the state had legislation passed through the synod at Zagorsk which effectively transferred ownership of church buildings to itself. This led to further closures and imprisonment of believers. Those in the Baptist Church who rejected state interference formed the 'Action Group' and attempted to win control of the churches main body, the ECB at a Congress in 1963. Their failure was as much to do with the imprisonment of many of their leaders as any other factor.

Foreign Policy 1955-61

Greater cultural freedom was overshadowed by foreign policy imperatives. In 1954/5 official visits were undertaken to China[9] and Yugoslavia[10] to build fraternal bridges. In 1955 also, the Austrian Peace Treaty was signed which led to the withdrawal of Soviet troops and Austria as a neutral state[11]. In response to the creation of NATO[12], the Warsaw Pact was signed in May 1955 which committed the signatories to a defensive alliance in the face of any aggression from the West. Improved relations with West Germany resulted from the release of all German POWs[13] in the summer of 1955 which was cemented by the visit of Chancellor Adenauer to Moscow. As part of the Soviet developing global ambitions, Khrushchev visited India and Burma in October 1955 and great power status was underlined by the explosion of a thermonuclear device in December. Better relations with Tito were cemented by a visit to Moscow by the Yugoslavian leader in April 1956. Further attempts to promote peaceful co-existence suffered a setback, however, with events in Poland and Hungary[14] which underlined the limits of the new policy. In October 1956 the Polish Communist Party elected Wladyslaw Gomulka as its leader and proceeded to demand a certain autonomy from Moscow, within the constraints of the Warsaw Pact. The government in Hungary led by Imre Nagy went one step further and declared neutrality which was followed four days later on the 4th November by a full scale Soviet invasion. Nagy was immediately arrested to be replaced by Janos Kadar. The invasion of Hungary heightened international tension and made very clear that peaceful co - existence was a policy which did not include the loss of Soviet power. The successful launch of the first space satellite Sputnik in October 1957 and the propaganda victory which followed were assertions of this power[15]. Even this achievement was overshadowed by the first manned space flight of Yuri Gagarin in April 1961.

Economic and social reform 1958-61

The more ambitious economic and social reforms of the Khrushchev era followed his installation as Prime Minister in March 1958, thereby gaining control of both party and government. It did not follow that proposed reforms would automatically lead to change as Khrushchev had to rely on the Stalinist bureaucracy and establishment generally to put these changes into effect. For the purpose of widening the technical elite and opening up higher education to the working classes, the 1958 education reforms were introduced. The reforms also intended to raise the status of manual labour by encouraging school students to spend considerable time in the factories observing Soviet work practices. All these reforms were unpopular, in particular with the elite who were horrified at the prospect of their children spending time learning about inertia and alcoholism then prevalent in industrial life! Simultaneously, Khrushchev embarked on a series of reforms to modernise agricultural and industrial production. The reforms were placed within the context of central planning but the plans were altered. As the sixth Five Year Plan (1956 -'60) became increasingly unrealistic, Khrushchev had it scrapped and introduced the Seven Year Plan (1959 -'65) at the XXIst Party Congress. The aim of this plan was to modernise the consumer and capital goods sector. Areas of the economy earmarked for expansion included the chemical industry which was to grow by 300% by 1965 and construction - there were to be 22 million flats and houses built. The prefabricated constructions which sprouted up in countryside and city alike were the most enduring monument to Khrushchev's reforms. In January 1960, Khrushchev introduced proposals with the aim of providing greater manpower for industrial and agricultural improvement. With the justification that nuclear weapons made ground forces relatively redundant, he slashed the number in the armed forces from 3.6 million to 2.4 million[16]. At the XXIInd Party Congress in October 1961, Khrushchev proclaimed that socialism had been achieved and the existence of a communist state was only just around the corner. A new party programme and a Twenty Year Plan were launched which promised to see this Communist state into existence and surpass the West[17]. Also at the Congress, further revelations were made about the excesses of Stalinism and, in consequence, Stalin's body was removed from Lenin's tomb.

Reform and unrest

The problem with many of Khrushchev's reforms was that they relied on new sources of investment by which all the aims would be fulfilled. To compensate for the lack of new investment, a series of administrative reforms were introduced in ad hoc fashion over the period. The Machine Tractor Stations (MTS) were phased out in January 1958 and the machines sold to the *kolkhozes*. The aim of this change was to place decision making in the countryside with one body[18]. However, a series of setbacks in agriculture precipitated further change. Despite an excellent harvest in 1958, subsequent production did not match expectations and in March 1962 the whole of the agricultural administration was reorganised. The new system consisted of a host of agricultural committees dominated by the party. These committees were to oversee the work of the Territorial Production Administrations (TPAs) whose job it was to ensure that the *kolkhozes* met their targets as set out by the plan. A more controversial reform was the raising of prices to meet the investment needs in agriculture which was introduced in June 1962. The reaction across the Soviet Union was negative, in some cities open protest against the measures developed into rioting. In Novocherkassk, the demonstrations began with a walkout by the workers of the Electric Engine Works which was the Soviet Union's largest railway factory employing over 10,000 people. The demands of the strikers were for better housing and food to be more widely available. As they moved to the local party offices to present their petitions they were met by soldiers who fired into the crowds killing perhaps hundreds. This incident was of critical importance for social unrest on such a scale was unheard of for some considerable period in Soviet Russia.

Other reforms were equally unpopular amongst the groups they affected. To improve efficiency in the management of agriculture, Khrushchev proposed the division of the party into two wings, one to be concerned with industry, the other with agriculture. The measure was introduced in January 1963 and was applied similarly to trade unions and Soviets. To the party bureaucrat, the *apparat*, this was a reform too far. Their position, previously seemingly secure, was increasingly being placed under threat. On the one hand, Khrushchev had increased their importance by raising the status of the party. Yet the influence of the *apparat*[19] was undermined by the drive to recruit more peasants and workers to the party, numbers increasing by 4 million between 1955 and 1964. Similarly the party hierarchy at local level, the *oblast* and *raions*[20] lost influence to the new bodies created to supervise the economic system, e.g. the TPAs. At the XXIInd Party Congress, Khrushchev introduced measures which insisted on regular deselection of party members from important posts and committees by elections.

Reforms under threat

Many of Khrushchev's agricultural reforms were born of an untrained but fascinated mind. The consequence was that the early sixties saw some spectacular catastrophes which gave ammunition to his enemies. The extension of his beloved maize[21] into areas unsuited for its growth such as the Ukraine led to poor harvests. In 1963, a spring drought in the virgin soil lands saw the drying out of the topsoil which was them blown away in the early summer with the consequence that the harvest failed. Around half of the virgin lands of Siberia and Central Asia were turned into a dust bowl. The grain harvest that year was only around three fifths of the 180 million tonnes target and the Soviet Union had to import 20 million tonnes from North America to make up the shortfall. Right to the end of his leadership, Khrushchev proposed change in how agriculture was organised. In the summer of 1964 he proposed the abolition of the TPAs to be replaced by organisational bodies in Moscow. Such chopping and changing increased his unpopularity.

Foreign policy tension

From 1958 the policy of peaceful co-existence came under even greater pressure until any pretence that it still existed was laughable. In fact, Khrushchev's foreign policy became one of argument, confrontation and brinkmanship. Despite initial attempts at reconciliation, the Soviet Union repeatedly clashed with non-satellite Communist states, of most importance being China led by Mao Zedong. In 1957, the Peking government was led to believe that the Soviets would help China become a nuclear power with technical and financial aid. Such a step was seen as risky by Khrushchev who maintained a frosty relationship with Mao and in 1959 all offers of assistance were withdrawn. The Soviet leader's attempts to woo the west also riled the Chinese leadership as did their tacit support for the Indians in the Sino-Indian border disputes of 1960. The following year at the XXIInd Party Congress, Khrushchev delivered a stinging attack on the Albanian leadership of Enver Hoxha to whose defence rushed the Chinese. All of this was dwarfed by the increasing tension with the West. Although a visit to the USA in 1959 had helped build a warmer relationship, any prospective co-existence was shattered by the shooting down in May 1960 of a US spy plane piloted by Gary Powers. At the United Nations in September 1960, Khrushchev recorded a vintage performance which included banging his shoe on the table during a debate at the General Assembly[22]. In Berlin, Soviet pressure on the Western powers to leave West Berlin was increased, culminating in the construction of the Berlin Wall in August 1961. This happened against an ever intensifying arms race which saw the Soviets claim superiority in nuclear capabilities. To prevent further attempts by the Americans to remove Fidel Castro's Communist government in Cuba, Khrushchev proposed the placing of missiles on the island in October 1962. For a few days at the end of this month the stand off between the two superpowers seemed to make nuclear war likely. In the end the Soviets backed down and promised to withdraw their missiles from Cuba in return for a promise from the Americans that they would not invade.

Khrushchev's Fall, 1964

With the economic reforms failing, foreign affairs proving to be an embarrassment and the cult of the Khrushchev personality being developed, his enemies planned a coup. Most importantly, he had few allies remaining in the establishment and at the CC plenum in October 1964 there were few voices to back his protestations at being removed from office. Khrushchev was ousted by the forces which he had antagonised and were disturbed by the developing personality cult. In attempting to reform, he had offended practically all the country's elites and his replacement by Brezhnev and Kosygin as First Secretary and Prime Minister respectively was swift and unopposed.

ANALYSIS.

Introduction.

Events in the Soviet Union at the end of the 1980's have led to a reappraisal of Khrushchev's role in the end of communism, portraying him as a de-Staliniser - one who through reform attempted to overhaul the Stalinist system. However, one should argue that he did not de-Stalinise the Soviet Union, just as it is inaccurate to present him as the reformer who wished to do so. Khrushchev denounced Stalin and the excesses of Stalinism yet reformed to perpetuate the system he built. There is evidence to suggest that he condemned many of its practices in such a manner as to distance himself from its crimes and for political motives. The structure within which he worked in terms of institutions, policy and vested interests provided the limitations to his reformist zeal. It should not be forgotten, however, that Khrushchev used that structure to gain power and to implement reform. His stated aims were often similar to those up to 1953 at their core, i.e. the maintenance of state and party power. The real de-Stalinisation was the promotion of those loyal to the new leader but that should be seen again as a rejection of the individual rather than the apparatus of control he built. There was a cultural thaw but that was linked to this process of rejecting the memory of Stalin the individual. He did this to create a regime with its own identity and credibility - that based on his own personality. So it is probably more accurate to describe the years from 1956 - '64 as de-Stalinisation only in terms of the discrediting of the personality of Stalin. Further reforms undertaken were done so within the Stalinist system and very much shaped and often limited by that system. The mainstays survived, the centrally planned economy, the role of the party, the central and restricted control of culture. Power lay within and was dominated by the structures Stalin had created, the greatest proof being Khrushchev's downfall.

The rejection of Stalin?

At one level, the Soviet Union saw a significant de-Stalinisation following the dictator's death in 1953. The denunciation of Stalin's crimes by Khrushchev at the XXth, XXIst and XXIInd Party Congresses in 1956, '59 and '61 made headline news around the world as well as shocking the Soviet population. The greater condemnation came in the speech in 1961 in which the new Russian leader detailed the mistakes made by Stalin in 1941[23], thereby shattering the myth of the leader in the 'Great Fatherland War'[24]. The subsequent removal of Stalin from Lenin's tomb in Red Square was seemingly the final act in his posthumous disgrace. Similar condemnation of the shortcomings of Stalin the leader of the party were made in 1956. The tone of this speech was to condemn the injustices served on the party and military during the great purges between 1934 - '39. However, there were limitations to the condemnations and one should be very careful not to equate the damnation of Stalin with his system. In 1956 the speech dated Stalin's excesses from 1934, i.e. after the process of collectivisation and industrialisation had been initiated. The speech was also specific in targeting the purge of the military[25] and the Bolshevik 'Old Guard'[26]. Stalin was condemned for his crimes against the party and not so much against Soviet society at large. There was no condemnation of the crimes against the *kulaks*[27] or different nationalities. This in part can be explained by the blood which was on Khrushchev's hands. As a subordinate of Stalin in the 1930's, first as Moscow Party leader then as acting Party leader in the Ukraine, Khrushchev was personally responsible for the death of thousands[28]. After the war Khrushchev continued to terrorise groups within the Ukraine including Jews and nationalists[29]. Similarly, there was no rehabilitation for the leading Bolsheviks such as Bukharin, in fact in June 1956, Khrushchev backtracked somewhat and praised Stalin's revolutionary ardour and service to the communist party. It is clear that Stalin was damned to place a distance between the new aspiring leader and his bloody past. Perhaps most significantly, the 1956 speech also served as a political weapon against those who opposed Khrushchev e.g. Molotov or Malenkov who were more closely identified with Stalin. By distancing himself from Stalin's crimes, Khrushchev was able to redefine the party line. In doing this he was therefore able to denounce those who opposed the party line as being 'anti-party', i.e. his political opponents. There were numerous examples of this including the backlash from the attempted coup in the summer of 1957 whereby Molotov, Shepilov and Malenkov amongst others were labelled as the 'Anti-Party' by the CC plenum. It is true that Khrushchev did not treat his opponents with the violence of Stalin but again this should be seen as much of a political

tactic as of behaviour stemming from conviction. So one should note that de-Stalinisation had its political ends and its limits. In particular, it was a policy to damn the individual not the system. There are even numerous examples when Khrushchev was moved to praise Stalin, either out of political expediency or when he feared that the party was being undermined. In the spring of 1963, Khrushchev spoke at length of Stalin's service to party and communism as a whole! This rehabilitation showed the limitations to de-Stalinisation. When the system was threatened as it was by 1963 with economic problems and the Cuban fiasco, it reverted to type to shore up its foundations. This made any attempts at significant de-Stalinisation seem somewhat superficial.

A cultural thaw?

It is similarly misleading to conclude that cultural de-Stalinisation resulted in censorship being was dropped and free expression permitted. Much of the 'new' literature which was published during 'The Thaw' shared a common anti-Stalin theme and in that became acceptable. There was a dividing line between art and literature which damned the excesses of Stalinism and that which openly criticised the system, the revolution or questioned the legitimacy of either. To put it bluntly, Khrushchev was only interested in literature if it shared the same critique of Stalin the individual. Therefore, Solzhenitsyn's *One Day in the Life of Ivan Denisovich* (1962) was acceptable as was Alexander Tvardovsky's poem *Tyorkin in Paradise* (1963). The former work was a damnation of the

Gulags set up by Stalin, the latter a satire on the problems of society post 1945. The common theme they both shared was that they blamed the Stalin the individual for the phenomena they criticised and in that they were acceptable. The treatment of Boris Pasternak after the publication of *Dr Zhivago* (1957) reflects the subtleties of the new cultural 'freedom'. Awarded the Nobel prize in 1958, the book attacked the Bolshevik Revolution of 1917 and its aftermath. The intensity of the campaign against Pasternak led to his rejection of the Nobel Prize but also broke him as a writer. The book was not published in the Soviet Union and Pasternak died in 1960 having not published another word since the affair. Khrushchev was only prepared to accept a cultural 'thaw' if it placed Stalin in a poor light. He himself despised modernism and most art forms which strayed from the socialist realism of the Stalinist years. The most telling episode which reflects this was his terrorising of the modern artist Boris Zhitovsky whose work he surveyed at an exhibition in Moscow in 1962. After studying one picture he pronounced to all present that it looked like the contents of a baby's nappy! No writers were sent to the *Gulag* and many of those who had criticised Stalin pre 1953 were released but 'the Thaw' was always precarious. It was a reflection of the new regime's rejection of Stalin and used to highlight that fact but the rejection only went so far.

There was much in Khrushchev's other cultural policies which was very much Stalinist in nature. The violent suppression of all religions is a clear reflection of 'The Thaw's' limitations. There is little explanation for the closing of the churches and monasteries, the 1961 legislation altering the churches' legal status or the widespread imprisonment of believers other than Khrushchev's personal dislike of religion which was carried over from his Stalinist past. Just as he had been instrumental in the suppression of the Ukrainian Catholic Church in the late 1940's, so he moved to use the power of the state to crush all organised religion. This included the Russian Orthodox Church which had become tolerated during and after the war years as it was unquestioning of the state's actions. The contradictions of the Khrushchev era are well summed up by the imprisonment of large numbers of believers between 1960 -'64, in particular Baptists. The main charge levelled against them was that their activities were incompatible with communism. This contrasts with the emptying of the camps in 1956 of those who had been wrongly accused of anti - state activities. The same level of intolerance was shown towards the nationalities within the Soviet Empire. Khrushchev continued to act with the same contempt for the nationalities as had his predecessor. This stands in significant contrast to the actions of Beria in his brief period of influence after Stalin's death in 1953. The feared head of political police, Beria, recognised that political survival necessitated some distancing from Stalin (it is generally accepted that Khrushchev followed Beria's example after his downfall). Within a short space of time he was to reintroduce the native languages into official business in the Baltic States and Belorussia, promote native officials in the Ukraine and end general repression of nationalist expression. These measures were wider reaching than any which followed - until 1964 - since Khrushchev's understanding of the nationalities issue was framed by a centralist mentality. Therefore, he insisted that Russian be used as the official language throughout the Empire; those areas including Latvia and Azerbaijan which resisted saw their governments purged. It is true that a freeing up of censorship saw the growth of nationalist sentiment but this was despite the regime. Many of the nationalities which had been incarcerated under Stalin were released in 1956 under the general amnesties but still ethnic Germans and Crimean Tatars had to wait until after Khrushchev's removal from power before they were granted full rights. As with so much else, the limitations of his rejection of the Stalinist legacy are clear to see.

Economic de-Stalinisation?

The main aims of Khrushchev's economic reforms were to improve an inefficient administrative system thereby increasing both production and productivity. However, there are two important points to make. Firstly, this reformism was undertaken within the Stalinist structure and secondly Khrushchev continued to use the tools of Stalinist planning. Therefore reform was only ever allowed to go so far - it was contained by the systems and structures it attempted to change. The policy of decentralisation was a constant theme of the Khrushchev era. Under Stalin, economic decision making was very much in the hands of the central ministries in Moscow which were run by the party *apparat*. Numerous reforms in both industry and agriculture attempted to move the

shift towards local initiative, it was this which Khrushchev saw as essential for improved economic performance. Therefore, the *sovnarkhozy* created in 1957 pushed the centre of much decision making away from Moscow. This is not to say that the party lost its influence, on the contrary the *sovnarkhozy* were controlled by local party committees - the *oblast*. The division of the party in 1961 into two agricultural and industrial wings had the aim of improving specialisation in the party and the quality of decision making in agriculture. Again, however, it should be stressed that reform was undertaken with the basic idea that the party was the main instrument of economic management left unchallenged. The division in the party failed to achieve its end of greater efficiency in management because the party bureaucracy was an unwilling partner. Another obstacle to reform being successful was that they were often ill thought through and ended up creating another layer of decision making. An example of this was the creation of the TPAs in March 1962 whose role in running collective farms had to be co-ordinated into an overall scheme by local management committees. All the attempts to improve agriculture through administrative reform hide the important fact that Khrushchev failed to transfer capital from the traditionally dominant industrial or defence sectors. Despite his own interests, despite initiatives such as the 'Virgin Lands' scheme the Stalinist priorities remained. The consequence was that investment had to be raised through other means, in 1962 an increase in prices was attempted with the consequence being the tragedy at Novocherkassk. Still agriculture remained inefficient and the failure of successive harvests after 1958 was compounded by the usual problems of supply. The *kolkhoznik*[30] remained reliant on his/her private plot to make ends meet and, although there was improvements in living standards, the *kolkhoznik* remained a second class citizen with personal income in 1964 still 20% less than the average state employee. The importation of wheat from North America in 1963 was an indication of the failure of Khrushchev's agricultural reforms. Yet these reforms were tinkering with a system rather than attempting to transform that system. Such radical action, however, was unlikely to be either desirable to Khrushchev or possible within the context of the system.

At no point in his period in office did Khrushchev attempt to reject the Stalinist levers of economic organisation, that of central planning. In fact Khrushchev attempted to rejuvenate his regime through the use of planning as Stalin had done in the late 1920's. The aims of the Seven Year Plan launched in 1959 and the Twenty Year Plan of 1961 were more than economic, the latter initiative being introduced as part of a reform of the party. They both aimed to increase production of capital and consumer goods which would surpass that of the US, Khrushchev's benchmark of economic success. The former plan was centred on a growth in chemicals and modern technologies, production overall to rise by 80% in the course of the plan. The latter's stated aim was to reach a communist utopia, the means being an increase in production of 10% p.a.. The planning system remained, unaltered with all its inefficiencies.

Perhaps the most impressive achievement of the Khrushchev years was the growth in house building which responded to the desperate needs across the Soviet Union. Similarly state expenditure on social benefits grew by 8% p.a. between 1956-'65 and the restrictive labour laws of the Stalinist period e.g. against absenteeism or changing jobs were repealed. However, these measures were all part of the drive to make the system more efficient, but not to alter it.

At the centre of this revolutionary drive was to be the party which was to be more 'accountable'. The 'indispensable' leadership would remain untouched but all other ranks in the party would have only limited tenure of office e.g. one quarter of the Presidium and CC were to be replaced at each Congress. The motive for this move is clear, it strengthened the influence of Khrushchev and his control over the decision making within the party. In 1961 the decision was promoted as one which would make the party more effective. The consequence was to further the careers of those who supported Khrushchev. It also greatly unsettled large sections of the party bureaucracy which felt their security threatened. Yet such insecurity was the most important weapon of control of Khrushchev's predecessor the main difference being that Khrushchev did not use terror to reinforce such changes. In fact many of the means of gaining and holding on to power were used by Khrushchev as they had been by his predecessor. As head of the CC Secretariat from 1953, he manipulated the party hierarchy as Stalin had done in the 1920's. When power was achieved after the failed coup against him in 1957 he was able to pack the Presidium with his own supporters as Stalin had done after 1934. In both cases the opposition were labelled as anti - party. The main difference, as has already been stated was Stalin's added ruthlessness. Khrushchev aimed to make the newly formed KGB accountable to the party and prevent the chaos of Stalinist times.

Foreign limitations

The area of foreign policy played an important part in the limiting of de-Stalinisation and showed why Khrushchev played a dangerous game in even denouncing Stalin. The context of Soviet foreign affairs was completely dominated by the systems created by or in response to Stalin. Therefore, the condemnation of Stalin in 1956 unleashed forces in Hungary and Poland which provoked a Stalinist response, i.e. Soviet suppression. It is interesting to note that above the protestations of peaceful co - existence, the reality of Soviet affairs was a Stalinist one. In Hungary, the ending of the uprising with Soviet tanks on the order of Khrushchev stands uneasily with the rhetoric of the 'secret speech' of the same year. Similarly, despite the sparing of the leaders of the attempted 1956 coup, the fate of the Hungarian leader, Imre Nagy, was not so lenient - he was executed in 1958. It is unlikely that Khrushchev didn't know of such an execution as it is unlikely that he couldn't have stopped it if he had wished to do so. The condemnation of Stalin in 1956 brought a division in the communist world with China under Mao Zedong emerging as a rival to the Soviet Union's claim to be the sole leader of that world. At the XXIInd party Congress in 1961, the dispute with China was apparent for all to see. Such a division weakened Khrushchev as party leader and the image of the Soviet Union in the world at large. The Twenty Year Plan of 1961 or the speech praising Stalin in 1963 should be seen in the light of Khrushchev's attempts to deflect the Chinese criticism that he and the Soviets were 'revisionists'. The worsening of relations between the two communist superpowers reflected the tension in the communist world after the death of Stalin. To Mao, as with many other leaders who followed his example, Stalin methods and systems of government were the model for their own. Khrushchev's criticism of Stalin, therefore were implicit criticisms of them.

Despite all the talk of peaceful co-existence and the visits to the US, France and Britain in 1959, Khrushchev's legitimacy as leader of the Soviet Union lay in his ability to protect Soviet interests abroad and provide economic growth at home thereby protecting the revolution. It was clear by 1960 that the economy was not developing as was planned, growth falling well short of targets. Despite the rhetoric, it was Khrushchev's responsibility to defend the Stalinist legacy - hence the building of the Berlin Wall, the Cuban crisis or improving relationships with India and the Third World. Khrushchev believed that communism would triumph in peaceful competition with capitalist forces and pronounced as such on many occasions - it was the rationale for the Twenty Year Plan. Yet one must divorce rhetoric from the power situation in which Khrushchev operated. The pursuit of foreign policy highlights the limitations on Khrushchev to effect fundamental change, even if he desired it. His foreign policy failures and dismissal (partly as a consequence of those failures) also reflect the underlying precariousness of his situation and how he worked so tightly within a party and structure created by Stalin. In October 1964 when he was dismissed by a CC Plenum from his posts, the prepared report justifying this action, damned his foreign policy failures.

Conclusion - Khrushchev's motives - reformer or political operator?

In judging the extent of de-Stalinisation it is useful to discover Khrushchev's motives for reform. It has been shown that much of the criticism of Stalin was used as a political tool firstly to place a distance between himself and Stalin's excesses (in which he played a full part) and secondly to place distance between himself and his political enemies who he could then manipulate out of influence. Yet Khrushchev's criticisms of Stalin had their limits. It is true that there were outward signs of a rejection of the Georgian, his removal from Lenin's tomb and the dismantling of many a statue yet Khrushchev's aims in this were to create an identity for the new regime. Another charge levelled at Khrushchev in 1964 was his development of an excessive personality cult - yet it was that which he criticised Stalin for in 1956. The most significant de-Stalinisation of the period was in the opening up of the *Gulags* and the limited cultural freedom which followed - yet those released were enemies of Stalin and those who were

published, damned Stalin's legacy. This is not to belittle the 'Thaw', no writer was imprisoned for his or her beliefs between 1956 -' 64 yet the Pasternak incident shows how fragile the freedom was. It was Khrushchev's aim to bring about the victory of communism through peaceful co-existence if possible. Yet the realities of the Soviet Empire and the Cold War resulted in a very different style of diplomacy which led the world to the brink of a nuclear war. Despite reforms of the party and constant administrative restructuring, Khrushchev failed to diminish the power of the party *apparat*. It is unlikely that he wished to do so - the party, as with Stalin, was the base of his power - but in his attempts to make it administratively more effective he managed to alienate large sections of it. Khrushchev attacked Stalin, to a point, but not the fundamentals of his system. He attempted reform as a means of securing that system, and allowed dissent with the past as a means of securing his own future. One should argue that he de-Stalinised only to the extent that he denounced the Stalin personality cult and his excessive methods of rule - yet even that was for his own political ends. Neither his past or his actions in government ever suggest that Khrushchev wished to dismantle the Stalinist system. Therefore, de-Stalinisation as a term to be applied to the period 1956 - '64 has to be used in the narrow sense only of a rejection of Stalin and his excesses, too much else survived and remained intact for it to be applied otherwise.

[1] Central Planning being the organisation of the economy and the setting of targets to be fulfilled. This role was undertaken by the central ministries in Moscow.

[2] There were three sources of power in Soviet life. The party's policy making body was the Presidium (later to be known as the *Politburo*). The Central Committee (CC) of the party directed and controlled its organisation. The Secretariat of that body made the important decisions regarding membership. The next important source of power was the USSR government and its bureaucracy. The third was the MVD or Ministry for Internal Affairs which merged with the MGB in 1953 to become the KGB. Khrushchev's power base was in the party organisation.

[3] The Stalinist system had bestowed power on those groups which worked within the organisations listed in footnote 2.

[4] Russification was the supression of non Russian nationalities within the Empire.

[5] Unrest in East Germany was the result of a forced collectivisation and industrialisation programme initiated by the East German leader Walter Ulbricht. This involved demanding increased industrial production of 10% without higher pay. the workers took to the streets in June 1953 and were crushed by Soviet tanks.

[6] This was the first major reform to decentralise economic administration.

[7] Zhukov was perhaps the most influential soldier of the Second World War. The acclaim he received after 1945 led to his posting in the Odessa military district and his demotion from the CC.

[8] In 1958 there were nearly seventy monasteries and convents in the Soviet Union and around 20,000 churches. The Russian Orthodox Church had avoided direct persecution after 1945 as a result of its role in the war and its reluctance to criticise the regime.

[9] The People's Republic of China was created in 1949 and led by Mao Zedong. Although he was a Stalinist, there was tension between the two leading communist powers from the outset.

[10] The creation of a communist republic in Yugoslavia in 1945 did not automatically lead to it falling into the Soviet sphere. Its leader, Marshal Tito, was determined to remain independent of Moscow and was banished from the international communist movement (Comitern) in 1948.

[11] This was the first withdrawal of Soviet troops from any territory occupied in 1944/5.

[12] The North Atlantic Treaty Organisation (NATO) was created in April 1949. The original signatories were Northern European nations including Britain and France and the United States and Canada. The expressed aim of the organisation was to provide for mutual assistance against aggression (presumed to be Soviet).

[13] These were the remains of the German invasion forces of the Second World War. It is estimated that only 3% of German prisoners survived capture and the *Gulag*.

[14] Both Poland and Hungary were under Soviet influence from the end of the war. Under the Yalta agreement of 1945, Poland was placed under Soviet influence and in 1948/9 the country was transformed into a Communist dominated Soviet satellite. Hungary had been an ally of Nazi Germany during the war and was controlled by a Soviet army of occupation. In August 1949 a new constitution was proclaimed, following very closely that of the Soviet Union.

[15] Sputnik was the world's first successfully launched artificial satellite. It's impact was to spark off the space race with the US.

[16] Many of those who were demobbed from the army were officers who were given insufficient training before being transferred back into civilian life. This was a strange oversight as the rationale for the move was to bolster the labour force. It made Khrushchev many enemies in the military.

[17] This was mainly in response to Mao Zedong's 'Great Leap Forward' launched in China in 1958 with similar stated aims.

[18] The reform caused immense problems in the short term as few in the *kolkhozes* had any idea how to repair the rather antiquated machines they were forced to by.

[19] The *apparat* being the technical term for an administrative officer of the Communist Party.

[20] Both the *oblast* and *raion* were administrative areas such as a council district in Britain.

[21] Khrushchev had a fascination with maize that went beyond the comprehensible. On his visit to the US in 1959 he considered the highlight a visit to a successful maize farm!

[22] This visit to the UN was a vintage Khrushchev performance. The shoe banging followed cat calling and heckling of other delegates. He attacked the Secretary General of the UN, Dag Hammarskjold as being an agent of the imperialist powers. The President of the General Assembly, F.H. Boland had to exert considerable patience and diplomacy to prevent uproar from other representatives outraged by Khruschev's antics.

[23] The mistake was the failure to accept the intelligence that the Germans were about to invade in June 1941 and to fail to react when they did.

[24] This is the Soviet term for the Second World War.

[25] The military purges of 1937 -'8 had shattered the command of the armed forces leaving them weakened until the early forces. The greatest indictment against Stalin was that the purges were undertaken at such a moment when Nazi Germany threatened.

[26] The 'Old Guard' were the original Bolshevik Party of 1917 which was wiped out by Stalin.

[27] The *kulaks* were the rich peasant class which was eliminated in the process of collectivisation.

[28] Around 60,000 members of the Moscow Party were arrested and shot between 1937-'8. All of their death warrants had Khrushchev's signature on them.

[29] In 1938, Khrushchev had acted as party leader in the Ukraine purging all around him. After the war his bloody purging continued and he rightly aquired the nickname the 'Butcher of the Ukraine'.

[30] A *kolkhoznik* is a collective farm worker.

Khrushchev

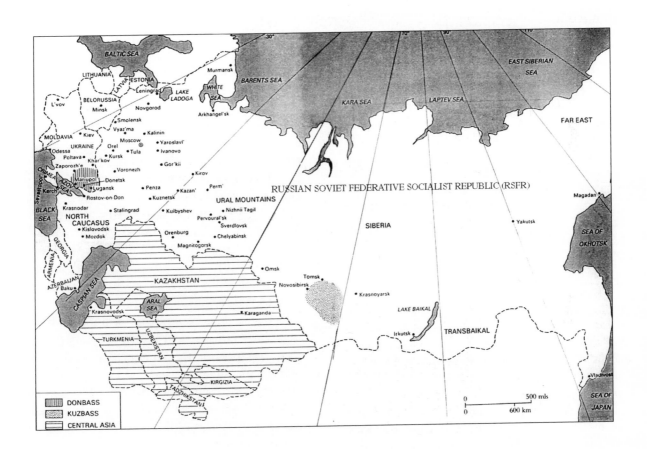

MAP OF SOVIET UNION POST 1945

WHY WAS THE FRENCH THIRD REPUBLIC COMPARATIVELY STABLE BETWEEN 1871-1929?

Introduction.

There are certain factors which seem to point to the structural instability of the French Third Republic. Most obviously, it suffered periodic crises which seemed to question its very existence. Ministerial instability and the opposition of both the Church and the Right to the Republic are further factors which at least superficially point to a lack of stability. Born out of a humiliating defeat at the hands of Prussia and her allies and marred by the brutality of the suppression of the Paris Commune, the Republic was overshadowed by the widespread desire for revanche[1]. Whilst these factors should not be ignored, however, one should argue that whilst the Third Republic did suffer crises of the system it was essentially stable and became ever increasingly so. The main cause of this stability was the conservatism of French republicanism which resulted in government which rarely divided or polarised the political nation. Without doubt, the exception to this was the issue of anti clericalism and the role of the church within France. By 1905, however, even this was to an extent, resolved. The Republic was legitimised by a successful foreign and diplomatic policy which enhanced its stability as did economic growth and prosperity. Even those crises such as the Dreyfus Affair which highlighted the ideological and social tensions within France played a role in defining the Republic. Even the political system served to promote stability, the threat from the left and right was marginalised and government essentially non ideological. That the Republic survived challenges to its continuity,

in particular the Great War, serves testament to its structural durability and underlying stability.

Defeat and humiliation 1870-71

On September 1st 1870, the French forces of Napoleon III were defeated at the Battle of Sedan by a tactically superior and better equipped Prussian army. The following day the Emperor surrendered and three days later a republic was declared at the Hôtel de Ville in Paris and a Government of National Defence was formed with General Trochu as President. From late September Paris was besieged by the German armies and after considerable hardship it surrendered on January 28th 1871. As part of the armistice between the two sides, elections were called as means of choosing an assembly which could then negotiate with the victorious Germans. Held in early February, the result was a victory for the conservative forces which pushed for an early peace settlement. The new National Assembly elected Adolphe Thiers as chief of the executive and it was he who negotiated the terms of surrender with the Germans. By this, the French were to pay reparations of five billion francs and the Germans gained control of the economically important Alsace Lorraine. These terms were accepted by the National Assembly on 1st March although 107 deputies registered their opposition including Gambetta and Clemenceau.[2]

The Commune 1871

The level of discontent with the humiliating peace terms was most keenly felt in Paris which had suffered a siege and then occupation by German troops. Anger was directed at the conservative National Assembly which was perceived as unrepresentative with hostility heightened by its failure to pay the troops of the National Guard. In response, the guardsmen seized 400 cannon belonging to the regular army which prompted Thiers to send troops to retrieve them. On March 18th the troops were dispatched from Versailles but ended up fraternising with the Parisian mob which then promptly executed their leaders Generals Thomas and Lecomte. The army retired and the city was left in the hands of the Central Committee of the National Guard which promptly called elections for March 26th. Out of a register of 485,565, there were 220,167 registered a vote and the triumphantly named 'Commune de Paris'[3] was installed at the Hôtel de Ville on the 28th. The newly formed Commune had little ideological coherence or cohesion, its membership including Jacobins[4], Blanquists[5], moderate Republicans and numerous individuals with various political affiliations. Almost immediately, however, it began issuing decrees on a variety of issues from the banning of gambling to a rent act which cancelled rent arrears. At Versailles, Thiers had assembled an army of some 60,000 soldiers which took the offensive on April 2nd. The fighting of the following two months was brutal in the extreme. As the Commune's forces faced defeat, so the decision was made on April 28th to elect a Committee of

Public Safety. Almost immediately that body created a Revolutionary Tribunal which began to try enemies of the Commune. The individual most commonly associated with this process was the police chief Raoul Rigault who on April 4th had arrested the Archbishop of Paris, Mgr. Darboy. From the beginning of May, Paris entered another state of siege to be broken on May 21st by government troops entering the city. The fighting which ensued in what became known as 'La Semaine Sanglante' resulted in the death of some 20,000 including the Archbishop who was executed[6] with other hostages. Whilst many of the leaders of the Commune escaped, thousands were arrested and tried, around 4,500 being deported.

The foundation of the republic, 1871

With the Commune crushed, the conservative majority in the National Assembly set about creating new structures which reflected their interests. The majority of deputies in the Assembly wished for a restoration of monarchy but it was very much divided as to which brand. Those so called Legitimists who wished for a return of the Bourbon family which had ruled pre-1789 pressed the claim of the pretender to the throne, the Count of Chambord[7]. They were opposed by the Orleanists who supported the Count of Paris's claim (he being descended from Louis Phillipe who had been king from 1830-'48) and the Bonapartists who desired a return to the Imperial regime of Napoleon Bonaparte and Napoleon III. The monarchist cause was significantly harmed by the Count de Chambord's declaration in July 1871 that he would refuse the throne unless he was accompanied in his reinstatement with the Bourbon flag as opposed to the revolutionary tricolour. More important matters were attended to by Thiers who, despite being a monarchist aimed to regain some semblance of stability and thereby set about working within the developing framework of the Republic[8]. Declared *Président de la Républic* in August 1871, Thiers had already set about effecting a return to normalcy by the raising of government loans in June 1871 to pay off the German indemnity. In July the following year a further loan was secured and in September 1873 the last German soldier left French soil. The desire of many within the Assembly was still to attempt a restoration of the monarchy and to that end, Thiers was ousted as President in May 1873 to be replaced by Marshal MacMahon. A soldier by trade, MacMahon showed little interest in his new found prominence but he had been chosen as a mere stop gap to prepare the way for a restoration. The whole issue again foundered in October 1873, on the Count of Chambord's insistence on the Bourbon flag. As a consequence, the Assembly chose by the Law of the Septenate of November 1873 to give MacMahon presidential powers for a further seven years[9].

Constitutional affairs 1875-79

The introduction of a constitution in 1875 was the work of the conservative forces led by MacMahon and the prime minister the Duc de Broglie. Their main aim in passing through piecemeal legislation was to maintain their political advantage but leave sufficient

flexibility within the system which might allow a monarchy to return. This tactic almost immediately backfired in January 1875 as the Law on the Organisation of the Public Powers was amended by one vote to state that the President of the Republic was elected by the National Assembly, thereby formally accepting the existence of the Republic[10]. Other laws followed which together made up the constitution and gave the President executive powers to make war, choose officials, dissolve the Chamber of Deputies etc. There were limitations on these powers including the counter signature from ministers on presidential orders. The Senate was constructed to be a conservative body with 75 life members and the remaining 225 to be elected for nine year periods of office by a complicated system of indirect election. It had the powers to introduce legislation apart from finance bills which were the sole preserve of the Chamber of Deputies. This was to be elected by universal male suffrage[11]. The new Assembly met in March 1876 but the elections for that Assembly produced a conservative majority in the Senate but an overwhelmingly Republican Chamber[12]. This was due to the fading of the issue of the war and the growing acceptance of the Republic as a factor for stability. The consequence, however, was a trial of strength between republican and monarchist forces, the battleground being the constitution and the relative power of the legislature and executive. Matters came to a head in the so called '*Crise of Seize Mai*', 1877 when President MacMahon forced the resignation of Prime Minister Jules Simon who he considered to be too accommodating towards the anti-clerical left. Such an action offended the majority within the Chamber which in June passed a vote of no confidence against MacMahon's chosen cabinet led by the Duc de Broglie[13]. As the constitution allowed, MacMahon proceeded to dissolve the Chamber[14] and called for new elections. Despite intense campaigning, the election of October 1878 resulted in only a 36 seat Republican loss, thereby ensuring a continued substantial majority in the Chamber. The following month, de Broglie's cabinet suffered another resounding vote of no confidence (312 votes to 205) and its successor led by the equally conservative Rochebouet fared no better. On December 13th, MacMahon conceded defeat and appointed the Republican Jules Defaure to the post of Prime Minister. The issue of ministerial responsibility and the power of the president was resolved in favour of the Chamber. In January 1879, an election to the Senate produced 58 new Republican senators and a majority hostile to MacMahon who proceeded to resign.

Reform and the issue of anti clericalism 1879-1884.

Despite the conservative republicanism of the new President Jules Grévy (1887-'94), the period of his being in office is associated with the reformist ministries and the anti clericalism of Jules Ferry who was either Minister of Public Instruction (education) or Prime Minister through from 1879 to 1885. There are numerous examples of the tension between Church and Republican forces in the formative years of the Republic, from the execution of Archbishop Darboy in 1871 to the vigorous anti clerical electioneering of leading Republicans such as

Gambetta in 1878. This culminated in a series of anti clerical laws from 1880 onwards. In March of that year, decrees were issued giving the Jesuit Order[15] three months and all other religious teaching associations six months to disperse as well as instructing all religious associations to register with the state. These moves were accompanied by education reform which was at least implicitly anti clerical. In March 1882, the Primary Education Law stipulated that primary education was to be compulsory, free from change and secular, i.e. there was to be no religious instruction in state run schools. This was followed by a law re-establishing divorce in July 1884. Such measures aimed at bringing about laicity[16] provoked considerable opposition and reinforced clerical anti republicanism. These were not the only reforms introduced in this period. In 1881 the press was allowed greater freedoms and a law was passed in July of that year provided an amnesty to virtually all Communards. Because of the growth of trades unions and in response to the formation of socialist dominated parties[17], the Trade Union Act of 1884 was passed which legalised unions despite the fact that they had been tolerated since the latter part of the Second Empire. Such reformist legislation had its limits, however, and there were divisions within Republican ranks of the extent to which anti clerical reforms should go. On the one hand, the Opportunists who were moderate/conservative Republicans (as epitomised by Grévy) believed that, by 1885, reform had gone far enough. The Radicals[18], however, believed that the issue could only be resolved by a complete separation of Church and State. This view was strengthened by the result of the

1885 election which produced gains by the anti republican right and forced the Opportunists into relying more on the Radicals for support[19]. A consequence was further anti clerical legislation including the expulsion in 1886 of all teaching orders from state funded schools.

The Boulanger Crisis 1886-'9

Widespread discontent with the conservative republicanism of the early 1880's manifested itself in the movement centred around General Boulanger. As the election of 1885 had strengthened the Radicals, so Boulanger was made Minister of War as a representative of that strand of republicanism. Immediately he introduced popular reforms including the shortening of military service, improvement of living conditions for servicemen and compulsory service for clerics. Such popularity was enhanced by numerous public appearances in 1886 and the Schnaebele Incident of April 1887. A French army officer on the Alsace Lorraine border was arrested and condemned by the Germans as a spy. The rousing condemnation of the Germans by Boulanger served to raise his status further as the epitome of *revanche*. In May 1887, however, the government was overthrown by a coalition of moderate republicans, monarchists and those who wished to avoid the provocation of war with Germany. Boulanger was perceived as a potential liability by the new cabinet led by Rouvier[20] and therefore dispatched to Clermont-Ferrand to be commander of the XIIIth Army Corps. His departure from the Gare de Lyons in Paris was an emotional affair as thousands of Radicals and nationalists from the Ligue des Patriotes[21] gathered to bid him farewell. They did not have to wait long to wreak their revenge for the new ministry was beset by scandal.

At the end of 1887 it became apparent that Daniel Wilson, son-in-law of President Grévy, had been trafficking in Legion of Honour ribbons and medals - France's most prestigious reward. The subsequent uproar resulted in the resignation of Grévy, the appointment of a new President, Marie Francois Sadi-Carnot, and widespread disillusionment with the Republic. Boulanger now became the focus for both Radical and monarchist aspirations. The former put him up as a candidate in a series of consecutive by-elections for the Chamber of Deputies. His reformist platform, demanding a revision of the constitution brought him widespread popular support culminating in a striking victory in a Paris by-election in January 1889[22]. Boulanger, with his popular rejection of republican institutions, also became the focus for monarchist aspirations and those who hoped that through the undermining of the Republic a monarchy could be restored. At the peak of his popularity, when a *coup d'état* seemed a distinct possibility, Boulanger's nerve failed and he fled to Belgium in April 1889[23]. The collapse in the support for Boulangerism was swift as was the response of mainstream republicanism in preventing any similar resurgence. In July 1889 standing in more than one constituency simultaneously was banned[24] and the general elections at the same time resulted in victory for the Republicans and the Boulangists being reduce to a rump of 40 seats.

Ralliement - 1890-'92

As an ally of the monarchists, the Church was forced to reassess its attitude towards an ever more secure Republic, in particular in the light of the failure of Boulangerism. In November 1890, the Primate of Africa, Charles Cardinal Lavigerie, delivered a speech in Algiers[25] to French naval officers in which he argued that it was the duty of all to 'rally' to the side of a popularly accepted government. Despite this countering the view of the majority of monarchists and republicans - the need for a ralliement was supported by Pope Leo XIII. In his encyclical *Inter innumeras* of February 1892, it was declared that once a government had been established it was deemed legitimate. Such a sentiment introduced a period of relative harmony in Church-State relations. The ministry of Méline from 1896-'8 saw a flowering in the relationship and a period of what might be called 'clerical republicanism'.

The Panama Scandal - 1892

Attracted by the previous success of the engineering ventures of Ferdinand de Lesseps[26], thousands of French citizens invested 1,500 million francs in the project to build a Panama Canal. Because of mismanagement and corruption, the company collapsed in February 1889 leaving the investors out of pocket. Investigations in the following years revealed that de Lesseps' company[27] had bribed senators and deputies[28] in an attempt to ensure the passage of legislation permitting a stock lottery to raise capital. It was not until November 1892 that legal action was taken against de Lesseps, a fact which heightened the suspicions of an attempted cover up. The court of appeal sentenced de Lesseps and his associates (which included Gustav Eiffel) to pay fines and serve prison sentences but this was quashed by the higher court, the *cours de cassation*[29]. Numerous politicians were tried for their role in the affair but only three found guilty.

The Dreyfus Affair.

Of far greater significance was the affair surrounding a Jewish *stagiaire*[30] on the general staff, Captain Alfred Dreyfus. In September 1894 it was discovered that military secrets were being passed to the Germans. The proof of this claim was said to be a list of military documents (known as a *bordereau*) found in the waste paper bin of the German military attaché in Paris. On the bordereau was claimed to be the handwriting of Dreyfus who was arrested in October, condemned and sent to Devil's Island despite pleading his innocence[31]. The matter was seemingly settled and the army's integrity regained but Dreyfus's family would not accept his guilt and in late 1896 they gained the support of intellectual Bernard Lazare who produced a pamphlet supporting Dreyfus entitled *Une erreur judiciaire*. In March 1896, the new head of the intelligence service, Colonel Picquart, received an intercepted letter (the *petit bleu*) from the continuing traffic of documents being sent to the Germans. This new evidence was addressed to Major Count Esterhazy whose handwriting matched that on the bordereau. Picquart took the evidence to General Gonse who was second in command in the general staff. Their response was to order his silence on his findings and transferred him to Tunisia. The new intelligence chief, Major Henry, set about doctoring the evidence to cover Esterhazy although the army was forced to investigate and try him in January 1898. Not surprisingly, the trial lasted a matter of minutes and ended with Esterhazy's full acquittal. On January 13th, the novelist Emile Zola published *J'accuse*, an open letter to President Faure in which he named some of those on the general staff who had conspired in the condemnation. The reaction to Zola's letter and his subsequent arrest and trial for defamation in February[32] raised the profile of the case considerably.

The continuing denial of wrong doing on the part of the army was weakened by the discovery that documents had been forged by the now Colonel Henry. In August he admitted his guilt and the chief of the general staff, General de Boisdeffre was forced to resign. By now the affair had polarised French politics, the Dreyfusards interested in protecting the Republic, the anti-Dreyfusards associated with its destruction. The death of President Faure in February 1899 removed an opponent of a retrial for Dreyfus, replacement President Emile Loubert and new Prime Minister, René Waldeck-Rousseau (who came to office in June of that year) both accepting the need to reopen the case. In August 1899, Dreyfus was brought back to mainland France but the following month he was again found guilty by a military court at Rennes. Under the direction of Waldeck-Rousseau, however, a presidential pardon was immediately granted to Dreyfus. It was not until

12th July, 1906 that the *cours de cassation* overturned the Rennes verdict declaring it to be 'wrongful'. The next day, Dreyfus was decorated and raised to the rank of major.

Separation of Church and state.

The Dreyfus Affair had a profound effect on the Republic's political landscape, part of which was the resurgence of Radicalism as the dominant force in government[33]. The defeat of the anti-Dreyfusards was a defeat for the Church and a victory for those who wished to see greater control of the church on the one hand through to suppression on the other. Whilst Waldeck-Rousseau very much favoured the former course of action in dealing with the church, many in the Republican Bloc (formed to defend the Republic in 1900) urged more radical action. In 1900, a religious order - the Assumptionists - were banned. The following year, in July 1901, the Associations Law was passed after being hijacked by Radical deputies. Its terms ensured that all religious 'congregations' could only be formed after appropriate legislation had been passed and that they had to be authorised thereafter by parliament.[34] The elections of 1902 served to strengthen the Radicalism, the Republican Bloc winning 370 seats of which 219 were radicals. This drift to the left resulted in the resignation of Waldeck-Rousseau and his replacement with Emile Combes. Known for his fierce anti-clericalism, Combes' government proceeded to enforce the Association Laws vigorously. In all over 3000 schools were closed until they applied for authorisation which many were refused. On July 7th

1904, all teaching by religious orders was banned which added to the growing diplomatic rift between France and the Vatican[35]. Growing animosity resulted in the publication of a bill in for the separation of Church and State which was prepared by Socialist deputy Francis de Pressensé. It was not the intention of Combes to allow matters to progress that far, despite his anti-clericalism he was still in favour of preserving the Concordat of 1801[36]. This caution resulted in the fall of Combes' government in January 1905 and its replacement by one led by Rouvier who at least tacitly supported separation. The bill was steered through parliament by the socialist Aristide Briand and it became the Separation Law on 5th December, 1905. By the terms of the Separation Law, all liberty of conscience was guaranteed and the state was to have no role in the appointment or payment of clerics. All state relationships with religious denominations were curtailed and church property was to be passed into the hands of so called 'cultural associations'. The papacy raged against such legislation, Pius X issuing encyclicals *Vehementer* and *Gravissimo* in 1906, both strongly attacking the Republic. This contrasted to the widespread acceptance of the legislation in France as represented by the May 1906 election results in which those who opposed separation only gained 175 seats.

The development of the left.

The growth of socialism in France was marked by internal division and debate amongst those on the left. What united them was a critique of a society and anger at such events as the Massacre of Fourmies on May 1st 1891 at which a demonstration was fired upon by troops killing some of its number. However, those who believed themselves to be the representatives of labour and standard bearers of the left, took many political forms. The main division was between those who accepted that they could work with the republican system, the so called 'possibilists', and those who could not. The latter group was represented by the Marxism of Jules Guesde with its rejection of the reformism[37] of the 'possibilists'. In 1882, the Guesdists had withdrawn from an alliance with the more moderate 'possibilists' to form the *Parti Ouvrier Francais*. However, the most potent force of revolutionary expression was that of syndicalism. A rejection of all existing institutions and parties, syndicalism was based on a belief that working class advancement could only take place with the destruction of such institutions. These views spread rapidly through the newly formed *syndicats* (trades unions) and *Bourses du Travail* (bodies which represented different trades in one area)[38]. There were many ideological strands which together shaped syndicalism, one of which being anarchism which became increasingly prominent in the 1890's. In 1892, an anarchist Ravachol carried out a series of bombings in France to be followed a year later by Auguste Vaillant who exploded a bomb in the Chamber of Deputies. On June 24th, 1894, President Carnot was stabbed to death by an Italian anarchist, Santo Caserio which was in the same year that the Trade Union Congress at Nantes voted to accept the principle of the general strike as a legitimate course of action. The following year the *Confederation Generale du Travail* (CGT) was formed as a national union dominated by syndicalist methods of direct action. This was to take the form of boycotts, sabotage, strikes and assassination - the collective theory of which was eloquently summarised by Georges Sorel in 'Reflections on Violence' in 1908.

All forms of French socialism paid homage to the Revolution of 1789 and laid claims to be its successor. Close to syndicalism was the party created by Jean Allemane in 1890, the *Parti Ouvrier Socialiste Revolutionnaire*. This group criticised those who 'collaborated' with 'bourgeois' government including the so called 'independents'. Most prominent in their ranks was Jean Jaurès and Alexandre Millerand. At St Mande in 1896, the latter set out a programme for socialism within the context of parliamentary rule and he actually joined Waldeck-Rousseau's coalition government in 1899. Such a move polarised the socialist movement, Guesde denouncing all such 'reformism' whilst Jaurès supporting Millerand's actions. As a consequence the movement divided into two distinct parties, Jaurès leading the more moderate *Parti Socialiste Francaise* whilst Guesde headed the anti reformist *Parti Socialiste de France*. The Amsterdam Congress of the Socialist International in 1904, strongly condemned actions such as that of Millerand, a decision which Jaures accepted. In 1905 the socialist movement was reunited with the creation of the *Section Francaise de l'Internationale Ouvriere* (SFIO) which was based on a revolutionary Marxist ideology.

Political change 1906-'14

The Radical government led by Georges Clemenceau from 1906-'9 took a strong stance against the unions in general. With the issue of anti-clericalism defused by the Separation Law, the Radicals turned to economic[39] and social reform but with minimal effect. In 1906 the Western Railway was nationalised, but the promises Clemenceau made regarding the reform of pensions, taxation and the working day came to very little. Instead the government became fully involved in energetically suppressing working class protest. In May 1906, Clemenceau sent troops to the Northern coal fields to put down strikes and leaders of the CGT were arrested. The following year, troops were again called up to break a strike of Parisian electricity workers. In 1908, workers were fired upon and killed by police at Villeneuve St Georges and Draveil. Clemenceau came under attack from those to the left of the Radical movement and socialists (most notably Jaurès) who objected to his harsh treatment of labour. From April-May 1909 saw a strike amongst Paris postal workers who, as civil servants, had been denied by Clemenceau the right to affiliate to the union of their choice, the CGT. The considerable sympathy for the strikers from many within the Radical Party was reflected in the vote of the party's executive in May which condemned the government's stance. This was also in part due to the government's failure to enact reform or even successfully alter the taxation system so reform could take place. In March 1909 a system of income tax was accepted by the Chamber of Deputies which would do away with the mixture of antiquated direct and indirect taxes on which the state relied. The proposals were deeply unpopular amongst the more conservative who would have had to have paid more. Therefore the proposals were defeated in the Senate. Clemenceau accepted this decision to the disgust of those on the Radical left. In July 1909, Clemenceau's ministry fell after criticism of its decision to only build light cruisers rather than the more threatening battleships. The new government was led by the ex socialist Aristide Briand who showed himself to be the match of Clemenceau in harshly repressing unruly labour. In October 1910, Briand responded to a strike of the North-Eastern railway workforce by calling out the troops. Despite the call of a general strike from the railway unions, the government held out as it did against the action of vineyard workers in the Champagne region in 1911[40]. The governments led by Caillaux (June 1911-January 1912) and Raymond Poincaré (January 1912-January 1913) which followed Briand were mainly concerned with foreign affairs. In August 1913, the short-lived ministry led by Louis Barthou passed a law increasing military service from two to three years. This legislation angered the Radical left and socialists, raising the possibility of a pact between the two which was a cause of some worry to those on the right. Leading the campaign to repeal the Three Year Law, Joseph Caillaux seemed a real threat to those on the right to the extent that the newspaper *Le Figaro* began to publish compromising material about his private life. The response of his wife was to shoot the editor of *Le Figaro* dead in March 1914, an action which somewhat damaged her husband's promising career. The election of 1914, however saw a victory for the Radicals in alliance with the left but the government led by Viviani was still able to operate without repealing the law.

The eve of the Great War saw a revival of French royalism, nationalism and the fortunes of the right in general. Known as 'integral nationalism', the doctrine which developed in the wake of the Dreyfus Affair was stridently racist, anti-Semitic and aggressive. Structured by the writings of Charles Maurras in the pages of the newspaper *Action Francaise* (founded in 1899) and the novelist Maurice Barres, the new ideology was based on an uncompromising nationalism. This contrasted with the more traditional conservatism of *Action Libérale Populaire* (ALP) founded in 1902 by Jacques Piou and Albert de Mun to combat Republican anti-clericalism. Although it had limited impact at the ballot box, in the 1906 election it won only 64 seats despite the Separation Law, the ALP became part of a broad anti Radical/Socialist alliance - the Republican Federation of France founded in 1903 and highly successful in blocking collectivist social reform after 1906. The election of Raymond Poincaré as Président and the passage of the Three Year Law in 1913 marked the resurgence of nationalism as a force in central politics.

Foreign and colonial policy - 1871-1914

The defeat by Germany and the humiliation of the peace treaty signed in Frankfurt in May 1871 overshadowed French diplomacy throughout the period. This was also a period of colonial expansion which was resumed in 1881 with the occupation of Tunis and the Treaty of Bardo in May of that year establishing a French Protectorate over Tunisia. The initiative had been taken by Jules Ferry who, as a keen imperialist, feared Italian expansion in that region. Colonial rivalry was at its peak in the 1880's and the British occupation of Egypt in 1883 led to an estrangement between Britain and France. A consequence was the loose *entente* arranged by Ferry and Bismarck in 1884 which saw the establishment of Germany as a colonial power. Attempts by France to expand her empire in the Annam and Tonquin regions of China suffered a setback in March 1885 with the defeat at Langson which led to the resignation of Ferry. Despite this, the Treaty of Tientsin signed in June recognised Annam as a French protectorate. Colonial success did not prevent growing demands for a more aggressive anti German stance which manifested itself in the popularity of Boulanger and the Schnaebele Incident in 1887. In 1891, the mother of the German Emperor, the Empress Frederick, visited Paris to be greeted by anti-German demonstrations. In March of the same year, Germany, Austria and Italy renewed the Triple Alliance which with a growing friendship between Germany and Britain, had the effect of edging Russia and France towards a formal alliance. In July 1891, a French naval squadron under the command of Admiral Gervais made a visit to the Russian base at Kronstadt and the August Convention the following month moved the two countries closer to an agreement on action if either was threatened. The formal acceptance of anything more concrete was postponed by the Panama scandal and famine in Russia. In late 1893 and January 1894, the two governments agreed a military convention which promised full support if either were attacked or threatened by a country of the Triple Alliance. The instability of the Austrian Empire led to an extension of this alliance in 1899 during a visit by the foreign minister Delcassé to St Petersburg, the two countries agreeing to lend each other support in the maintenance of the balance of power. In response to

an Anglo-Japanese alliance in 1902, the Franco-Russian agreement was extended to the Far East.

By the turn of the century it was not only Russia to whom the Republic's ministers extended the hand of friendship. In December 1900 an agreement was signed with Italy by which the French were given a free hand in Morocco in exchange for turning a blind eye to their neighbour's expansion in Libya. Better relations between the two countries were sealed by the Italian-French *Entente* of November 1902 and assurances from Italy that she would not support an attack on France. A successful colonial policy became dependent on better relations with Britain, especially after the Fashoda crisis of 1896. Both countries laid stake to land about the Nile south of Egypt and sent missions to the area, the British led by Lord Kitchener, the French by Colonel Marchand. In the end the latter withdrew after thinly veiled threats of war were issued by the British and the French given poor land in the Sahara in return for their renunciation of territory along the Nile[41]. Such a humiliation postponed better relations between the two nations, but the desire to secure Morocco within the French sphere of influence led to diplomatic overtures and, in 1903, the visits of King Edward VII to Paris and Président Loubet to London. In April 1904, the *Entente Cordiale* was concluded by which British interests in Egypt were recognised in return for a French *carte blanche* in Morocco[42]. This was confirmed by a Franco-Spanish treaty in October which detailed secret plans for partition of the country. Such obvious designs on Morocco and the new understanding with Britain worried the Germans who attempted to test

French resolve by arranging a visit by the Kaiser to Morocco which occurred in March 1905. At Tangiers, Wilhelm proclaimed German support for the principles of independence and demanded an international conference on the future of Morocco. Whilst the foreign minister, Delcassé argued that closer alliance with Britain would be sufficient to overcome the German threat, he was outvoted in cabinet and resigned in June. At the Algeciras Conference in early 1906, Morocco's independence was recognised but French interference in some matters accepted[43]. Importantly, the affair failed to damage the Anglo-French understanding but the issue of Morocco had not been resolved. In February 1909, another agreement between France and Germany hinged on the latter's acceptance of the former's 'special interest' in the country but guaranteed the protection of German interests in North Africa. Tension increased in April 1911, however, with the advance of French troops into Fez to quell anti foreigner disturbances. The German foreign ministry objected to what it saw as a breach of the Act of Algeciras and the 1909 agreement. In July 1911, the German gunboat Panther arrived at Agadir which acted to worsen the crisis and pushed the two countries towards the brink of war. After much diplomatic discussion, however, a Convention was agreed in November 1911 by which Germany gave the French a free hand in Morocco in return for land in the French Congo. From 1911 to the eve of the Great War saw an improvement in relations with Britain, in November 1912 both countries agreeing to consult in the event of an threat from another power. The German declaration of war on France in August 1914 was partly undertaken with the knowledge that France would come to Russia's support in any case. It also helped precipitate a British declaration of war the following day.

The Great War 1914-'18

a. The military war

Plans for the invasion of France, the Schlieffen Plan, had been drawn up in 1905. In August 1914, the main thrust of the German forces was through Belgium, wheeling down to Paris. The advance was rapid and spectacular, by the beginning of September, the French government withdrew to Bordeaux and the French forces had retreated to the Marne River. Here the advance was halted by the forces under the command of General Joseph Joffre and the line of the Western Front for the next three years was established. The tactic of attacks on the enemy line in the belief that a breakthrough was imminent became the norm but at a horrific cost to French lives. In 1915, the French pounded the German lines and undertook large scale offensives such as the Second Battle of Artois (May-June) and the Second battle of Champagne (September-November). Both battles resulted in huge losses of men (the former alone producing 400,000 French casualties) but with little to show in terms of land gained. The following year was a watershed, the French army undergoing the horrors of the Battle of Verdun which began in February 1916. Fought around forts which the French had abandoned, Verdun became the symbol for French resolve, General Pétain promising of the Germans that they 'shall not pass'. The blood bath which followed between January and June accounted for 350,000 French lives, the battle at the end of the year in Verdun acting to correct the line back to where it had been at the start of the campaign. The forts of Douaumont, Vaux and Thiaumont were to become monuments to the slaughter. In the summer of 1916, the French also contributed 14 divisions to the Somme offensive which saw the decimation of the Kitchener's volunteer army. The end of the year saw Joffre replaced by General Nivelle who launched an obvious and outdated offensive on in April 1917. The Second Battle of the Aisne and Third Battle of Champagne saw huge losses, the French only succeeding in capturing the Chemin des Dames. By May 1917, mutiny was rife in the ranks, at least 40,000 troops refusing to fight. Nivelle was sacked and the 'hero of Verdun', General Pétain appointed to restore discipline. In all 27 *poilus* were shot and nearly 3,000 imprisoned but conditions and rations were improved in response to the grievances expressed by many mutineers. Against the background of continuing discord between the British and French, the Germans launched an offensive in March 1918 in the Somme region which broke the British line and forced a retreat of 40 miles. Although this advance was halted, two months later the German army broke through at the Third Battle of the Aisne and advanced to within 37 miles of Paris. The Allies under General Foch regrouped and counter attacked, by September the Germans had been pushed back on all parts of the front and with a worsening domestic situation they sued for peace. In all 1.38 million French servicemen were killed, another 3 million wounded.

b. The home front

On 4th August 1914, President Poincaré appealed to politicians of all persuasions to form an *union sacree* to defeat the hated enemy. In consequence, the first wartime cabinet led by René Viviani included members from across the political spectrum including Jules Guesde and Theophile Delcassé. However, as it became apparent that the war was not going to end as soon as had been hoped, so old political enmities re-emerged. The issue in 1915 which became most pressing was General Joffre's tactics and his treatment of fellow commanders[44]. Suspicions that Delcassé was protecting the General led to his resignation from the post of Foreign Minister in October 1915 and suspicions of his leaning too far in favour of pro-clerical officers caused the collapse of Viviani's government the same month. The new Prime Minister Briand created a better political balance and initiated administrative reform including a war cabinet created in December 1916. In March 1917, Briand's government fell after the newly appointed Minister of War, General Lyautey, managed to infuriate the Chamber of Deputies by challenging their right to discuss the war. The new Prime Minister, Alexandre Ribot, was equally short lived in office. Not only did his government have to deal with the failure of Nivelle's offensive in 1917 but it managed to infuriate the Socialists who left the coalition after delegates were refused passports to travel to the international peace conference in

Sweden. As a consequence, Ribot's government fell in September followed by a two month interim administration led by M. Painlevé. In November 1917, Georges Clemenceau formed a new government and immediately proceeded to hunt down all those who had begun to suggest a negotiated peace[45]. From this date to the end of the war, Clemenceau dominated government and centralised authority in his quest for victory.

Versailles and foreign policy 1918-'29

The signing of the Treaty of Versailles in the Hall of Mirrors in June 1919 was a humiliation for defeated Germany. The treaty returned Alsace Lorraine to France, gave her mineral rights in the Saar for 15 years, boosted her empire with the acquisitions of the Cameroons, Togo, Syria and the Lebanon and set out the structure for reparations payments to be paid by Germany as compensation. It was the aim of Clemenceau to ensure the future security of France against a resurgent Germany. To that end a defensive treaty was negotiated with Britain and the USA in June 1919 but was not ratified. Therefore the French looked for alliances elsewhere, in February 1921 they signed a defensive treaty with Poland. When the Germans failed to pay an interim cash payment in February 1921, the French occupied Düsseldorf, Duisberg and Ruhrort such was the level of mistrust between victors and vanquished. This harsh line was again followed in January 1923 when French troops were sent to occupy the Ruhr in response to Germany being declared in default of her payments. Such a tactic essentially backfired, the French franc suffering

a 25% devaluation and the local German population frustrating the French attempts to seize coal with a policy of passive resistance. The Dawes Plan of 1924 which reorganised the payment of reparations was a victory in that payments were to be continued but a failure in that it ended the policy of containing Germany through enforced economic hardship. In April 1925, Aristide Briand became French foreign minister, the constraints of the international situation pushing him towards agreement with Germany as the means by which security could be assured. The Locarno Treaties signed in October 1925 guaranteed the borders of Versailles, confirmed the demilitarisation of the Rhine and saw the signing of mutual assistance treaties between the French and Poland as well as France and Czechoslovakia. It was Briand's hope to cultivate the relationship between France and Germany, in 1926 a trade agreement being signed. It was also his desire to see a concerted effort to build structures whereby war could be avoided in the future. The resultant Kellogg-Briand Pact of June 1928 was not much more than a statement renouncing aggressive war but won its authors universal praise. In September 1929, as part of this policy, Briand proposed a European federal union the creation of which was to be discussed by the League of Nations. Nothing came of the plan.

Domestic politics 1918-'29

Politics post 1919 was dominated by the same interests and concerns as pre 1914. A new Electoral Law passed in July 1919 introduced limited proportional representation and voting by list. This had the effect of making an absolute majority of one party even harder to achieve and the two wings of French politics formed themselves in to two coalition blocks. That revolving around Clemenceau and those on the right, the *Bloc National*[46], won a resounding victory in the November elections - winning two thirds of the seats in the Chamber of Deputies. Their opponents, the *Cartel des Gauches* were soundly and convincingly beaten. Nevertheless, Clemenceau failed to win the Presidency in the January 1920 election, the victor being Paul Deschanel[47]. Whatever the rightward appearance of the new government, it was dominated by the moderate Republicans of the centre ground *Alliance Democratique*. Therefore legislation was more moderate than might have been expected. Concessions were made to the church, in 1921 links were re-established with the Vatican and in 1924 the was allowed to reoccupy former property but these were little more than cosmetic. Successive governments were highly effective in dealing with labour militancy. Strikes were endemic in the 1918-'20 period, culminating in a general strike on May 1st 1920 led by the CGT[48]. The government suppressed the strike and the CGT was dissolved by court order. Without doubt, the most important priority for government was to restore the battered economy and that in real terms meant securing reparations and increasing taxation. The latter option was extremely unpopular and attempts by Poincaré (Prime Minister from 1922-'24) to force through a package of tax increases in 1923-24 to combat a growing financial crisis failed in the Senate. As highlighted above, attempts to extract revenue from

Germany proved to be similarly difficult.

In May 1924 the election for the Chamber of Deputies saw victory for the *Cartel des Gauches*, winning 328 seats and the new cabinet led by Herriot dominated by Radicals. The following month, President Millerand was forced to resign due to his links with the right and Gaston Doumergue chosen in his place. The issue of anti-clericalism did re-emerge but with less urgency than in previous years. In February 1925, the Vatican embassy was again closed but reopened in May after a considerable outcry. Of far greater significance was the financial crisis which saw the collapse in the franc and resultant government turmoil. In July 1926 the Chamber turned to Poincaré to form a 'National Union' government. As a result, taxation was finally increased and the budget balance. Financial confidence, which had been absent, finally returned and the franc stabilised. In April 1928 Poincaré and the right won a majority in the Chamber.

ANALYSIS

Introduction

Despite its problematic birth, the Third Republic was relatively stable, its political institutions surviving unchanged up until 1929. Similarly, the periodic crises which seemingly threatened the Republic should be seen less as indicators of instability and more as manifestations of the traditional divisions within French politics. Indeed the Dreyfus Affair acted as the conduit through which the Republic became more clearly defined. Whilst other countries suffered political turmoil in this period, the Republic was increasingly accepted as a factor which ensured stability. The key reason for this was the conservatism of republicanism and the negativism of its ideology. This endeared the Republic to the majority of the political elite which increasingly identified the Republic's survival with their own interests. It was only the issue of the Church which polarised the political nation sufficiently to fundamentally threaten the Republic, yet this issue was more or less resolved by 1906. Opposition from the left and right was hindered by internal division, the moderation of government policy and in the case of the former, effective repression. The threat from both was therefore diminished. Political stability was also a product of a developing economic structure and social peace. The Republic gained significant legitimacy through a successful foreign policy and in particular victory in the Great War. So a variety of factors together produced stability in what were turbulent times elsewhere Europe.

The issue of anti clericalism

What threatened the stability of the Republic more than any factor was the issue of the influence of the Catholic Church. It was this more than any other which threatened to become the factor around which the enemies of the Republic would rally in their desire to destroy what they termed 'la gueuse'[49]. Similarly laicisme (the creation of a lay society) was at the core of republicanism, the attack on Church privilege and influence was commonly accepted by republicans of all persuasions. This was strengthened by the conviction that the Church was central to the attempts to restore the monarchy in the early 1870's. To those who believed in progress and reason, the Catholic Church was embodiment of reaction and superstition. The threat from the clerics was perceived to be very real, in the Syllabus of Errors of 1864, Pope Pius IX claimed for the Church universal control over all education and science, seemingly declaring war on all forms of liberal thought. This was reinforced by the dogma of papal infallibility proclaimed in July 1870 by which the papacy claimed moral supremacy over all secular bodies. This then was the ideological justification for the anti republican stance taken by the church after 1870 but also the attacks on church interests made by successive republican governments. Therefore the reforms of Ferry's Opportunist dominated governments from 1880-'85 acted to polarise opinion, the dissolution of teaching orders after the 1880 legislation provoking significant opposition. It should be remembered that a Catholic education was perceived as desirable by large portions of the population, in particular the middle class. Yet there was a limit to the extent of anti-clerical legislation and it is this which prevented significant instability for whilst the church was attacked, those social groups which relied on it to provide quality education were not threatened. Therefore, even though Catholic teaching was removed from all state primary schools in 1882, teaching congregations were banned for all state supported schools in 1886 and so on, the fact remains that an elitist educational system was maintained. Still after Ferry's reforms only 3% of boys were sent to secondary schools i.e. those who could afford the fees. In 1900, 43% of secondary school students were at private Catholic institutions. The reaction against republican anti-clericalism in the early 1880's can be seen in the 1885 election in which the right won significant gains (202 seats against the 80 won in 1881).

The issue was tempered by a more menacing threat to both Church, Opportunists and establishment generally - the spread of Socialism. It was this reason more than any other which prompted the *ralliement* of 1892, Leo XIII reflecting the perceptions of many Catholics that the threat to the Church in the long run came from a socialist left which promised to bring down not only the church but the classes which supported it. The *ralliement* was not universally popular in some quarters in France but it did give the Republic legitimacy and at least temporarily defused what had been the issue around which opponents of the Republic were able to rally and find some popular support. It was the attack on the Church in the wake of the Dreyfus Affair which acted

to resolve the issue to the extent that separation of Church and state marked a victory for the forces of anti-clericalism. Although many French Catholics and the Church hierarchy preferred to stay neutral during the Dreyfus affair, the intervention of certain orders such as the Assumptionists on the anti-Dreyfusard side was the excuse for the anti clerical action which followed. The Dreyfus Affair was a serious a defeat for the Church as was the subsequent election in 1902 which was a landslide for the Radical strand of republicanism. It is ironic that the issue of the role of the church should be to all intents resolved by the victory of one side but this was the case. This also was the opportunity as the Dreyfus Affair had temporarily discredited the church. Therefore, as the legislation of Combes was passed and enacted it was the Church in Rome which protested most vehemently, the French ambassador to the Vatican being recalled in May 1904. Similarly, the reaction to the Separation Law was to be seen as most furious in the papal encyclicals rather than in the population at large. There was some resistance from Catholics who tried to prevent state officials making inventories of Church property in 1906 but in fact, the relative poor showing of the Catholics and Nationalists in the May 1906 election (they gained 175 seats between them as opposed to 321 Radicals and Socialists) reflects the degree of acceptance that separation had resolved the issue.

It is wrong to claim that the issue of the role and influence of the Church disappeared after 1905 for it still managed to raise passions. However, the stability of the Republic after this date can be partly attributed to the fact that the issue was no longer as politically sensitive. The fact that the Church was now forced to register as 'cultural associations' was not an issue which offended a population of which by 1900 some 75% were non-practising Christians. After 1906, the issue itself had become less fundamental, it was less about the role of the Church within the state as time had moved on. One should see the anti-clericalism of the 1880's -1900's as a response to the culture of the Church of papal infallibility, the *Syllabus of Errors* or *Vehementer* and *Gravissimo* (both 1906)[50]. Even before the Great War attitudes had begun to shift. The first ministry of Briand between 1909-'10 implemented the Separation Law in a far more conciliatory manner. It was not the issue of the Church which was at the centre of Poincaré's 'nationalist revival' right wing government of 1912 and presidency from 1913 but nationalist sentiment. Similarly, the legislation which raised most controversy and division between left and right on the eve of the war was the Three Year Law and not one related directly to the Church's role. Those political groups closely associated with the Church such as the *Action Libérale Populaire* continued to lobby on its behalf but concentrated on preventing the spread in the influence of the left. Further evidence of the decline of the issue of the Church can be seen with the victory of the *Bloc National* in the elections to the Chamber in 1919 and the Senate in 1920. Despite its overwhelming majority, the *Bloc* enacted legislation and initiated reforms which were to an extent superficial, e.g. in 1924 it gave the Church the right to reoccupy some of its former property as ' diocesan associations'. It is true that

diplomatic links were restored with the Vatican in 1921 and Alsace was exempted from the Separation Law. However, when Herriot attempted to suppress the embassy in Rome in February 1925 after the triumph of the *Cartel des Gauches* in May 1924 the uproar forced him to back down. The Church by the mid 1920's was very different to that of the 1880's. Most importantly, the views of the papacy had significantly changed, Pius XI prepared to negotiate with the French state as shown in 1923-'24. So the stability of the state was very much related to the resolution of the issue of the relation of Church and State. Although friction remained between clerical factions and their opponents, the spectre of socialism acted as the grounds for some common interest. Without such an issue to polarise France as it promised to do until 1906, there developed a greater degree of consensus within the political nation.

Political conservatism.

As shown above, political stability was achieved with the resolution of the outstanding issue which tried the republic. Anti-clericalism apart, Republicanism was ideologically neutral, a force for conservatism. Whilst there were different strands of Republican thought, they were united in their desire to create a lay state and protect the Republic from the forces of reaction. Whilst the Radicals were identified as being to the left on some issues, in particular their ferocious anti clericalism, they did not share with socialism a class based analysis of society. More moderate Republicans, the so called Opportunists who dominated government between 1879-1899 were even less inclined towards active reforming government. This is the key to understanding the stability of the Republic, neither strand acted to substantially offend the establishment or to unite anti republican opposition apart from when dealing with the issue of the Church. In fact the conservatism of Republicanism attracted support across the social and political spectrum. As mentioned above, even the so called reformism of Ferry between 1879-'85 were not radical in a social sense. Perhaps the best example of the negativism of Republicanism was the lack of social reform post 1906. Despite an impressive list of proposed reforms presented by Clemenceau in October of that year including pensions and tax reform-none were to become law. The reason was simple, Radicalism depended on the votes of a propertied class which opposed any reforms which would increase the financial burden or which smacked of collectivism. A lack of Radical reformism can also be seen with the *Cartel des Gauches* government of 1924. It is true that it was hamstrung by financial crisis, but it was not in the nature of Radicalism to initiate change which would create tensions. In fact instability and tension were caused more when Republican governments which leaned to the right were in office. An example was Poincaré's 1912 ministry which provoked controversy with the passage of the Three Year Law. However this legislation was passed with the aid of Radicals and the opposition centred around the socialist left led by Jaurès. Despite much posturing, there was a decree of consensus amongst Republican politicians of all inclinations.

Such conservatism was a product of the nature of elected politicians of the Third Republic. The first past the post system used (apart from an interlude between 1919-'28) created a Chamber of Deputies with local allegiances as often the most impressive dignitary was elected. Although certain Presidents attempted to make the post an effective one (in particular Poincaré from 1913-'20 and Millerand 1920-'24), the lack of a strong executive was a factor for stability. After the 'Crise de Seize Mai' in 1877, the executive became less important - in line with the Constitution - in directing political life and affairs. The result was that the Chamber of Deputies could bring down governments with ease. That is what they did, there being 60 administrations between 1871-1914. This very much encouraged conservatism for any government which had pretensions to fundamental reform did not last long, e.g. that of the Radical, Léon Gambetta, lasting only 3 months in 1881. A Radical ministry in 1895 attempted to reform the taxation system with the introduction of the taxation system[51] was brought down in the Senate. The ministry which lasted longest, that of Méline which survived a staggering two years from 1896-'8 was particularly conservative. The crises such as Boulangerism were as much reaction against the resultant inertia of such a system, its corruption, nepotism and stagnation. Yet such a system had strength, for all those within it were prepared to act to protect the system. The response to Boulangerism was swift, outlawing the standing of candidates in multiple constituencies. Similarly, the formation of a government of 'National Union' in 1926 and led by Poincaré was not as unlikely a political feat as many of the members of the Cabinet such as Herriot did not greatly differ in outlook.

The conservatism of Republicanism appeased the country's elites. Economic policy as explained below was conducted in their interests. The Republic survived and prospered as its leaders identified themselves more with the interests of capital and consistently acted to crush the left and labour whenever it threatened. In return, the challenge from the right progressively weakened from the monarchist heyday of 1873. Although it re-emerged during the Dreyfus Affair, the extreme right of *Action Francaise* or the Catholic groups such as the ALP were essentially marginalised. This greatly enhanced the stability of the Republic as it was on the right where the most implacable opposition to the Republic was to be found. However, even the *Bloc National* government from 1920-'24 was dominated by the centre, the *Alliance democratique* which was less interested in ideology and more preserving the status quo. All governments from 1871 were patriotically based and many such as Poincaré's of 1912, overtly nationalist. This undermined any threat from the extreme right as support for the 'integral nationalism' and its clear anti semitism and racialism was limited to a fringe of French society, even if it was an influential one. What appealed to the ruling class as much as any other factor was the ruthless suppression of labour unrest by successive Republican government. The consequence was that the Republic became the bulwark against socialism, the defender of vested interests against the threat of syndicalism. It therefore won at least the tacit

acceptance of many who were otherwise against it. There are numerous examples to back this up, not least the *Ralliement* or the restoration of diplomatic links between France and the Vatican in May 1921. The instances in which it was shown that Republicanism was far more concerned with social control than reform are numerous. Some of them reflect an astonishing lack of ideological thought. Most obvious was the attitude undertaken by Aristide Briand, Prime Minister from 1909-'10, towards striking railway workers in October 1910. Despite his socialist background, Briand did not hesitate to use force to crush the strike and arrest its leaders. His predecessor, Clemenceau, acted with a ferocity towards labour which greatly heartened the propertied classes (just as the crushing of the Commune in 1871 had). The examples are many, the general strike, 1906, the miners' strike of the same year, the Paris postal workers' strike 1909. That he became the focus of socialist hostility, in particular from the leader of the SFIO, Jean Jaurès, simply raised Clemenceau's status amongst those who feared the implications of collectivism. Post war, moderate Republicanism stood resolutely against the advances of labour. Despite widespread unrest in 1919-'20 the state did not hesitate to use force to crush strikes such as that in the metal industry in 1919 or of the railwaymen in 1920. Republicanism stood firm against the threat from the left and won considerable support for that. It also managed to include the reformists within socialists ranks who supported the Republic, in particular during the Dreyfus affair but also during and after the war. The fact that there were many within the CGT hierarchy post war who wished to work with the Republic, such as Léon Jouhaux (secretary general since 1909) helps to explain why the Republic was not undermined by the left. It also shows how broad the appeal of the Republic was which is central to explaining its stability.

Divisions within the left

It was not only the constant repressive policy of Republicanism against the left which helps to explain its marginalisation. The Republic was not so threatened by the left as the left itself was decidedly fragmented. Most fundamental was the division between the so called possibilists/reformists i.e. those who were prepared to work within the system such as Millerand or Jaurès and those who believed that such a view was class collaboration (the views of Guesde, Allemanists and Blanquists). Although attempts to resolve divisions resulted in the creation of SFIO in 1905, the decision that it was to be a revolutionary Marxist party (and therefore strictly anti-reformist) reduced socialist political influence. Similarly, the syndicalism of the largest union, CGT led to tensions between it and the SFIO which meant that the labour movement overall was critically divided. Perhaps Jaurés more than any individual had the ability to unite all groups but his assassination in 1914 and the intervention of the war prevented any progress in that direction. After the war, the left again was riddled with divisions, the tensions remaining from those who had wished for a negotiated peace (such as Faure) and those who continued to support the *Union Sacrée*. In 1920, the SFIO split between those who wished to tow the Bolshevik line (thereby forming the communist PCF) and those who did not. Such division caused marginalisation, such marginalisation acted as a factor for the Republic's stability

Economic stability

The stability of the Third Republic was much enhanced by the style of economic development which was particular to France. Instead of the rapid changes and large scale industrial concerns which so typified the British or German economic development, France experienced a more gradual transformation in which small scale business dominated, a form of *petit capitalism*. This structure was underpinned by a social system which was closely related, that of the small business owner or artisan peasant. Successive Republican governments did little to alter this structure, in fact quite the opposite, policy was made with its preservation in mind. In 1878 the government introduced the Freycinet Plan which was essentially a centrally planned attempt to improve infrastructure e.g. rail, canals and ports. The money raised for the project came from public loans. The benefits of the Plan won for the Republic widespread approval from business interests. Much the same can be said about the imposition of protective tariffs on imported grain - the Méline tariff of 1892. Whatever the advance of industry, France remained a predominantly agrarian country and the peasantry were a primary factor for stability. The tariff brought security for the countryside, even if it prevented necessary modernisation through offering false security. There were examples of rural unrest, in particular in wine growing areas in 1907 which suffered a fall in prices due to over production. Despite the level of violence and the threat presented the *Confederation des Vignerons*, this instance was more of an exception to the rule. Generally the countryside was conservative as the structure of land holding (much of it subsistence farming) remained unchanged. Despite some remarkable changes in industrial production in the period there was also considerable continuity. During the Third Republic the economy experience a dual development. On the one hand there was entrepreneurial success and change, especially in the new industries such as cars, engineering and steel. In fact individuals such as Renault, Citroen and Michelin created a motor industry without rival in Europe and contributed to an industrial growth figure of some 5% p.a. between 1906-'13. However, many industries retained their distinct small scale characteristics, often as they were linked in with the agricultural sector, most obviously textiles. Prosperity within the constraints of traditional economic and social boundaries was very much a factor promoting stability. To maintain such stability, the economic status quo, was at the heart of successive government's negativist approach to economic policy, hence the lack of social or fiscal reform.

Much the same can be said of the stabilising effects of the economy during and after the war. Although French industrial growth was not as comprehensive or as dramatic as in Britain or Germany, it was sufficient to provide the basis of an efficient war time economy. Whilst much of industry was shaped by the dominant agricultural sector, those essential in wartime were not. The munitions industry grew rapidly during the war, by 1918 it employed some 1.7 million workers. Throughout it was directed from the Ministry of Munitions, first by Albert Thomas and then by Louis Loucher. It was the latter who first attempted (as Minister for Industrial Reconstruction) to deal with the massive post war economic problems faced by the Republic. The fact that the economy, and the Republic withstood such a shattering blow as the war dealt it - the complete destruction of ten departments, 1.3 million dead, 3 million wounded, a 175 billion franc national debt, 400% inflation since 1914- is testament to their underlying strengths built up in the pre war years. Loucheur attempted to rebuild by reverting to a pre war economic system of minimal state intervention and tariffs. The assumption that reparations (and not increased taxation) would pay for reconstruction was a mistake that produced near permanent financial crisis in the 1920's. Yet again, despite the seeming structural instability of the Republic (between April 1925 and July 1926 there were five governments formed), the style of Republican government made possible the creation of a government of 'National Salvation' with widespread support. The fact that the franc was in freefall between 1924-'26 was not because of weaknesses in the economy but because of its mismanagement in the post war period. With a stabilisation of the currency (through devaluation) at a fifth of its 1914 level by Poincaré, the inherent strengths of the economy re-emerged (buoyed by strong exports), from 1926-'9 growth running at 5% p.a. Economic confidence was restored but also that in the Republic's politicians. There is a strong relationship between the economic well being of France between 1871-1929 and political stability. That the Republic survived was due to the flexibility and durability of an essentially prosperous economic structure.

Social stability underpinned the political stability of the Republic - there was a close relationship between these factors and gradual economic change. The slow rate of population growth in relation to other industrialising countries (France had a birth rate of 19.5:1000 from 1900-'13 in contrast to a German rate of 29.1 in the same period) reflected the different pattern of economic growth. Whereas in Britain and Germany migration patterns into cities had increased fecundity and lowered the marriage age, in France population growth was very much dictated by a peasantry which wished to limit sub division of land. The consequences of this fact were plain to see for all those who feared German expansionism. Whilst the French population grew at an annual rate of 0.1% p.a. from 37.4 million in 1881 to 39.1 million in 1911, that of Germany increased by 1.2% p.a. from 45.2 million to 64.9 million in the same period. Most worrying for French military analysts was the fact that by 1910, 34.1% of the German population were under fifteen whereas in France that figure was only 22.5%. Yet population stagnation was not a product of economic problems but more a reflection of a desire to improve living standards across all classes. The slaughter of the Great War, the death of 1.3 million, the collapse of the birth rate in the war years

(down to as low as 9.5 in 1916) created a shortfall of labour after the war which threatened economic recovery and, therefore, political stability. This was resolved by the attracting of foreign labour from Southern and Eastern Europe in the post war years, from 1920-'30 around two million in total. Although this migrant force was not made welcome, neither did it disturb a French social structure which remained resolutely unchanged throughout the period, even after the trauma of war. The class system, rigidly reflected and perpetuated by the education system remained unchallenged, the role of women in society unchanged despite their significant role in the war effort[52]. Indeed, the Senate's rejection of a bill giving women the vote in 1922 reveals much about prevailing conservative social attitudes.

Crises

The periodic crises suffered by the Third Republic have often been held up as evidence of the chronic instability and weakness of the political system. This is too much of an oversimplification for each of the crises had distinct causes which more often than not were based on short term discontent. They also often reflect the inability or unwillingness of the conservative political system to react to populist desires. Yet this same conservatism was a key factor for stability at other times. A clear example of this was Boulangerism and the desire of the Opportunist government to avoid war with Germany at all costs despite the public clamour for *revanche*. Yet the whole Boulanger affair should be seen in the light of the Daniel Wilson scandal and the widespread revulsion at what was, at least temporarily, seen as a corrupt system. This drew in support from left and right, but the measure of the permanency of that support can be measured by the speed at which Boulangerism faded away in 1889. It was the perceived level of corruption which was also responsible for much of the outcry over the Panama Canal Company yet again this was not long in lasting, many of those politicians implicated were re-elected in 1893. Indeed, the fact that the central campaign against the system led by Edouard Drumont in the newspaper '*Libre Parole*' the was based on anti-Semitism reflects that there was little threat to the Republic itself.

The same cannot be concluded about the Dreyfus Affair yet even here one should argue that the incident should be seen less in the light of an attack on the Republic and more a reflection of the deep intellectual, political and cultural divisions in France. It was these divisions, between clerics and anti-clerics, monarchist and Republicans and so on which shaped the political conservatism of the Republic. Yet the Dreyfus affair acted as a conductor for the defining of the Republic in positive terms. Just as the opposition was based around anti-Semitism, so those who supported the Republic did so in the name of liberty and justice. To this banner flocked individuals and groups as diverse as Jean Jaurès to the right wing *Ligue de la Patrie* Francaise. This gave the Republic a wider base of support than it had previously enjoyed and help to further isolate those on the extreme right. Therefore, although the Dreyfus Affair rocked the Republic to its very foundations,

it was central in its definition. In that it became a factor for stability.

Foreign and colonial policy

The importance of foreign policy in legitimising and by that stabilising the Republic should not be underestimated. Such a process was essential because the Republic lacked legitimacy, being born out of a crushing and humiliating defeat in 1871. This is not to say that a successful foreign policy won the Republic widespread popular support for that was not the case, public interest in foreign affairs being somewhat limited. What it did was restore the image amongst the governing classes of France as a 'great power', a factor which was essential if the Republic was to withstand the pressure from its internal as well as external enemies. The issue of *revanche* became less powerful in its ability to stir French emotions as time passed, but the need to ensure French security did not. Of great importance, was the Franco-Russian alliance in the shape of the military convention which was finally ratified in 1894. This gave France the promise of support in case of attack by Germany and her allies and redressed the balance in Europe to an extent. The Russian alliance became the cornerstone of a diplomatic policy which attempted to contain the obvious expansionist ambitions of the German Empire. This was a policy which gained widespread popular support and on the eve of the war, the support of an army recovering from the setback of Dreyfus. Foreign policy was to all intents and purposes made by the Président and Foreign Minister alone. It was important that those interests which were a potential threat to the Republic, especially the army, were not alienated however. As war approached, the opposite is true. In fact as President, Poincaré promoted accepted the views of the army on a number of issues including three year service and General Joffre's 'Plan 17'[53]. The former policy caused controversy but few questioned the need to create a policy which guarded against Germany, particularly after the Agadir crisis of 1911. This even went as far as general acceptance of the *Entente Cordiale* signed with historic foe and colonial rival Britain in 1904.

Whilst French colonial policy did not win the Republic substantial popular support, it served two particular ends very well. Firstly, the creation of Empire in Africa and Indo-China, served to reinforce the impression that France's 'great power' status was assured, despite its inability to enact *revanche*. Secondly, imperialism offered an outlet to business and investors from which rich pickings could be made. The main outlet for the vast foreign investment pre 1914 was Tsarist Russia, but there was money to be made in such projects as the railway constructed eastwards into the African interior from Senegal in the 1880's. Imperialism did create tensions at home, in particular the creation of the Tunisian protectorate in 1881 (with the approval of Bismarck) provoked Radicals into creating the *Ligue des Patriotes* with the expressed aim of maintaining revanche as the priority in foreign policy. Indeed, the level of opposition to an expansionist colonial policy can be seen in Ferry's fall over the Tonkin question in 1885, brought down by Radicals and the Right

who believed it to be wasteful. However, the key point is this, whilst there was opposition to imperialism, for France to have allowed others to plunder alone would have been a mortal blow to the country's prestige in an era when 'greatness' was measured by the extent of a nation's ability to colonise others. There was considerable support amongst influential groups within society to press France's imperial claims against Britain, witness the creation of colonial pressure groups in the early 1890's. The strength of opinion can be measured by the outburst of anti-British sentiment after the Fashoda incident of 1898. Similarly, the importance of Morocco was clear to French national prestige, attempts by Germany to prevent French influence extending and to humiliate her neighbour acted to rally support for the Republic in its attempts to defend French interests.

Without doubt, the most obvious example of foreign policy acting to stabilise the Republic was the Great War. There was hostility to the war, especially in the latter years as the extent of the slaughter took its toll. Strikes took hold in important areas of production, in the Loire metal industry in 1918 or the unrest in munitions factories the previous year. Similarly, a minority of socialists led by Jean Longuet began to call for a negotiated peace. Despite that, a political consensus just about survived (if not a *union sacrée*) into 1917 to be followed by Clemenceau's government which, although it opened up political divisions, reflected the majority popular opinion that the war should be waged until Germany had been defeated. In what was seen as the ultimate test, the

Republic became identified with the national interest. Just as the 'nationalist revival' of Poincaré before the war had reconciled many otherwise indifferent sections of society to the Republic, most importantly the army, this process continued during the war. The fact that General Joffre was allowed such an extensive role in the decision making process from 1914-'16 was astonishing when one considers the antipathy between army and Republic at the turn of the century. That the war was won, that Clemenceau's government was prepared to take the measures it did to suppress opposition to the war meant that by 1918, the Republic was more established and secure than at any time previously. This was reinforced by Versailles, despite the opinion in some quarters that the Germans had been softly treated. Despite the failure of the policy of containing Germany through reparations, the Republic was bolstered by the successful diplomacy of Aristide Briand in his attempts to ensure French security. The Locarno treaties of 1925 were popularly seen as the best means of restricting any future German resurgence. Similarly, the Kellogg-Briand pact of 1928 and its inherent pacifism reflected a general mood fuelled by stories of the horrors of the trenches.

Conclusion

That the French Third Republic was essentially stable has been a source of some historical debate but should not be questioned. The factors which ensured this stability are many, most important of which was the conservatism of Republicanism, the absence of ideology which produced consensus and

gave the Republic a broad base of political support. This was reflected in the absence of ideologically inspired legislation apart from in the topic of the role of the Church. Economic and social stability acted to reinforce the political institutions rather than undermine them yet this was reciprocated in that the Republic's politicians acted to reinforce rather than reform. The threat to the Republic from the right was limited by the conservatism of government and from the left by divisions in the ranks of the representatives of labour. Added to this was the resolute stance taken by successive administrations against labour demands and unrest which won the Republic the support of many who believed it to be an effective bulwark against socialism (including the papacy) . Legitimacy came also through success in foreign policy, in particular the break out of isolation after 1871 and victory in the Great War. Through such legitimacy, the threat from those who opposed the Republic was reduced. There were numerous crises within the political system yet these should be seen in the context of the deeper divisions within France and their own immediate causes. The stability of the Republic is particularly outstanding in an age when other more seemingly secure regimes were toppled. Its institutions and vulnerabilities mirrored those of France itself but for that ensured their survival.

---

[1] *Revanche* was the demand for revenge against Germany for the defeat and settlement of 1871.

[2] The treaty was formally signed in Frankfurt on May 10th.

[3] The term 'Commune' was an emotive one for all radicals and revolutionaries. The 'Commune de Paris' had ruled the capital city in 1789 after the fall of the Bastille. It was replaced by the Revolutionary Commune which executed Louis XVI and laid the foundations for the Republic.

[4] Jacobins believed in the concept of 'political liberty' as espoused by their forebears in 1793.

[5] Blanquist ideals included decentralisation, the dismantling of the army and the separation of Church and State. The Commune passed legislation aimed at achieving the last of these on April 2nd.

[6] In retaliation for the death of the Archbishop, 147 communard prisoners were shot.

[7] The Count of Chambord was the grandson of Charles X who had reigned from 1824-'30, and the great nephew of Louis XVI who had been executed in 1793.

[8] Thiers was an Orleanist but more fundamentally, a conservative.

[9] It was hoped by monarchists that by this time the elderly and childless Chambord would have died leaving the way clear for the accession of the more pragmatic and flexible Count of Paris.

[10] This amendment was called the Wallon amendment (named after its sponsor Henri Wallon) and was passed by 353 to 352 votes, in the main due to division amongst the monarchists.

[11] Deputies were elected in single member constituencies as in Britain today. The hope was that this would produce the election of local dignitaries who would be naturally conservative.

[12] The balance of deputies after the election was 360 republicans and 153 monarchists (including Bonapartists).

[13] The vote of no confidence was passed with 363 for and 158 against.

[14] This was and could only be done with the consent of the conservative Senate.

[15] Founded by Ignatius de Loyola in 1534, the Society of Jesus or Jesuit Order was organised on military lines to counter the spread of the Reformation. It remained the most belligerent force within the Catholic Church and was often the first target for anti clerical action.

[16] Meaning control by laymen rather than clerics.

[17] The *Parti Ouvrier Français* was founded in 1882 and dominated by the followers of Jules Guesde who was a Marxist. In contrast, those on the left who believed that change could be effected through non revolutionary means formed themselves into the *Parti Ouvrier Socialiste Revolutionnaire Français*, also in 1882.

[18] Radicals strongly believed in the creation of a secular republic. They also stood for *revanche* against Germany.

[19] The 1885 election saw gains for the anti republican right, up from 80 seats in 1881 to 202. The broad republican movement still had a majority with 372 seats but this movement was diverse.

[20] Rouvier's cabinet was dominated by Opportunist republicans.

[21] Founded by Paul Deroulede in 1882, the *Ligue* was concerned with promoting the cause of *revanche* which explains its support for Boulanger.

[22] In 1888, Boulanger won six out of seven by-elctions pulling votes from radical left and anti- republican right.

[23] Boulanger was very much committed to his mistress, Mme de Bonnemain, and it was on her grave that he committed suicide in Brussels in September 1891.

[24] Part of Boulanger's successful campaign was due to multiple candidacy - on August 19th 1888, he stood in and won three constituencies simultaneously.

[25] This incident is known as the Algiers Toast.

26 De Lessep's most famous venture being the construction of the Suez Canal.

27 The company was known as the *Company du Canal Interoceanique*.

28 The names of those accused of accepting bribes ranged from the Radical Clemenceau to the Finance Minister Rouvier. Suspicion of widespread corruption was heightened by the suicide of the company's intermediary with the politicians Baron Jaques Reinach, the day before he was due for trial.

29 As the crimes had been committed over three years beforehand, the cours de cassiation ruled that the sentences were invalid under the criminal statute of limitations.

30 A *stagiaire* was a junior probationer officer.

31 Dreyfus was an Alsatian Jew and therefore provoked animosity from the overwhelmingly anti-Semitic, conservative and royalist general staff of the French Army.

32 Zola was sentenced to a year imprisonment but escaped to England.

33 The 1890's had been dominated by conservative republicanism with radicalism very much damaged by its association with Boulanger and individual politicians' dealings with the Panama Canal company.

34 The Radical deputies had altered the legislation to make parliament the authorising body rather than the Council of State.

35 In 1903 Pope Leo XIII died and his replacement Pius X was less inclined to accept such overt attacks from Radical inspired governments.

36 Agreed between Napoleon and the papacy of Pius VII, the Concordat agreed that bishops and archbishops should be appointed by the state but their appointment confirmed by the Pope. Other articles included the state paying the clergy.

37 Reformism is accepting reform as a means of improving the lot of the working classes.

38 The unions has been legalised by the Trade Union Act of 1884.

39 The postal workers were not the only public service workers to be denied that right, in 1907 Clemenceau forbade primary school teachers to affiliate to the CGT.

40 These years saw considerable unrest in the wine industry caused by a fall in prices. Violence in rural areas was common and in 1907 a union of vinyard workers, the *Confederation Generale des Vignerons* was formed.

41 Such a backdown was due to the growing domestic crisis caused by the Dreyfus Affair and the lack of Russian support for war against Britain.

42 *The Entente Cordiale* also settled disputes over Newfoundland, Siam, Madagascar and the new Hebrides.

43 The Act of Algeciras accepted Franco-Spanish control of the police and French influence over the running of the state bank.

44 Joffre was criticised in particular for his sacking of General Sarrail who was well connected with many Radicals and whose treatment was perceived as being politically inspired.

45 Apart from the Socialists, many leading politicians were moving towards the idea of a negotiated peace, especially in the light of the 1917 mutiny. This included Caillaux and Louis Jean Malvy, the Radical ex Minister of the Interior.

46 This included figures such as Clemenceau, Briand, Millerand and Poincaré.

47 Clemenceau's defeat reflected discontent with Versailles and the fact that his anti-clericalism was not forgotten.

48 Agitation for a general stoppage had been considerable, in particular in the metal and rail industries.

[49] Loosely translated this means 'a slut'.

[50] The *ralliement* (1892) and *Rerum Novarum* (1891) were a shift in attitudes and did bring a reconciliation between Church and Opportunists, i.e. more conservative republicans. To radicals, socialists and many others, however, the Church was still the main enemy.

[51] Repeated attempts to reform the taxation system were the product of need rather than ideology. The existing taxation was complex and cumbersome, relying on indirect taxes and direct taxation being organised through the local government.

[52] As in Britain, women played a significant role in the wartime economy with large numbers working in munitions.

[53] 'Plan 17' was the army's outline of how it would wage war against a German invader. Authored by Joffre it stressed the need for attack as being the best form of defence.

Dreyfus

M. Briand

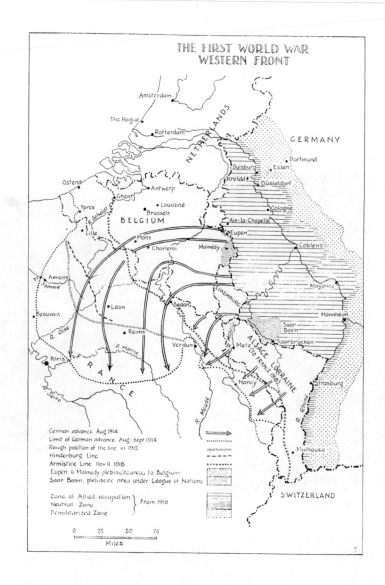

FRANCE: FIRST WORLD WAR AND AFTER

EUROPE 1870-1980 - INDEX

[Greenwich Exchange/Martin Collier]